THE US–KOREA ECONOMIC PARTNERSHIP

The US–Korea Economic Partnership

Policy directions for trade and economic co-operation

Edited by
YOUN-SUK KIM
KAP-SOO OH

Avebury

Aldershot • Brookfield USA • Hong Kong • Singapore • Sydney

Published by
Avebury
Ashgate Publishing Limited
Gower House
Croft Road
Aldershot
Hants GU11 3HR
England

Ashgate Publishing Company
Old Post Road
Brookfield
Vermont 05036
USA

British Library Cataloguing in Publication Data

US–Korea Economic Partnership: Policy
Directions for Trade and Economic
Co-operation
     I. Kim, Youn-Suk   II. Oh, Kap-Soo
     337.519073

ISBN 1 85972 022 6

Library of Congress Catalog Card Number: 95 75558

Printed and bound by Athenæum Press Ltd.,
Gateshead, Tyne & Wear.

Contents

Editors' Note

Founded in 1985, the Korea-America Economic Association is a nonprofit academic and professional organization. Its objective is the encouragement of economic research and professional communication among Korean economists residing in North America, who share research interests in economic relations between North America and Korea, and among the Pacific Rim nations in general.

1993

President:	Youn-Suk Kim, Kean College of New Jersey
Vice-President:	Hae-Shin Hwang, Texas A&M University
Secretary-General:	Dong-Kuen Jeong, North Carolina A&T State University
Treasurer:	Kap-Soo Oh, Drexel University

1994

President:	Chong-Soo Pyun, Memphis State University
Vice-President:	Suk Hi Kim, University of Detroit
Secretary-General:	Hun Young Park, University of Illinois
Treasurer:	Yoon Kuen Song, University of Detroit

1995

President:	Kwan Suk Kim, University of Notre Dame
Vice-President:	Yoon Kuen Song, University of Detroit
Secretary-General:	Hong Yul Park, Saginaw Valley State University
Treasurer:	Hoon Park, University of Central Florida

Regional Coordinators

Liaison:	Semoon Chang, University of South Alabama
Northeast:	Yeomin Yoon, Seton Hall University
Southeast:	Cheol Soo Eun, University of Maryland
Midwest:	Hy Sang Lee, University of Wisconsin
Southwest:	Baek In Cha, University of Texas, Arlington
South:	Don Lee, University of Alabama
West:	Yung Y. Yang, California State University
Canada:	Jong S. You, Algoma University

Figures and tables

LDC-MNCs

Acknowledgements

The editors wish to thank the many people who made this book possible and who contributed to the success of the conference on which this volume is based. We greatly appreciate the assistance and guidance provided by Byung-Tae Whang, P.H. Koo, Duck Woo Nam and Jang-Hee Yoo. We are particularly grateful to the sponsors of the conference for their generous support: Anam Group, Federation of Korean Industries, Korean Airlines, Korea Chamber of Commerce & Industry, Korea Development Institute, Korea Foreign Traders Association, Korea Foundation, Korea Institute for International Economic Policy, Korea Sanhak Foundation, Korea Securities Dealers Association, Korea-US Economic Council, and *Meil Kyungje* - The Economic Daily.

Contributors

Peter Cashman is former Deputy Assistant Secretary for East Asia and the Pacific at the United States Department of Commerce.

Rajan Chandran is Professor of Marketing and International Business at Temple University in Philadelphia, PA, USA.

Thomas Chiang is Professor of Finance at Drexel University in Philadelphia, PA, USA.

Joonmo Cho is Professor of Economics at Soong Sil University in Seoul, Korea.

Soon Cho is the former Deputy Prime Minister, Republic of Korea. He is currently the Executive Advisor to the Bank of Korea.

Jongmoo Jay Choi is Professor of Finance and International Business at Temple University in Philadelphia, PA, USA.

Young Back Choi is Professor of Economics at St. John's University in Jamaica, NY, USA.

Myung-Gun Choo is Chairman of the Sejong Institute of Economics in Seoul, Korea.

Hae-Wang Chung is Vice-President of the Korea Institute of Finance in Seoul, Korea.

James M. Devault is Assistant Professor of Economics at Lafayette College in Easton, PA, USA.

E. Djimopoulos is Professor of Economics at Fairleigh Dickinson University in Teaneck, NJ, USA.

James H. Fall III is Deputy Assistant Secretary for Developing Nations, United States Department of the Treasury.

Bang Nam Jeon is Assistant Professor of Economics at Drexel University in Philadelphia, PA, USA.

HongYul Han is Senior Research Fellow at the Korea Institute for International Economic Policy in Seoul, Korea.

Seung-Soo Han is the President's Chief of Staff, The Blue House, Republic of Korea. He is the former Korean Ambassador to the United States.

Dong K. Jeong is Professor of Economics at North Carolina A&T State University in Greensboro, NC, USA.

Stanley Judd is formerly an attorney with the Division of Investment Management at the Securities and Exchange Commission in Washington, DC, USA.

Kwang W. Jun is Senior Financial Economist in the International Economics Department of the World Bank in Washington, DC, USA.

John Kendrick is Professor Emeritus of Economics at George Washington University in Washington, DC, USA.

Jin-Ouk Kim is Chief Executive Attorney and Partner at the law offices of Kim, Shin and Yu in Seoul, Korea.

Kyoung Kim is Assistant Professor of International Business at Keimyung University in Taegu, Korea.

Youn-Suk Kim is former President of the Korea-America Economic Association. He is Professor of Economics at Kean College of New Jersey in Union, NJ, USA.

Lawrence R. Klein is the Benjamin Franklin Professor of Economics at the University of Pennsylvania in Philadelphia, PA, USA.

Jae Won Lee is Professor of Economics at Baruch College, City University of New York in New York, NY, USA.

Catherine Mann is a Senior Economist in the International Finance Division at the Federal Reserve Board of Governors in Washington, DC, USA.

Marcus Noland is Senior Fellow at the Institute for International Economics in Washington, DC, USA.

Timothy J. O'Brien is a Partner at Coudert Brothers, Attorneys at Law, in New York, NY, USA.

Kap-Soo Oh is President of Management Development Institute in Seoul, Korea.

Woo-Hee Park is President of the Korea Economic Association in Seoul, Korea. He is Professor of Economics at Seoul National University.

Woong-Bae Rha is a member of the National Assembly, Republic of Korea. He chairs the Foreign Affairs and National Unification Committee.

Preface

The United States and Korea have entered into an era of renewed economic activity and a commitment toward closer bilateral ties. Discussions in recent years at the Uruguay Round and the APEC Conferences have amply demonstrated how a close coordination between the two countries' policies are bolstering a more promising economic relationship.

This book aims to expand the dialogue on the Korean economy, particularly in respect to its ties with the United States. Korea's economic development continues to be based on outward-growth policies. Korean economics are both complex and contentious, and the US-Korea economic partnership is a relationship of ever increasing significance. The contributors to this volume discuss important bilateral economic issues to highlight economic cooperation and policy options for enhancing trade and improving economic relations between Korea and the US. They identify and examine the new policy directions for trade between the US and Korea, how Korea can liberalize its financial market and improve its investment environments, and how the US and Korea can strengthen industrial cooperation and business relations.

In publishing this book, the Korea-America Economic Association hopes to present constructive and mutually advantageous economic options for the two countries. To meet the challenges of a rapidly changing Pacific-Rim economy, an effective US-Korea economic partnership has become essential.

Youn-Suk Kim
1993 KAEA President

Introduction

This book grew out of a conference sponsored by the Korea-America Economic Association, entitled 'US-Korea Economic Partnership: Policy Directions under the New Administrations,' held on July 29-30, 1993, in Philadelphia. It includes a broad-based discussion of the following: (1) trade and economic cooperation issues, examining new policy directions for trade between the United States and Korea; (2) financial issues, looking at how Korea can liberalize its financial market and improve its investment environment; (3) industrial issues, including how the United States and Korea can strengthen industrial cooperation and business relations in areas such as investment and technology transfer between the two countries. Many of the original papers have been revised by their authors for this publication so as to reflect responses to conference discussants' comments on the respective articles.

The conference focused on the heightening international interdependence in the US-Korean economic partnership. Patterns of international trade, finance, industry and technology have been changing dramatically in recent years, with serious consequences for economic and financial policy as well as for industry strategy. These changes are especially important for those countries seeking to benefit from their own ties to a US-Korea economic partnership. Furthermore, recent developments on both sides of the Pacific indicate that the US and Korea are entering into an era of renewed activity and commitment toward bolstering bilateral economic ties. Indeed, it is now imperative for the two countries to construct dynamic and mutually advantageous economic plans of action to meet the challenges of the changing Pacific-Rim economy.

Despite a history of a strong political and military alliance which dates to the 1950s, the US-Korea economic partnership is neither generally discussed nor widely understood. The extraordinary asymmetry that characterized this relationship in the beginning has blurred the new circumstances surrounding this economic partnership. A world order dominated by two superpowers has given way to the changing multipolar global economy of the post-Cold-War years, shaped in part by the Uruguay Round agreement, the expanded European Community, the North American Free Trade Agreement and APEC discussions. In this context, Korea has fully emerged as a newly industrialized country with a burgeoning and increasingly self-reliant middle economy. US approaches to Korea must deal with these changes in Korean orientation.

Fundamental to an understanding of Korea is an appreciation of its history. Korean history is widely estimated to be about 4000 years long, much of it under the cultural influence of China, followed by 36 years as a colony of Japan. It has ended up a divided country, separated into North Korea and South Korea. At partition Korea was a very poor nation by every economic measure. The South's backward and traditional agrarian sector employed more than two-thirds of the labor force during the 1940s and 1950s, and its industrial base was small. Even before the South could establish any foundation for economic independence, the Korean War broke out, wiping out whatever industry had survived liberation from Japan. By the time the conflict ended in 1953, the US saved South Korea from communist takeover, but at a cost of some 34,000 lives and more than $18 billion.

In the critical postwar years, US aid played a key role in sustaining the Korean economy, supporting the ravaged country as it recovered from the war's damage and began to undertake industrialization. During the 1953-1960 period, US aid to Korea was about $1.7 billion. However, Syngman Rhee's newly formed government concentrated on policies opposing communism and the Japanese, giving those ideological campaigns top priority and allowing the stagnant economy to languish throughout Rhee's tenure.

Until 1961, the Korean economy could be called a US client economy; in other words, Korea was economically dependent on US assistance for its survival. For instance, combined US economic and military aid accounted for about 10 percent of Korea's GNP in the period from 1954 to 1970. However, after 1961 Korea instituted drastic economic measures, which established a new track of industrial and trade policies that drove the country toward its current status of an economic partner, instead of merely a beneficiary.

The rise of Korea's economy began in the mid-1960s. Since the early 1960s there has been rapid growth and tremendous structural transformation. Real GNP has increased more than eight percent a year on average, and export earnings average about 30 percent per year. Korea has followed a strategy of export-led high economic growth which in turn has transformed it from a traditional agricultural society to a newly industrialized country and has led to its current rank as the world's twelfth largest trading nation. It is now the largest producer of color TVs in the world and is the largest maker of microwave ovens with about 40 percent of the global market. It also controls 30 percent of the global VCR market and has become the world's largest producer of color picture tubes and the second-largest monitor manufacturer.

Until recently, Korea's economy was managed by its government, which consciously sought to maximize exports and growth through a strategy that depended on an authoritarian political and social order. The government set goals for economic growth and sought to mobilize the whole energy of the nation to support it. Economic policies such as macro-management, labor, sectoral and financial policies were all geared toward the promotion of economic growth. Even though it cannot be assumed that a strong government will allocate resources efficiently, it must nevertheless be acknowledged that the Korean economy has achieved industrialization as a result of strong government intervention.

There are, indeed, certain characteristics of the Korean economy which resemble those of contemporary or historical Japan. But Japan is a seasoned modern industrial world power, and has expanded its net external assets to become the largest creditor country in the world. In contrast, Korea has needed substantial resources in order to transform itself from a developing country into an industrial country, and its economy has been industrialized with the assistance of foreign capital, technology and markets.

As a country which depends on foreign trade for more than half of its GNP, Korea stands exposed to the changing patterns of the world economy. Its manufactured products have not only been the major components of Korea's production and export, but also played a major role in contributing to its production and export expansion. As soon as Korea completed its economic takeoff, it undertook production transformation toward heavy and chemical industries, reflecting the need of the changing international economy. This has paved the way for a frontier of continuous and expanding production possibilities. Korean industrialization integrated international product cycles into aggregate production functions so as to realize a dynamic competitive advantage by mixing endogenous inputs with imported capital goods and technology. In essence, Korea successfully realized the crucial transformation to a newly industrialized country in a remarkably short time.

But a greater problem lies in the fact that economic relations between the United States and Korea have changed from dependence to partnership status, and have become increasingly contentious as Korea has assumed a more

3

prominent role in the global economy. The US-Korea economic partnership has been propelled by market forces, which have been an outgrowth of the former status of protector-client linkage. The bilateral economic relationship has been restructured, reflecting the changing nature of the partnership. How did this come about? Four basic factors were operative: (1) trade, (2) finance, (3) industries, and (4) policy.

With respect to these factors, the papers in this book point to the many academic and policy issues which help frame the discussion on contemporary economic relations between Korea and the United States.

Lawrence R. Klein's 'US-Korea Trade and Economic Relations' briefly assesses the overall performance of Korea's economy since World War II. Klein emphasizes the leader-follower relationship between Japan and Korea on the path of economic development and growth, underlining the advantages of an open economy which could offer lessons to other developing countries.

Woong Bae Rha's 'The Future of US-Korea Economic Cooperation in the New Asia-Pacific Era' discusses how economic cooperation between the US and Korea has been placed as having the most important logistical role in the Asia-Pacific Basin arena for the respective policy objectives of the two countries.

Peter Cashman's 'New Policy Directions for US-Korea Economic Partnership' explains what the US expects to achieve through the Dialogue for Economic Cooperation and other objectives of US trade policy towards Korea for strengthening bilateral commercial relations.

Myung-Gun Choo 'Economic Regionalism and US Trade Negotiation Strategies: Rationale for a World Free Trade Agreement' argues for free trade by proposing a global agreement which reflects the post-Uruguay Round reality, addressing the merits for such a pact from the vantage points of Korea and the US in particular.

Marcus Noland's 'Asia and the NAFTA' presents a series of models to analyze prospective trade diversion effects due to the NAFTA. While Asian countries may suffer losses due to trade diversion in the medium-run, in the long-run the NAFTA may actually be to their advantage, to the benefit of both the US and Asia.

HongYul Han's 'Imbalances in the Asia-Pacific Economy and the Role of ANIES' examines the very dynamism of the regional problem of structural imbalance by analyzing structural problems. Emphasis is given to policy coordination to facilitate regional economic integration.

James M. Devault's 'The Republic of Korea and the United States: Trade and Trade Policy Issues' examines trade between the two countries and how

4

it is affected by trade barriers. The article then discusses prospects for elaborating bilateral negotiations and the implications of the increasing integration of Korea with the rest of the East Asian economy.

Soon Cho's 'Financial Liberalization and Reform in Korea' presents a concise summary of Korean financial developments since 1962. He identifies the problems that arose in the early years because of financial recession and presents the main financial liberalization and reform measures since 1980. Looking ahead, he outlines the remaining tasks that will provide Korea with an efficient financial system for the 21st century.

Thomas Chiang, Bang Nam Jeon and Kap-Soo Oh's 'Financial Structures in Industrial Countries: Lessons for Reform in Korea' surveys financial system structures in major industrial countries which shed light on the ongoing financial reform in Korea. They discuss ownership linkages between banking and commerce, the scope of banking services, and the macroeconomic environment under financial liberalization.

Kwang W. Jun's 'Effects of Capital Market Liberalization in Korea: Empirical Evidence and Policy Implications' examines the impact of market opening, based on the recent experience of Korea. The major findings are that direct foreign investment had a significant positive impact on the equity market performance and that the impact of foreign investment on the volatility of stock market return was also positive, thus suggesting the benefits of more active external liberalization of domestic capital markets.

James H. Fall III's 'The US-Korean Financial Dialogue' discusses financial policies of the two countries by explaining the position of the US in regard to Korea. He emphasizes Korea's need for financial liberalization to allow the market to allocate resources more effectively, and to free the commercial banking sector in order to attract foreign investors.

Jongmoo Jay Choi, Kyoung Kim and Rajan Chandran's 'Foreign Direct Investments by Firms from Developing and Developed Countries: Stylized Facts and Theoretical Interpretations' discusses the patterns of foreign direct investment by firms from developing countries. In particular, they focus on investors from newly industrializing Asian countries, in comparison to investment by conventional multinationals from developed countries. They examine the existing theories of foreign direct investment for establishing a framework for interpreting this new phenomenon.

Youn-Suk Kim's 'US-Japan Technological Competition: Implications for Korea' discusses the technology policies in Japan and the United States and analyzes how technology has contributed to changing the respective trade-production patterns. The study looks into what bearing US-Japan technology

5

competition has on Korea-US economic cooperation.

Catherine L. Mann's 'Managed Trade, Direct Investment and External Balance' deals with the linkages among microeconomic policies, and the macroeconomic balances between savings and investment regarding exports and imports. Granted managed trade can change overall internal and external balance only temporarily, these policies can also affect the geographical composition of external balance by changing the costs of accessing certain markets.

Woo-Hee Park's 'Technological Policy and Development in Korea' surveys the growth path of the Korean economy since 1962. Korea has managed to reach a high level of manufacturing and has become competitive in several areas. In order to continue its progress, Korea must now move into the growth areas of the future.

Dong K. Jeong's 'Changes in Korea's Bilateral Trade Structure with Japan and the United States' examines Korea's bilateral trade patterns with Japan and the US since the early 1960s. The empirical testing showed that Korea's imports from the US and Japan were not responsive to prices of products from both Japan and the US, though Korea's import income elasticity of US products was roughly comparable to Korea's import income elasticity of Japanese products.

Finally Seung-Soo Han's remarks highlight a new partnership in the Asia-Pacific, the world's most dynamic region, by focusing on Korea as it expands its presence in the Asia-Pacific arena through bilateral relations and APEC.

Part I

TRADE AND ECONOMIC POLICY OPTIONS

1 US–Korea trade and economic relations

Lawrence R. Klein

One of the great success stories of the period since World War II has been the economic development and expansion of Korea. After the successful defense of the lower part of the Korean peninsula (below the 38th parallel), the economic and political development of the Republic of Korea was influenced by the United States, which provided strategic security, and Japan, which provided important economic and cultural influence.

Not only did the US protect the Republic of Korea, but we also invested significantly in order to get the economy moving forward. The fact that Japan was the main supply base of US forces in Korea contributed greatly to the takeoff of the Japanese economy, which was also aided by the US security umbrella, thus freeing up resources for the civilian sector.

In the Asia-Pacific area, Japan started to grow vigorously in the late 1950s and all through the 'income-doubling' decade of the 1960s. The key sectors for Japanese industrial growth were textiles, shoes, optics, electronics, steel, shipbuilding and cars. These and other labor-intensive activities formed the base for effective Japanese competition in the world markets at very competitive prices. Japan qualified in 1964 for OECD membership, marking a transition to advanced nation status.

There is, of course, much more to the recent economic history of Japan, but the stages related above are of particular importance in understanding Korea's recent economic history. Approximately one decade later, Korea entered a similar takeoff period. Korea was not alone in this stage but was accompanied by Taiwan, Hong Kong and Singapore. The four countries became known as the 'New Japans' or the 'Four Dragons.'

Wages rose in Japan, aspirations became elevated, lifestyles changed (very much towards Western ideals), and Japan could no longer serve the world market so cheaply at the lower technical end of her export menu. Korea and the other dragons filled the void with labor-intensive manufactures of good quality at relatively lower prices. Textiles, shoes, electronics, shipbuilding and construction were some of the early leaders in Korean exports. They are still important, but Korea, Taiwan, Hong Kong and Singapore now have higher costs and are challenged at the low end of the technological scale by China, Vietnam, Indonesia and other Asia-Pacific countries.

Japan shifted to very high technology but is still a formidable competitor in some of the world export lines of the 1960s; however, with a higher degree of technical input. Meanwhile, Korea advanced to motor cars, shipbuilding, world-wide construction and more sophisticated electronics. But just as Japan had to shift upwards on the technological scale, so must Korea. It is very unlikely that Korea can continue to make the impressive gains that were realized in the 1970s, based on the relative sophistication of the second generation of postwar technologies.

It must be pointed out that very few countries can expect to grow at annual rates in excess of 7.2 percent (doubling in 10 years) for very long periods of time. The four dragons, especially Taiwan and Korea, have been experiencing fast growth for about 25 years or so, but not without mishap. Korea had setbacks in 1979-1981 and again in 1992-1993. These are partly politically affected episodes but also related to changing income distribution, labor market pressures and world economic conditions. Korea's economic development is noteworthy in these important respects: (1) After the second oil shock (1979-1981) Korea, through an oil importer, did not let the deteriorating terms of trade in energy products generate an inflationary surge. There was great adaptablility and flexibility, especially in the labor market. (2) Korea incurred some debt, managed to service this debt, but started to experience a current account surplus and retired some debt. (3) Korea followed a pattern of export-led growth. Korea was not alone in these respects, but it should be stressed that these were important factors in the strong growth period.

If we consider the analogies and linkages with Japan, we can see that eventually Japanese growth slowed — from more than 10 percent annually at the end of the 1960s, to 5 or 6 percent in the 1970s, to 4 or 5 percent in the 1980s. Now Japan is in serious recession and is not expected to reach much more than 3 percent when the recovery takes hold.

Korea should also be prepared for slowing down. Growth has been less than 5 percent for two years running and is not expected to exceed 7 or 8 percent in the near term. The current account surplus has vanished, and the deficit must be financed. Inflation runs higher than formerly, and Korea can no longer rely on being a low-price supplier in many export markets that were formerly conquered.

The new strategy for Korea is to seek production and exports at a higher level of technology, maybe not up to Japan's level, but ahead of Korea's past level. There must be more attention paid to development of the home market. Korea, however, has two very important new markets on the horizon.

In the first place, Korea can develop ever closer ties with China and has virtually an unlimited market, for a few years at least, consisting of more than one billion people. This is of enormous importance. China can be a threat in some Korean export markets, but it is also a land of opportunity, not only for exports of goods and services but also for capital exports in the forms of joint ventures, licensing, financing and other types of foreign direct investment. China has developed unusually well in the southeast, with input from the other three dragons. Korea is well-situated to do the same thing in the northeast, which has been relatively neglected.

The second market is in Russia or, more generally, the whole former Soviet bloc (the former USSR and Eastern Europe). Exports and capital investment provide opportunities for Korea. In both cases — China and Russia — Korea has an opportunity for lasting development. China's growth has been underway since 1978, with very impressive performance. Russia's expansion is yet to be started, but when it does begin it has the possibility of enduring for some time. The large internal markets of China and Russia are not likely to mature so early, as did Japan's expansion or those of Korea and Taiwan. This present a unique opportunity for Korea and is less a threat than a benefit.

From the beginning of China's reform movement, in 1978, there was great admiration for the economies of Korea and Taiwan. The familiar refrain from Chinese officials and economists was,

> We are so backward and need to know how to modernize, taking lessons from whatever sources are available. The economies of Taiwan and Korea have done so well; please tell us how those two systems have developed.

This is not an exact quotation but is a paraphrase of Chinese remarks in 1979 to a visiting delegation of economists sponsored by the US National Academy of Sciences, the American Council of Learned Societies and the Social Science Research Council.

Not only did Chinese economists show great admiration for the achievements of the Korean economy as early as 1979, but also many

11

economists at conferences around the world expressed similar thoughts. I frequently heard the comment, 'Why can't we be like Korea?' Such searching questions came from economists of other developing countries. At an earlier stage, similar questions were asked about comparisons with Japan.

An appropriate answer to such questions in the case of Korea would be, 'You, too, can develop economically as Korea has done, but you must first do the following things:

1 adopt a very powerful *work ethic*;
2 achieve a high degree of excellence in education, at all levels — primary, secondary and advanced;
3 provide good working opportunities for well-trained young people, encouraging them not to join the brain-drain group;
4 live sparingly for many years, saving a high fraction of income;
5 be moderate and fair in wage demands, especially in the early stages of expansion;
6 be good hosts to foreign enterprises who can supply advanced technology;
7 seek out world markets.'

Needless to say, there are few countries that are willing to put in the required effort; that is why Korean performance stands out so prominently, in terms of excellence, on the world economic landscape.

While Korean progress has been reasonably good in agriculture, commerce, construction and industry, it has lagged in one respect; namely, in the opening up and liberalizing of financial markets. Korea and Taiwan, too, do not measure up to the achievements of the other two dragons — Hong Kong and Singapore — in the development, to the high degree of sophistication, of stock markets, foreign exchange markets, banking (commercial, merchant and investment), commodity markets and other forms of financial activity. In Korea's case, the reform in financial markets has often been promised and suggested as being nearly ready, but postponements keep occurring. Now it appears to be ready to start, and this can open a fresh avenue of economic activity. If it is successful, as in Hong Kong and Singapore, it can be a significant earner of foreign exchange.

Another kind of new prospect lies on the economic horizon in the form of increasing trade relations with North Korea, leading eventually to the prospect of unification. Large-scale changes in this direction have not occurred, but they could lead to the creation of a formidable economic power in the Asia-Pacific area. Fortunately, Korea has had the spectacle of Eastern and Western

12

unification in Germany and can benefit from having watched the major economic mistakes that took place there. Undoubtedly, South Korea will proceed cautiously in unification with North Korea if the event ever does take place and will not rush into an economically unfavorable set of relationships such as befell West Germany in the form of inflation, tight money and disapproval from associated economic partner nations.

Korea and the US have long been active trading partners. Until 1991, Korea had been enjoying a string of bilateral merchandise surpluses with the US. The balance suddenly turned, however, and the US ran a merchandise surplus with Korea during 1991, 1992 and the early months of 1993, for which data are available. The balance is presently not very large, and Korea's exports to the US are comparable in size to Korea's imports from the US, both flows running near $18 billion annually. This makes the US approximately a 25 percent partner in trade with Korea. With Japan, Korea maintains a large bilateral deficit of $8 billion to $9 billion per year. On Korea's import side, Japan is a slightly larger partner than is the US, but on the export side Japan is a much smaller partner, at about two-thirds the level of the US.

Together, Japan and the US are by far the largest national trading partners of Korea, but Korean trade with East Asian developing countries, including the expanding China market, is becoming a very large trading area. Trade among the developing countries of the Asia-Pacific area is growing very rapidly, and during the first four months of 1993 this region accounted for 30.4 percent of Korea's total exports, surpassing the US share of Korea's exports at 23 percent. This change has most probably not yet run its course.

Thus it might be concluded that the US has recently become more competitive with Korea, while Korea has been competitive with East Asian developing countries on a growing scale. If Korea is to turn the present deficit on current account into surplus, they will probably do this in East Asian trade rather than in trade with the US.

While commercial trading relationships with the US are shifting, somewhat in favor of the US position, there is one relationship that may stay in place for a while. That is the defense relationship with the US. As part of the downsizing of the US defense establishment after the end of the Cold War, it was assumed that the US would give serious consideration to the reduction of our presence in the Pacific area. By force of circumstances, brought on by the Mount Pinatubo volcano and political shifts in the Philippines, the US gave up the bases at Subic Bay and Clark Air Field. Japan has been quite generous in sharing the cost of support of our forces there, and little change is in sight,

13

especially after the re-occurrence of political disturbances in Russia. Nuclear facilities with sophisticated rocketry remain in the hands of Russians and former states of the USSR with no firm commitments yet on their disposition.

It seemed, at one time, that there might be a force reduction in South Korea, but this is becoming more and more questionable, as North Korea indicates no major tendency towards reconciliation, especially on the issue of nuclear weapons development. For the time being, it appears that the presence of US forces in South Korea will remain at present strength. There is no serious disagreement about this in discussions of economic relationships between the two countries.

In this brief summary, I have stressed the leader-follower relationship between Japan and Korea on the path of economic development. Just as Japan achieved advanced nation status, essentially on entering the OECD as a member of 1964, Korea can look forward to advancement in economic status. Many economists are confident that Korea will be upgraded before long, possibly during this decade. The Republic of Korea has the best chance of being the second country to make this achievement.

2 The future of UK–Korea cooperation in the Asia–Pacific area

Woong Bae Rha

The rise of East Asian economies

For the last decade or so, East Asian economies have emerged as the main engines of worldwide economic growth. This has been propelled by broad-based rapid development in the area over the last 10 years. Japan has clearly emerged as one of the world's leading economic superpowers, rivaling both the United States and the European Community. China has quickly taken advantage of a seemingly endless supply of cheap labor as well as economies of scale. The extent of China's economic influence may become even greater in the future with the possible spill-over effect reaching economies in close proximity or where Chinese emigrants reside. The newly industrialized economies, which include Korea, Taiwan, Singapore and Hong Kong, have displayed tremendous growth potential and dynamism over the last decade, and this trend of high economic growth is expected to continue into the next decade. Smaller developing economies in Southeast Asia are also experiencing phenomenal economic growth, including Thailand, Malaysia and Indonesia, which are successfully implementing industrialization efforts and are expecting continued rapid growth in the near future.

Because of such remarkable growth, the status of the East Asia in the world economy has improved considerably. The 10 East Asian economies – that is, Japan, China, the NIEs and ASEAN countries – account for a share of the world's total GDP which has increased from 12.9 percent in 1980 to 23.2 percent in 1992 (see Table 2.1). In addition, their share of the world's total trade volume rose markedly from 13.3 percent in 1980 to 25.4 percent in 1992 (see Table 2.2). This noticeable improvement among the East Asian economies may suggest a shift in the global economy, as many have come to acknowledge that the center may be gravitating away from the Atlantic and moving toward the Pacific region. Some major factors that have contributed to this phenomenon have been Asia's abundance of cheap labor and the strength of the US market for Asian exports.

Table 2.1
Shares of US, EC, and East Asia in world GDP

(Amount in billion US $)

Year	World Amount	World Share (%)	US Amount	US Share (%)	EC Amount	EC Share (%)	East Asia* Amount	East Asia* Share (%)
1970	3,704	100	1,011	27.3	694	18.7	351	9.5
1980	12,846	100	2,708	21.1	3,128	24.3	1,662	12.9
1987	19,003	100	4,540	23.9	4,305	22.7	3,204	16.9
1992	21,639	100	5,920	27.4	6,853	31.7	5,023	23.2

* East Asia includes Japan, China, NIEs, and ASEAN (except Brunei) countries.
  Source: *Foreign Economic Statistics Annual,* Bank of Japan (for 1970, 1980, 1987 statistics), *Major Foreign Economic Statistics,* Economic Planning Board of Korea, 1994 (for 1992 statistics).

However, such changes that seem to favor the Asia-Pacific region have created a backlash on the part of the world's most powerful economic heavyweights, including the US and Europe. Both powers have reacted defensively to these shifts in the global economy, often citing the negative externalities associated with East Asian economic growth.

Over the past few years, however, East Asia's dependence on the US economy has, in fact, clearly declined. The share of East Asia's exports to the US out of the area's total exports declined to 23.9 percent in 1992 after peaking at 35.3 percent in 1986 (See Table 2.3). At the same time, the share of intra-regional exports out of total exports in East Asia increased. For example, the percentage of intra-regional exports among China, NIEs and ASEAN countries increased from 23 percent in 1980 to 37 percent in 1992. Meanwhile, US exports to East Asia increased so significantly that the area has become a very important trading partner for the US. The share of US exports to East Asia out of total US exports increased from 21.7 percent in 1982 to 26.3 percent in 1992 (see Table 2.4). As a result of this clearly expansionary trend of US exports across the Pacific, smooth economic relations between the two areas have gained increasingly vital importance. In other words, neither side, especially the US, should jeopardize the bright future of both regions.

16

Table 2.2
Shares of US, EC and East Asia in world trade volume

(Amount in billion US $)

Year	World Amount	World Share (%)	US Amount	US Share (%)	EC Amount	EC Share (%)	East Asia* Amount	East Asia* Share (%)
1970	579.1	100	85.3	14.7	225.1	38.9	59.2	10.2
1971	646.7	100	93.3	14.4	254.3	39.3	70.1	10.8
1972	763.6	100	108.2	14.2	301.9	39.5	81.7	10.7
1973	1,058.1	100	144.0	13.6	416.0	39.3	124.1	11.7
1974	1,549.5	100	203.3	13.1	561.3	36.2	185.9	12.0
1975	1,605.6	100	208.1	13.0	582.9	36.3	185.3	11.5
1976	1,846.9	100	239.7	13.0	657.0	35.6	218.6	11.8
1977	2,114.6	100	274.3	13.0	750.6	35.5	256.5	12.1
1978	2,449.2	100	322.8	13.2	902.4	36.8	312.6	12.8
1979	3,094.1	100	401.4	13.0	1,155.3	37.3	395.5	12.8
1980	3,794.7	100	478.9	12.6	1,351.7	35.6	505.0	13.3
1981	3,739.5	100	504.1	13.5	1,228.5	32.9	539.6	14.4
1982	3,513.6	100	454.9	12.9	1,272.5	36.2	559.4	15.9
1983	3,419.8	100	470.4	13.8	1,226.9	35.9	571.8	16.7
1984	3,636.3	100	547.2	15.0	1,252.0	34.4	639.0	17.6
1985	3,701.8	100	554.8	15.0	1,308.3	35.3	658.6	17.8
1986	4,048.1	100	585.9	14.5	1,577.2	39.0	712.4	17.6
1987	4,772.4	100	662.2	13.9	1,914.4	40.1	865.9	18.1
1988	5,461.7	100	759.0	13.9	2,144.1	39.3	1,065.5	19.5
1989	5,910.6	100	827.9	14.0	2,302.0	38.9	1,174.3	19.9
1990	6,766.2	100	895.1	13.2	2,787.1	41.2	1,306.2	19.3
1991	7,019.5	100	929.8	13.2	2,827.2	40.3	1,473.1	21.0
1992	7,533.1	100	1,000.9	13.3	2,968.8	39.4	1,915.3	25.4

* East Asia includes Japan, China, NIEs, and ASEAN (except Brunei) countries.
  But Taiwan's trade volume is not included for 1970-1981 statistics.
  Source: Direction of Trade Statistics, IMF.

US trade policy

Despite the potential for rapid joint East-West economic development, the US and Europe seem to feel threatened by the growing importance of the East Asian economy, blaming high domestic unemployment rates on the rising market penetration by exports from East Asia. As a result, a tendency towards a protectionist stance has evolved in North America and Europe. The advent of organizations such as the European Union and NAFTA can be viewed as a direct result of such tendencies. While the world economy is rapidly moving towards further globalization, the US and the EU seem to be headed in the opposite direction, using a protectionist approach as the temporary cure-all to internal economic problems.

For example, at the end of the Uruguay Round negotiations, the US and the EU adamantly supported the Blue Round as a measure intended to check East Asia's abundance of labor. While such measures are clearly attempts at self-protection, they are neither beneficial to the US, the EU or the overall world economy. In fact, it is in the US's best interests to steadily improve economic relations with East Asia.

Nonetheless, the US also shows signs that it is beginning to realize the importance of the East Asian region. For example, US Under-Secretary of Commerce Jeffrey Garten recently stated that the US has a strong interest in Big Emerging Markets (BEMs) in the world economy, which include 10 developing countries: China, Indonesia, South Korea, India, Turkey, South Africa, Poland, Argentina, Brazil and Mexico. It is estimated that three-fourths of the world's growth in global trade over the next two decades is likely to take place in developing nations, mostly in BEMs. In particular, BEMs are likely to double their share of world GDP in the next two decades from today's 10 percent to 20 percent. Since almost half of the BEMs are Asia-Pacific countries, the best option for the US may be to utilize APEC. By taking a more active role in the strengthening of APEC, the US could effectively move in a positive direction toward improved US-East Asian economic cooperation.

The Clinton Administration's new trade policy has become a focal point of contention for developing countries. Globally, the US has made completing and implementing the Uruguay Round of negotiations an important objective, placing emphasis on new trade issues, environmental protectionism, labor issues as addressed in the Blue Round and a new competition policy. Concentration on such issues puts late developing countries with considerably fewer resources at a disadvantage. Bilaterally, or rather unilaterally, the US has revived Super 301. In other words, the US has taken a protectionist stance in its efforts to increase US exports of goods and services to overseas markets in order to boost its domestic economy.

Such an approach may help the US to improve internal economic conditions in the short run, but with major offsetting long-term consequences. The US justifies such blatant protectionism under the guise of free-trade principles,

18

arguing that it will eventually help the developing nations. While economic theory supports such a view, in reality there is more to international relations than pure economic gains. In fact, if the current US trade policy continues with strong trade pressure on global trading partners, it will degrade friendly relations with many countries – an unwanted result at a time when the US must rely on global relationships in executing important post-Cold War policy objectives.

The Korea-US relationship in the past

The US and Korea have had strong bilateral ties for the past 40 years. Historically, the US and Korea have been military allies in a relationship that has progressed considerably since the Korean War. The US has contributed significantly to the growth of the Korean economy by investing capital in Korea and by providing an extensive market for Korean exports. At the same time, the US has contributed to the progress of democracy in Korea.

In 1964, the per capita income of Korea was $103. Gross national product was $2.9 billion, and total exports stood at a mere $120 million. In 1994, Korea is expected to reach a per capita income of $8,196, a GNP of $364.3 billion, and total exports valued at $91.5 billion.

From being one of the poorest countries in the world, Korea has grown into an important industrialized country in one generation, ranking 13th in the world in trade volume, 12th in GNP, and 37th in per capita income. At the same time, Korea has become one of the world's major producers of automobiles, semiconductors, electronics, steel, and other manufactured goods. And what is particularly remarkable is that all of this was achieved despite the heart-breaking reality of the peninsula's territorial division, which has created tension and a confrontational atmosphere between South and North Korea.

The great economic success Korea has achieved during the past 30 years is indeed the fruit of strenuous efforts exerted by the Korean people, but it would have been impossible without US direct assistance and support.

When the Korean War broke out in 1950, the US provided military support which secured South Korea's existence and in the postwar era provided critical economic support and assistance. Furthermore, the US provided Korea with an important market for exports. At the same time, by providing educational opportunities to Korean youths, the US helped Korea to create a highly trained workforce, now a key factor in all sectors of society. In these ways, the US has greatly contributed to the economic success of Korea.

The current state of Korea-US relations

As Korea began to experience trade surpluses in the 1980s, however, trade friction developed between the US and Korea. By trying to resolve the problems through open dialogue, the two governments have been making efforts to reduce trade friction, to maintain an even balance of trade and to sustain economic cooperation between the two countries.

For example, the Dialogue for Economic Cooperation (DEC), launched by the two nations' presidents in July of 1993, was the product of the realization on the part of both sides that the issue-by-issue approach to trade in the past had not been conducive to the bilateral expansion of trade, investment and the transfer of technologies. As a result of DEC, noticeable progress has been made in various areas, including investment, competition policy and administrative procedures. The remaining areas, as well as recently emerging issues, will be further discussed in the near future to realize the full potential for economic cooperation. Consequently, the DEC has helped to enable the two governments to undergo deregulation and liberalization of their economies on a more equal footing, and with minimal strain on Korea-US economic relations. The DEC economic conciliatory framework is a model of how cooperative, bilateral efforts can work to advance the interests of both countries.

Korea's exports to the US, however, have decreased from a peak of $21.4 billion in 1988, to $18.0 billion in 1992. The major reason for this trend is, of course, the rapid increase of wages in Korea which, in turn, has resulted in a substantial loss of the US market share to other developing economies like China and Malaysia. For example, as Korea's exports to the US dropped, China's exports to the US rose significantly from $8.5 billion in 1988 to $31.5 billion in 1993. In addition, direct investment from the United States to Korea is certainly less active than before.

In other words, while the trade imbalance between the US and Korea has improved over the last five to six years, this improvement was achieved not through trade expansion, but through trade reduction. Both governments and the private sectors of the US and Korea share the belief that, to reverse this undesirable trend, it is of utmost importance to eliminate the hindering factors between the two countries, and to provide a new set of opportunities to revitalize economic cooperation for abiding mutual interests.

For Korea's part, the government under President Kim Young Sam has developed an extensive new economic policy under the Five-Year Plan for the New Economy that will help carry Korea into the 21st century on the back of internationalization and liberalization.

The new policy has been created to deregulate the economy in all sectors, particularly the financial sector. It also aims to improve the investment climate, especially for foreign investors. In general terms, the basic areas for economic reform range from fiscal reform, financial sector reform and the deregulation of administrative controls, to the development of a new pattern of economic behavior. The fundamental purpose of the Five-Year Plan for the New Economy is to provide strong work incentives and to distribute the burdens and benefits of economic development evenly, as well as to pursue economic development and democracy through voluntary participation and creative initiatives. To this end, the Kim Administration is in the process of implementing institutional reforms that will establish a new pattern of economic behavior. The reform effort has been geared toward securing Korea's economic growth potential through various liberalization measures, expanding foreign markets, strengthening internationalization and improving the nation's standard of living.

Future Korea-US economic cooperation

The future of US-Korean relations is a serious issue that must be given prudent consideration. Korea offers enormous potential as an important US partner in East Asian economic cooperation as both a platform for investment throughout Asia and a market for goods and services. That both countries have traditionally been strong allies is one important factor. Another is that potential for economic development and growth within Korea remains very promising.

With the ongoing economic reform measures, including the liberalization policy, the Korean economy shows strong growth potential and offers great opportunities for US businesses. Korea and the US can cooperate and produce goods more efficiently and export them to other Asian countries. Korea can provide high-quality labor, experience in economic development and marketing skills. The US can provide technology, financial resources and management know-how. By cooperating together in industrial activities, both countries can greatly benefit from such an alliance.

Korea's proximity to China, the up-and-coming economic powerhouse in

Asia and in the world, is another characteristic which will be helpful to the US in the future, especially once China and Japan vie for leadership in East Asia. By establishing close ties, the US and Korea together can keep China and Japan in check, with Korea acting as a buffer zone between the two Asian giants. Together, the US and Korea may also have the strength to penetrate the Japanese market and even capture a significant share of the ever-growing Chinese market, as well as participate in the joint development of Siberia, which is one of the most resource-rich regions in the world.

Such cooperation between the US and Korea can facilitate economic prosperity and help to maintain security and peace throughout Asia. Equally important, US-Korean cooperation should evolve into a much broader relationship to include political, security and military cooperation, among other things. Through closer ties and cooperation with Korea, the role of the US in East Asia can only be strengthened. Without such an advantageous relationship with Korea, the US may find efforts to remain a global superpower thwarted.

At this moment, the North Korea nuclear issue is perhaps the most pressing and important issue in the East Asian region. Ultimately, the US seeks denuclearization of the Korean peninsula. To resolve this dilemma, extremely close cooperation between the US and Korea is necessary. Once North Korea gives up the nuclear weapons development program in dispute and opens itself up to the rest of the world, economic cooperation between South Korea and North Korea can improve and accelerate, and peace and prosperity in this region can be secured. Korea and the US should therefore cooperate closely with the United Nations in order to bring North Korea out into the international arena.

The foregoing analysis underscores the vital importance of bridging East and West, particularly East Asia and the United States on economic, political and security levels. Into the 21st century and beyond, the United States will unquestionably be the world's leading economic and military power and, as such, it ought to play the most important role in further advancing the world economy. It is of utmost importance, however, that the US recognizes the growth potential and dynamism of the East Asian region. A close relationship with this region will prove to be indispensable in the near future for the United States.

Therefore, the US ought to lead this region towards lasting progress. In this context, Korean-US cooperation in particular will play the most important role in the ability of the US to achieve success in this area. With continuing emphasis on internationalization and liberalization and through the institutionalization of economic reforms, Korea for its part ought to seek domestic development as well as global progress for the benefit of all nations.

Table 2.3
Trend of East Asia's export dependency on US[*]
(Amount in billion US $)

Year	Total export volume		Export volume with US	
	Amount	Share(%)	Amount	Share(%)
1970	29.9	100	9.4	31.4
1971	38.7	100	11.4	29.5
1972	43.7	100	14.6	33.3
1973	61.9	100	17.1	27.6
1974	91.2	100	23.5	25.8
1975	93.7	100	22.7	24.3
1976	114.0	100	28.7	25.2
1977	138.0	100	34.4	24.9
1978	168.7	100	43.1	25.6
1979	202.3	100	47.5	23.5
1980	256.1	100	56.6	22.1
1981	284.3	100	67.2	23.7
1982	297.1	100	75.6	25.4
1983	308.5	100	86.7	28.1
1984	357.2	100	115.6	32.4
1985	375.6	100	129.7	34.5
1986	425.1	100	150.0	35.3
1987	509.7	100	168.4	33.0
1988	606.8	100	182.5	30.1
1989	657.7	100	192.3	29.2
1990	717.5	100	191.0	26.6
1991	813.4	100	199.3	24.5
1992	912.5	100	217.7	23.9

* East Asia includes Japan, China, NIEs and ASEAN (except Brunei) countries. Taiwan's trade volume is, however, omitted for 1970-1981 statistics.
Source: Direction of Trade Statistics, IMF.

Table 2.4 US trade patterns with the EC, East Asia and Korea

Year	EXPORT Total import	EC Amt	EC Share (%)	East Asia* Amt	East Asia* Share (%)	Korea Amt	Korea Share (%)	IMPORT Total import	EC Amt	EC Share (%)	East Asia* Amt	East Asia* Share (%)	Korea Amt	Korea Share (%)
1970	43.2	11.3	26.2	7.3	16.9	0.6	1.4	42.5	9.2	21.6	9.4	22.1	0.4	0.9
1971	44.1	11.1	25.2	6.8	15.4	0.7	1.6	48.4	10.4	21.5	11.4	23.5	0.5	1.0
1972	49.8	11.9	23.9	8.2	16.4	0.7	1.4	58.9	13.2	22.4	14.6	24.8	0.8	1.4
1973	71.3	16.7	23.4	13.5	18.9	1.2	1.7	73.6	16.5	22.4	17.1	23.2	1.0	1.4
1974	98.5	22.1	22.4	17.5	17.8	1.5	1.5	108.0	20.5	19.0	23.5	21.8	1.6	1.5
1975	107.7	22.9	21.3	17.2	16.0	1.8	1.7	103.4	17.8	17.2	22.7	22.0	1.6	1.5
1976	115.4	25.4	22.0	17.1	14.8	2.0	1.7	132.5	19.1	14.4	28.7	21.7	2.6	2.0
1977	121.3	27.1	22.3	18.2	15.0	2.4	2.0	160.4	23.7	14.8	34.4	21.4	3.2	2.0
1978	143.8	32.1	22.3	23.1	16.1	3.2	2.2	186.1	31.0	16.7	43.1	23.2	4.1	2.2
1979	182.0	43.5	23.9	32.4	17.8	4.2	2.3	222.3	35.8	16.1	47.5	21.4	4.3	1.9
1980	220.8	54.6	24.7	41.1	18.6	4.7	2.1	257.0	38.3	14.9	56.6	22.0	4.4	1.7
1981	233.7	52.4	22.4	42.0	18.0	5.1	2.2	273.4	43.7	16.0	67.2	24.6	5.5	2.0
1982	212.3	52.4	24.7	46.0	21.7	5.5	2.6	254.9	46.4	18.2	75.6	29.7	6.0	2.4
1983	200.5	48.4	24.1	47.0	23.4	5.9	2.9	269.9	47.9	17.7	86.7	32.1	7.7	2.9
1984	217.9	50.5	23.2	50.3	23.1	6.0	2.8	341.2	63.4	18.6	115.6	33.9	10.0	2.9
1985	213.1	49.0	23.0	48.0	22.5	6.0	2.8	361.6	71.6	19.8	129.7	35.9	10.7	3.0
1986	217.3	53.2	24.5	53.3	24.5	6.4	2.9	387.1	79.5	20.5	150.0	38.8	13.5	3.5
1987	252.9	60.6	24.0	61.1	24.2	8.1	3.2	424.1	84.9	20.0	168.4	39.7	18.0	4.2
1988	319.4	75.9	23.8	84.3	26.4	11.3	3.5	459.8	88.7	19.3	182.5	39.7	21.2	4.6
1989	363.8	86.6	23.8	97.5	26.8	13.5	3.7	493.3	88.8	18.0	192.3	39.0	20.5	4.2
1990	393.1	98.0	24.9	105.0	26.7	14.4	3.7	517.0	95.5	18.5	191.0	36.9	19.3	3.7
1991	421.8	103.1	24.4	111.9	26.5	15.5	3.7	509.3	89.4	17.6	199.3	39.1	17.7	3.5
1992	447.4	102.9	23.0	117.7	26.3	14.6	3.3	552.6	97.1	17.6	217.7	39.4	17.4	3.1

* East Asia includes Japan, China, NIEs and ASEAN (except Brunei) countries. But Taiwan's trade volume is not included for 1970-1981 statistics.
Source: *Direction of Trade Statistics*, IMF.

3 New policy directions for the US–Korea economic partnership

Peter Cashman

President Clinton's visit to Seoul in 1993 and the announcement of the 'Dialogue for Economic Cooperation' (DEC) provided a useful starting point for the discussion of new policy directions for the US-Korea partnership. The DEC replaced the 'President's Economic Initiative' as one of the principal fora for the discussion of economic and trade issues of mutual concern and the expansion of bilateral economic cooperation. This chapter will focus on what the United States expects to achieve through the DEC and other objectives of US trade policy towards Korea over the next few years.

Korea's place in US trade relations with Asia

It has become increasingly clear that the Clinton Administration has placed Asia at the top of its trade policy agenda – and for good reason. In 1992, countries in the East Asia-Pacific region imported $128 billion in goods from the US, accounting for a little less than one third of total US exports. The value of US exports to Asia has long passed Europe, and the gap grows wider every year. Some estimate that Pacific trade will double Atlantic trade by the year 2000. Asia is also rapidly becoming an important source of capital for the US.

In a speech given in Tokyo during the G-7 Summit, President Clinton articulated his vision for a 'new Pacific Community.' The new Pacific Community rests on the principles of open markets, more open and regional economies, supporting democracy, and reaffirmation of America's military presence in Asia. One of the key organizations which will be used to advance this vision is the Asia Pacific Economic Cooperation, or APEC. The President's participation in the APEC Ministerial Meeting in Seattle made him the first US President to attend an APEC event since the organization's establishment in 1989.

The Clinton Administration's approach to trade policy has much in common with previous administrations. That is, it has a determination to use the tools provided in US law to ensure market access and free and fair treatment for US goods and services aroad. However, unlike previous administrations, trade policy has taken center stage and, according to the President, 'will be fully integrated into domestic and foreign policy.'

Korea has and continues to attract significant attention in the formulation and implementation of US trade policy — both in the US Congress and the Executive Branch. Korea is currently the US's eighth largest trading partner, with overall trade in 1992 reaching $31.3 billion. US business has achieved some notable successes in the Korean market, particularly in areas such as cosmetics and electronics, agricultural products, computers, chemicals, pharmaceutical and medical equipment. Yet, despite significant steps to improve market access and the elimination of a number of import and investment restrictions, the market is not completely open and can still be quite difficult to penetrate. In fact, many US businesses continue to list Korea as one of the world's most difficult countries in which to do business.

President's Economic Initiative

For most of the last eight years or so, the US government has used a dual approach toward liberalizing the Korean market. It has attempted to upgrade and expand international trade disciplines through the Uruguay Round, integrating multilateral discussions wIth Korea into that process. Of more immediate impact, though, has been the bilateral approach, using negotiations and the threat of retaliation under US trade law. This approach has brought positive results. Using the Super 301, Special 301 and other provisions of US trade law, the US concluded a series of market-opening agreements with Korea over the period of 1986 through 1991, including agreements on insurance, agriculture, standards, telecommunications, wine, beef, cigarettes and motion pictures.

But by 1992 the bilateral relationship with Korea had advanced to such a stage that a solely confrontational approach was no longer appropriate. A new, or modified, approach was necessary to address the many secondary barriers which continued to restrict full market access for US firms. This new approach took the form of the Presidents' Economic Initiative (PEI), which

26

was announced in January 1992 by former Presidents Bush and Roh.

The PEI was based on the principle of cooperation rather than confrontation. The initiative addressed the trade concerns of both countreis, rather than just the US. Unlike previous initiatives, the final agreements contained non-binding recommendations, rather than legal commitments.

Four areas were covered by the PEI: customs, standards, investment and technology. Agreements were reached in each area in September 1992 that in the long run we believe will improve commercial relations. These improvements include: a reduction in the amount of time and paperwork needed to clear import; the establishment of more open, transparent and non-discriminatory standards-making procedures; stronger channels for commercial cooperation and the exchange of information on technology; and liberalization of Korea's investment climate.

Implementation of the PEI recommendations began immediately and will continue over the next few years. Preliminary indications show that the PEI has already had a positive effect on our commercial relations. One US firm took advantage of a new Korean regulation to save millions of dollars by importing used machinery and equipment for a new investment. Other US firms, encouraged by improvements made by the Korean government, are looking at entering the Korean market for the first time.

The Dialogue for Economic Cooperation

Now that the PEI is over, the US and Korea are looking at ways to build on the success of that initiative. The PEI showed for the first time that our two governments can work cooperatively in resolving trade issues, rather than having to resort to US trade law to force Korea to open its markets. The PEI also showed the usefulness of a broader, systemic level approach to our trade relations, rather than an approach that is solely focused on resolving company-specific trade disputes.

Over the past few months, we have held discussions about a new bilateral initiative to succeed the PEI. The objective of this new initiative would be to continue to strengthen the US-Korea economic partnership through economic deregulation and the enhancement of bilateral economic cooperation. During the Economic Subcabinet Consultations held on June 24, 1993, in Seoul, our governments agreed on a name for the initiative, the 'Dialogue for Economic Cooperation' or DEC, and began formal preparations for negotiations. The

DEC was then announced and endorsed by Presidents Clinton and Kim during the US-Korea summit meeting on July 11. During the closing press conference, President Clinton expressed his hope that the new initiative would 'resolve outstanding trade issues and build an even stronger economic cooperation' between the US and Korea.

The DEC has provided an umbrella framework under which the US and Korea hold discussions on economic deregulation. The discussions have addressed a variety of different areas such as trade, investment, technology, finance, distribution, agriculture, standards and administration. The umbrella group has reviewed progress on these areas and developed recommendations, where appropriate, to improve deregulation efforts. The group has also been charged with developing recommendations and possibly agreements for strengthening economic cooperation. The initiative is chaired on the US side by the Assistant Secretary of State for Economic and Business Affairs and on the Korean side by the Assistant Minister of Foreign Affairs. USTR and Commerce also participate, as well as other Korean ministries.

Kim Young Sam administration

With the commitment of the two administrations in the US and Korea, we expect to see significant progress in US-Korea trade over the next few years. President Kim has made strong appointments in key economic positions, with Kim Ch'ul-su at MOTIE, Hong Jae Hyong as Minister of Finance, and former trade minister Han Seung-Soo as ambassador to the US.

We are also encouraged by the strong public commitment President Kim has made to economic deregulation and reform, a commitment that has already been backed up by government action. In May 1993, Korea announced its Financial Liberalization Plan and the President's 100-Day Plan for Economic Reform. More recently, on June 22, the Ministry of Finance released a five-year investment liberalization plan. President Kim's five-year Economic Reform Plan is expected to be announced shortly, as well as several changes to trade regulations.

The US response so far to the new administration has been very supportive. We hope to work closely with Korea on its financial and economic reforms through the Dialogue for Economic Cooperation. But while these are all positive signs, I would emphasize that there has not yet been any evidence of actual change. Most of Korea's planned reforms in the key areas of trade, finance and investment are not scheduled until 1996 and 1997. Given the difficulties many US firms still face doing business in Korea, this may not be soon enough.

Some economies in the Asia-Pacific region, are far ahead of Korea in market liberalization. Others — such as Indonesia, Thailand and Malaysia — though perhaps still behind Korea, are liberalizing much more rapidly. If Korea does not move more quickly to open its markets to foreign firms, it is in danger of losing a great deal of business to these economies. In fact, the statistics cited above on disinvestment from Korea support this assessment.

So although Korea is undoubtedly headed in the right direction, there is a lot of work to be done. And it must be done while Korea's economy is still strong and while its markets are still attractive to foreign business. Indeed, Korea is ultimately the greatest beneficiary of an open, internationalized economy. More growth in trade and investment means more jobs for Koreans and continued economic growth. It means competitively stronger Korean industries, at home and abroad. It also means lower prices and higher quality products for Korean consumers.

We believe that many of the changes initiated by the US regarding Korea in the Presidents' Economic Initiative and other ongoing negotiations will help Korea along the road of reform, while continuing to strengthen US-Korea commercial relations.

Conclusion

While the overall aim of the DEC and other initiatives with Korea is to strengthen our economic partnership, it is important to remember that the Clinton Administration's trade policy also sets parameters for this cooperation. Where Korea is concerned, this will mean that the US government must ensure that past trade commitments are being adhered to and that progress is being made in key problem areas, even as we continue to move forward into new areas of opportunity.

4 Economic regionalism and US trade negotiation strategies

Myung-Gun Choo

The move toward economic regionalism

In the post-World War II area, the United States assumed the role of generous benefactor to the rest of the world. However, burdened with chronic deficits, its trade policies have become more protective since the 1980s. Initially, countries that enjoyed surpluses in trade with the US willingly opened up their markets. Unfortunately for the US government, the markets were not opening up fast enough. And, as the US constantly demanded its trading partners to liberalize imports with pressures of retaliatory measures, it brought the resentment of these countries, and thus, trade policies have evolved into sensitive political issues.

For half a century following the end of World War II, the world economy operated on the three principles of the Bretton Woods Treaty. The first principle stated that each country is responsible to take care of its deficit with loans from the IMF and the World Bank. Today, however, the US is saying that countries enjoying trade surpluses must share the burden. The second principle called for liberalization based upon nondiscrimination between domestic and foreign enterprises. This policy of equal treatment for domestic and foreign entities has also been replaced by the principle of reciprocity. The last principle dictated a multilateral approach in coordinating trade: rather than focusing on the balance in bilateral trade, efforts to solve problems in trade were to be multilateral, based on the overall balance. But this also gave way to more narrowly defined channels of bilateral negotiations between individual countries. Hence, the ideals of Bretton Woods were abandoned, and protectionist and reciprocal trade frictions continued to spread.

Since 1985 when the US began to enforce Section 301 of its trade law, market opening was accelerated but trade frictions intensified. In response to mounting pressure from the US, Asian markets were made more accessible, but the benefits from this move were enjoyed mostly by Japan and China. For the US, the opening of the Asian markets have only helped to increase the deficit in its trade with Japan, and have not resulted in any real profit. Riding on the US's drive to open up foreign markets, Japan was able to increase its share of the Asian market. Furthermore, using Southeast Asia as an export outpost, Japan strengthened its hold on the US market. Therefore, the US cannot hope to improve its balance of trade by trying to open foreign markets through bilateral negotiations, a move that has only helped to intensify conflicts with its trading partners. Particularly, with Japan no longer feeling that it must heed the demands of the US since the collapse of the Soviet Union, the US must seriously rethink its basic strategies in trade.

In 1992, the countries of the EC converged to create a more formidable economic bloc with a population of 340 million and a combined GNP of $6.3 trillion. Japan has come to surpass the US in international competitiveness in virtually all areas of trade. Under these circumstances, the US needed a radical measure that would help cuts its burgeoning trade and budget deficits. Thus, the US signed free trade agreements with Canada in 1989 and with Mexico in 1992. The resulting North America Free Trade Agreement is another economic bloc, with a population of 340 million and a combined GNP of $6.4 trillion, accounting for 35 percent of the world's GNP and 18 percent of its trade. But several factors work to undermine the advantages of this union for the US. First, Canada and Mexico are much smaller than the US in terms of economic size and thus lessen the integration effect. Second, imports between the three neighbors only account for 33 percent of the three-nation total. Third, 70 percent and 40 percent of Canada's and Mexico's trade, respectively, are already free of tariffs. Thus trade increases derived from additional tariff reduction will be negligible. Finally, Canada and Mexico rely on the US for 76.1 percent and 70.8 percent, respectively, of their total exports. Therefore, benefits of forming the NAFTA would be limited at best.

The negative consequences, on the other hand, are possibly many. If ratified, NAFTA would instigate regionalism and protectionist sentiments around the globe. The EC poses no new problem to the rest of the world since already 70 percent of its trade is internal and it has long enjoyed special privileges of regional economic integration in breach of the GATT. In fact since the Mexican government began to pursue an open-door policy in 1987, the EC has invested heavily in Mexico to secure a manufacturing base for exports to the North American market. However, for the countries that are neither part of NAFTA nor the EC, the pressure is mounting to form their own regional economic union. The countries of Latin America and Asia, in particular, have emerged as a new variable in world trade. Since Mexico is already trying to lower its economic dependency on the US, and since the US seems to be aiming ultimately at the establishment of a pan-American free-trade zone, NAFTA does not appear all that threatening to the Latin American countries. However, it would deal a fatal blow to the Asian countries that depend heavily on the US for their exports and are in a competitive relationship with Mexico. In the end, this would only help to intensify inter-regional frictions, perhaps even escalating them into ethnic confrontations.

The rationale for WORFTA (World Free Trade Agreement)

The global move toward regional trading blocs has fundamentally altered the basic framework of the world economy, making it impractical for the US to hope to solve the problem of its trade deficit through bilateral talks with its trading partners. Yet, the US is hesitant about aggressively pushing for a worldwide FTA, in fear of losing its leadership role to Japan. Meanwhile, nations around the world are seeking their own regional economic integration as a countermove against NAFTA and the EC. Malaysia, under Japanese guidance, has proposed the formation of an East Asian Economic Group (EAEG) that would encompass a population of 530 million and a combined GNP of $3.6 trillion. Since 41.9 percent of the export accounts in the region is already settled in Japanese yen, the EAEG proposal risks further subordinating the region to Japan, and could even incite divisive sentiments along ethnic lines. Yet, it is understandable for the US to be wary about proposing a global free trade agreement without any guarantee that Japan would open up its market. Therefore to establish a harmonious world economic order and maximize the benefits of economic union, it is desirable to gradually expand NAFTA into a World Free Trade Agreement, starting with the countries that are more willing to enter into the negotiations. In particular, South Korea, Taiwan, Australia and New Zealand are greatly dependent on the US for their exports and are mutually complementary with the US in their industrial structures. Therefore, creating WORFTA including these countries would be relatively smooth and convenient, and the benefits of the move would be immediate. As Table 4.1 clearly shows, the expansion from NAFTA to WORFTA, as outlined above, would boost intra-regional dependency on trade, expand the market size, and strengthen the negotiating power of the member countries vis-a-vis non-members. On this basis, the organization would be able to rally other countries that espouse open trade,

Table 4.1
WORFTA's economic power and degree of dependency on trade with US

(Amount in billions US $)

	Population (millions)	Fixed GNP	Gross export	Export to US	% of export to US	Gross imports	Imports from US	% of imports from US
US	250	5465	393			516		
Canada	26	528	131	95	72.5	121	75	61.9
Mexico	86	200	27	21	77.7	29	15	51.7
S. Korea	43	237	64	19	29.6	69	15	21.7
Taiwan	20	161	67	21	31.3	54	12	22.2
Australia	17	294	39	4	10.2	38	9	23.6
New Zealand	3	38	9	1	11.1	9	1	11.1
Subtotal	440	6928	730	161	47.8	836	127	39.7
Japan	124	2961	287	91	31.7	235	52	22.1
ASEAN	319	272	140	28	19.7	159	23	14.7
Total	888	10161	1157	280	36.6	1230	202	28.8

** The population and GNP figures for Canada are from 1989. The population figure for Taiwan is from 1989.
** The GNP figures for Australia and New Zealand are from 1989.
Source: IFS Yearbook (1991), DOT Yearbook (1991), IMF.

including those belonging to APEC, and to promote economic integration on a global scale.

Furthermore, as Table 4.2 shows, the industrial structures and trade patterns of these countries are complementary with the US. Their union would encourage other countries of the region to increase their trade dependency on one another, and thus heighten the effects of economic union. A free-trade agreement works best when there is an economic complementarily among the members. And thus the proposal for WORFTA was made to include the above-mentioned four countries as a starting point and by no means to limit it to a certain geographical region. Due to technological advances in transportation, the entire world, in all practicality, is in a one-day travel zone and because of relatively cheap transportation costs, the geographical distance factor is now almost negligible in trade. Therefore, since the ultimate goal is to create one global free-trade zone in gradual stages by encompassing countries that support the idea of WORFTA, no country should reject it or feel threatened by it.

International competitiveness is acquired when the domestic industrial structure is compatible with the manufacturing conditions, when businesses are able to produce quality goods at a fair price and when the workers are diligent. If one of these elements is missing, it is easy to fall behind in the increasingly fierce competition of the global arena. The difficulty arises as manufacturing conditions constantly change due to economic development, technological progress and rising income levels. Therefore, a country with a cheap labor force would start out by exporting labor-intensive products at a low price. With an increase in exports comes an improvement in income and higher labor costs, and the country starts to lose its competitive edge. At that point it must make the transition from a labor-intensive industrial structure to a technology- and capital-intensive one, or else its competitiveness in the international market would evaporate.

Also, countries with similar levels of capital accumulation would behave in different ways depending on their population density, natural resources, level of technology and corporate culture. Because it responded wisely and promptly to the fast-changing external and internal conditions, Japan was able to enhance its competitiveness in the global scene. But this is also a temporary situation, which could rapidly deteriorate if it does not adapt well to the constantly changing international climate and manufacturing conditions. Since it is virtually impossible for one country to keep up with this process indefinitely, the rise and fall of powerful nations is an inevitable phenomenon that has been repeated throughout history. At one time the US accounted for more than half of the global industrial output, and as the world's largest foreign-currencies holder, it was able to lend generous support to the postwar world economy. Now, 40 years later and following the collapse of the Soviet Union, the US can lay clam to being the only superpower. Its industries are now, however, as internationally competitive as they once were, and against a Japan that is no longer afraid of the Soviet threat, the US is seeing its negotiating power weakened considerably.

The prolonged rule of Japan's Liberal Democratic Party base on give-and-take compromises among the different factions, provided the country with political stability at least until the current turmoil triggered by the parliamentary vote of non-confidence in Prime Minister Kiichi Miyazawa. Active government support and guidance of the industries through MATTE, the voracious entrepreneurial spirit of the businessmen and the national aspiration to turn the war-defeated nation into an export-oriented economic superpower enable Japan to pour all its resources into strengthening its international competitiveness. Also, by strategically phasing out declining industries and aggressively supporting those that were more promising exportwise, Japan swiftly revamped its entire industrial structure. As a result, Japan has become the world's largest creditor nation. But by continuously dragging its feet on opening up its market, it is frequently frowned on by the international community. Although Japan may adhere to GATT regulations on the surface, while discouraging imports through government guidance and various non-tariff barriers, in reality, it seems that nothing can be done. In fact, the individual countries that protest against Japan's unfair trade practices are the ones that, in the end, suffer most from its retaliation. WORFTA would help overcome this problem by strengthening the negotiating powers vis-a-vis Japan and improving international competitiveness through market expansion.

Regarding the economy, the key issue is not the distance but the time and cost of the transport. Thus, practical economic ties, not geographic proximity, is the basis of an effective union. The US and East Asia already enjoy a close partnership and are highly dependent on each other. The amount of US trade in the Pacific region is already 150 percent of that in the Atlantic, and when considering population size and growth rate, the difference in trade volume is likely to grow. By pushing ahead with NAFTA and slighting its partners in the Pacific, the US weakens the potential for economic progress, and economic union might degenerate into a lightning rod for ethnic confrontation. It could propel the emergence of a 'yen bloc' and ultimately create an international climate more beneficial to Japan.

Table 4.2
Breakdown of US trade

Unit %

Country	Exports	Imports
Canada	21.1	18.1
Mexico	7.2	6
S. Korea	3.7	3.7
Taiwan	3	4.6
Australia	2.2	1
New Zealand	0.3	0.3
Subtotal	37.5	33.7
Japan	12.3	18
ASEAN	4.8	5.5
Total	54.6	57.2

Source: DOT Yearbook (1991), IMF.

The strategic value of WORFTA

WORFTA has several advantages over NAFTA. First, among the three countries in NAFTA, only Canada enjoys a trade surplus with Japan and most of the countries in WORFTA suffer deficits in their trade with Japan. Accordingly, WORFTA would make it possible to replace a considerable portion of their existing imports from Japan with intraregional imports, thereby strengthening their negotiating powers vis-a-vis Japan. As Table 4.3 shows, Japan relies on the countries in WORFTA for 48.2 percent of its exports. This is 17 percent higher than the US alone, thus strengthening the bargaining leverage. In particular, for its 10 largest export items, its dependency on this region reaches above 50 percent, thus proving that while as individual countries they may not be so strong, as a combined group they can possess formidable negotiating powers. This also applies in dealing with the EC and can deter it from turning into an economic fortress. And since WORFTA is not region-specific like the EC or NAFTA, there should be no reason for any one country to resent it or to go against the movement toward global economic union.

Table 4.3
WORFTA's weight in Japan's 10 largest export items
(Unit: Millions of US $)

Country	Exports	Share (%)	Imports	Share (%)
US	91	31.7	52	22.1
Canada	6	2.1	8	3.4
Mexico	2	0.6	1.9	0.8
S. Korea	17	5.9	11	4.8
Taiwan	15	5.2	8	3.4
Australia	7	2.4	12	5.1
N. Zealand	1	0.3	1.7	0.3
Subtotal	139	48.2	94.6	39.7

Source: DOT Yearbook (1991), IMF.

Second, cheaper production costs through market expansion and reduced uncertainty and risk factors in international trade can be realized. Also by promoting constructive competition among the region's private enterprises, WORFTA would lower consumer prices and increase employment and bring about technological innovations. Furthermore, it would protect consumers from the tyranny of the monopolistic companies that dominated small-scale domestic markets. Table 4.4 clearly shows that the bulk of trade barriers will greatly amplify the effects of the economic union. All too frequently, trade barriers are put up in the name of patriotism, setting the consumer prices of protected goods several times higher than the international rate. A world economic union is an effective way to protect the consumers from being forced to purchase items at such unfair prices.

Table 4.4
Trade within WORFTA zone

	US	Canada	Mexico	South Korea	Taiwan	Australia	New Zealand	Total
Export	34.9	74.4	84.7	35.1	40.0	26.4	38.8	44.7
Import	32.4	66.1	70.4	28.9	27.3	36.7	44.3	42.1

Source: DOT Yearbook (1991), IMF. Unit: %.

Third, by removing trade barriers among the member countries, WORFTA would accelerate international specialization based on comparative advantages. When the US's technological know-how and capital are successfully combined with the other member countries' strong production factors, the benefits such as lower costs and improved quality could be enjoyed globally. Thus the effects of economic specialization are greater among countries with different resources, endowments and WORFTA's initial memberships as proposed represent a degree of economic complementarity that is greater than any other combination of nations.

Fourth, WORFTA would stimulate trade expansion and conversion. If realized, WORFTA would substantially expand trade and ultimately provide the momentum for global economic integration. Especially among the countries where imports were widely regulated, the effects of trade expansion would be quite substantial. This would put pressure on Japan to open up its domestic market. Ironically, for items that cause the greatest trade frictions, the blame was put on the smaller, developing countries during negotiation processes, when more often than not Japan was the real responsible party.

In addition, even though it may start out with only seven countries, the ultimate goal of WORFTA is nothing less than the integration of the world economy, based on the ideas of GATT. Therefore, it would be an effective deterrent against any country that may try to close off its domestic market with non-tariff barriers, while capitalizing on global open markets. The greatest trade barriers today are non-tariff such as unfair quotas, anti-dumping suits and self-imposed regulations. The real problem lies in the fact that usually the most important trade items are heavily restricted by a confusing web of regulations and control. Therefore, WORFTA must move beyond tariffs and direct its energy to breaking down non-tariff barriers. In this sense, in the earlier stages of WORFTA, it could bring effective pressure to bear upon Japan which has the highest non-tariff barriers, by tentatively excluding it from membership. The real reason the US does not feel comfortable with converting APEC into a free-trade zone seems to be that Japan overly protects its market through various non-tariff barriers while its export industry capitalizes a global open market.

Fifth, with WORFTA, free-trade negotiations can be conducted in a more cooperative climate and thus be more fruitful than bilateral talks over individual items. Bilateral negotiations can easily be a source of conflict and more often than not the results are unsatisfactory to both sides, causing resentment among all parties involved. If such an unproductive relationship between two countries is prolonged it can cause irreparable damages beyond economic losses. But with WORFTA, the countries involved would understand that even if they make concessions in one area, they would be sufficiently rewarded in others and thus feel that it is beneficial to maintain steady cooperation. In contrast, if the US, through bilateral talks, manages to force a concession on a particular item from one of its trading partners, that country could use all means at its disposal to inflict the same damages on the US, and this tug-of-war could easily escalate into an international confrontation.

Sixth, WORFTA guarantees the US an expanded market. In contrast, because of the MFN (Most Favored Nation) status, the bilateral negotiations that the US actively pursued in the past ended up being more beneficial to Japan, an idle bystander, than to the US which actually exerted more sincere efforts to open its markets. Furthermore, they gave rise to new forms of trilateral trade, prompting Japan to use the Asian countries as an export outpost. There countries for their part felt that in order to reduce their deficits with Japan, they had to increase their exports to the US. But WORFTA would not only expand regional markets, it could also be a driving force for the expansion of exports to Japan.

Finally, due to low tariff barriers, the US is already the greatest market for foreign goods. If it cedes a few additional steps through WORFTA, it would have access to a much larger market than it can hope to gain through bilateral negotiations. Without giving many new concessions, the US has much to gain because it is easier to win compromise from other countries if they feel the US has made sincere efforts.

Conclusion

In 1992 trade between the US and Asia was $345 billion, of which US exports totalled $128 billion, up 9.1 percent from the previous year. This is 150 percent of the amount the US traded with Europe and accounts for the employment of more than 2.57 million American workers. Therefore, Asia is an important region that the US cannot afford to ignore or antagonize. Yet, the US seems to feel awkward about forming a pact such as WORFTA that includes Japan since it would only strengthen Japanese superiority. On the other hand, the bilateral negotiations on individual items run the risk of triggering anti-American sentiment and would, in the end, only provide Japan with another new market. The fact is the opening of the Asian markets have not brought substantial benefits to the US and only intensified anti-American sentiments, resulting in a boost of Japan's trade surplus. Therefore, the most effective policy would be for the US to advance into Japanese markets by utilizing countries such as South Korea and Taiwan as it export base. Initially, the US could effectively expand its exports to the Asian markets, by establishing South Korea and Taiwan as its bridgehead. Ultimately, however, WORFTA would open up the world markets by gradually expanding its membership on a global scale and strengthen its negotiating position vis-a-vis the EC and Japanese market.

The greatest obstacle to WORFTA lies, however, in the domestic arena. For example, in order for WORFTA to be realized, it needs an aggressive push from the US. Yet, the domestic political climate is influenced by a handful of special interest groups that are more concerned with protecting declining industries rather than increasing the overall national benefit. As it was well-demonstrated 150 years ago when the British government boldly abolished the Corn Law, the artificial protection of agriculture and other declining industries is a burdensome and futile task. Thereafter, Great Britain was able to become a strong player in international trade because it could import food at the most favorable rates and thus, stabilize domestic price and wages, creating a firm foundation for a competitive manufacturing industry. On the other hand, any attempt to use food as a weapon is a reckless act of self-destruction, as Napoleon found out in 1807 when he declared the continental blockade against Great Britain. The results were similar when the US restrained grain exports to the Soviet Union in 1960. And this is true of any country or industry.

The US cannot survive on the principle of self-sufficiency, detached from the global economy. It should strive for market expansion and greater income by signing a free trade agreement with the APEC countries that account for more than 50 percent of the country's total exports. Concurrently, the US should not let Japan's irregular trade practices get in the way. Admittedly, this is not an easy task because Japan is reluctant to loosen its control on ASEAN countries, as we have witnessed recently. Thus the US should strengthen its negotiating powers by expanding its free-trade partners starting with those countries that are supportive of the idea. This move would ultimately provide a firm basis for establishing global free trade. Such an agreement would be far more effective and constructive than waiting for the success of the UR talks or conducting bilateral negotiations.

References

Ardnt, Sven and Willett, Thomas (November 1991), 'EC 1992 From a North American Perspective,' *The Economic Journal.*

Baker, James A (Winter 1991-1992), 'America in Asia: Emerging Architecture for a Pacific Community,' *Foreign Affairs.*

Balassa, B. (Spring 1986) 'Japanese Trade Policies Towards Developing Countries,' *Journal of International Economic Integration,* Vol. 1, No. 1.

Bank of Korea (May 1991), 'Promotional Status of the US Free Trade Agreement and Its Prospects,' Bank of Korea, Seoul.

Brand, Diana (March-April 1990), 'Free Trade in Latin America: A Successful Way out of Crisis?' *Intereconomics.*

Bernhard, Fischer (March-April 1990), 'Development Countries in the Process of Economic Globalization,' *Intereconomics.*

Harrison, Selig and Prestowitz, Clyde (Summer 1990), 'Pacific Agenda: Defense or Economics?' *Foreign Policy.*

Gray, Peter (Spring 1990), 'Free Trade, Economic Integration and Nationhood,' *Journal of International Economic Integration,* Vol. 5, No. 1.

Institute of World Economy (January 1992), 'New International Order and Economic Cooperation in North-Eastern Asia.'

Korea Institute for Economics and Technology (January 1991), 'Effects of the North American Free Trade Agreement on Our Industry,' Seoul.

_____ (December 1990), 'Promotional Policies for Korea-US Industrial Cooperation,' Seoul.

_____ (1991), 'The Formation of a Free Trade Agreement by the US and Our Countermeasure,' Seoul.

Korea Trade Association (December 1990), 'Trends and Prospects in the North American Free Trade Agreement,' Seoul.

_____ (1991) 'North American Free Trade Agreement,' Seoul.

Shinha, Radha (September-October 1990), 'Are EC-Japan Trade Relations at the Crossroads?' *Intereconomics.*

Spencer, Edson (Spring 1990) 'Japan as Competitor,' *Foreign Policy.*

US International Trade Commission (March 1989), 'The Pros and Cons of Entering into Negotiations on Free Trade Area Agreements with Taiwan, The ROK and ASEAN, or the Pacific Rim Region in General.'

Welfens, Paul (November-December 1989) 'The Globalization of Markets and Regional Integration,' *Intereconomics.*

Yarbrough, Beth and Robert (1990), 'Economic Integration and Governance,' *Journal of International Economic Integration,* Vol. 5, No. 2.

5 Asia and the NAFTA

Marcus Noland

Upon receiving ratification by the federal legislatures of Canada, Mexico and the United States, the North American Free Trade Agreement (NAFTA) went into effect January 1, 1994. Among its provisions are a phased elimination of most border impediments to intraregional trade, commitments to liberalization of investment rules, and the extension of the US-Canada trade dispute resolution mechanism to Mexico. The pact is of analytical interest because it is the most ambitious trade integration among such disparate economies ever attempted. It is of policy interest for several reasons.

For one thing, the NAFTA represents an attempt by the participating governments to lock in Mexican economic reforms undertaken since the mid-1980s. Mexico has cut its maximum tariff from 100 percent to 20 percent, and its average tariff from 23 percent to 10 percent, liberalized its highly restrictive investment regime, and engaged in wholesale deregulation, privatization, and reform. As a result, Mexican growth has accelerated from around 1 percent per annum in the 1980s to 3 or 4 percent in the 1990s; the rate of inflation, which was over 70 percent annually for the decade of the 1980s has now dropped to near single-digit levels; and the debt service to export ratio has fallen from 50 percent in 1980 to 28 percent in 1990. For the Mexican government the NAFTA is a way of insuring that future governments cannot without extreme difficulty go back to the bad ways of the past. For the US government, the NAFTA is a way of bolstering desirable reforms in its large neighbor to the south with which it has had problematic relations throughout its history.

At the same time it is worth recalling that the NAFTA grows out of the earlier US-Canada Free Trade Area (FTA), which was in no small part motivated by a desire to create bargaining leverage in the Uruguay Round of multilateral GATT negotiations. With possible — daresay likely — failure of the Uruguay Round, the NAFTA potentially represents the first step in the construction of a non-GATT second-best policy by the US. In this respect, the NAFTA may have pronounced effects on countries outside the agreement. The focus of this chapter is on the NAFTA's implications for Asia and, as such, does not attempt to review the agreement in any comprehensive manner.[1] Rather, the paper will highlight the issues of greatest importance to Asia, namely the latent possibilities for adverse trade results and investment diversion. Several models of trade diversion are developed and applied to Korea. The results indicate that trade diversion could ultimately be on the order of 1 percent to 3 percent of Korea's global exports, with the impact on the more labor-abundant economies of Southeast Asia even larger. The chapter concludes with some reflections on the implications of these results.

Overview of the NAFTA

Under the NAFTA, tariff and most non-tariff barriers on intraregional trade are to be eliminated within 10 years, with some import-sensitive products granted a 15-year phase-out period. Rules of origin are necessary to identify which products qualify for this treatment and to prevent intraregional trade and investment diversion when there are significant differences in external barriers among the member states. From an Asian perspective, concern over extraregional trade and investment diversion center on two sectors, motor vehicles and textiles and apparel, where external barriers are high and the rules of origin are stringent.

In motor vehicles, the goal of the US and Canadian negotiators was to open the highly protected Mexican markets. At the same time, they were under pressure from the Big Three US automakers to ensure that firms with existing operations in Mexico (which had been developed under a strict domestic content regime) would not be disadvantaged relative to new entrants unburdened by the old regulatory structure, and that these new entrants would be unable to use Mexico as an 'export platform' to penetrate the US and Canadian markets.[2] The eventual agreement was for a rule of origin stipulating that autos must contain 62.5 percent North American content to qualify for duty-free treatment. This would appear to be somewhat more stringent than the 50 percent rule in the US-Canada FTA (though the two are not directly comparable since parts produced in Mexico did not count as local content under the US-Canada agreement). The NAFTA also provides for a simplified way of calculating the regional content share, though given the experience of the US-Canada FTA and other trade pacts, one doubts whether any system of assessing local content could be implemented in a fair and unburdensome way.

Modeling work by Lopez-de-Silanes, Markusen, and Rutherford (1992) confirms that the rules of origin will have a disproportionate impact on non-US firms. They conclude that

> The North American firms rely heavily on North American made parts and engines. Liberalization within North America then allows these firms to capture significant gains from rationalization. The foreign firms either do not rely as heavily on North American parts and engines, or in the case of foreign firms in Mexico, source their engines and parts primarily in Mexico. The foreign firms thus do not receive the same opportunities from rationalization that liberalization provides to North American firms. A failure to receive the same advantage becomes a competitive disadvantage and foreign firms contract their overall North American operations. (p.35)

In other words, the NAFTA rules of origin afford the Big Three and their unionized workforces an effective weapon to strike back at Japanese (largely non-unionized) transplant production in the US and Canada. Interestingly, while Lopez-de-Silanes, Markusen, and Rutherford conclude that foreign *producers* are hurt by the agreement, the pact actually accords minor benefits to the rest of the world as a whole when consumer interests are taken into account.

The other sector of major concern is textiles and apparel. The agreement eliminates tariffs and quotas on intraregional trade. These benefits are limited however, by what Hufbauer and Schott (1993a) term 'ultrastrict' rules of origin. To qualify for preferential treatment, 'textile and apparel goods must normally pass a 'triple transformation test,' which essentially requires that finished products be cut and sewn from fabric spun from North American fibers in order to qualify for NAFTA preferences' (*Ibid*, p. 44). North American-made products that do not meet this test can still qualify for preferential treatment up to specified import levels. Hufbauer and Schott describe the overall impact as 'schizophrenic': on the one hand the agreement eliminates virtually all barriers to intraregional trade, while on the other hand imposing rules of origin that could potentially nullify the impact of the nominal liberalization.

Other sectors of interest to Asian countries, such as agriculture and telecommunications equipment, are those by which the NAFTA significantly liberalizes intraregional trade and thus raises the specter of trade diversion.

In the case of telecoms, however, Mexican commitments under the NAFTA to liberalize telecoms *services* access, along with ongoing reform efforts may create a rapid growth in Mexican demand in telecoms equipment. Asian producers may stand to gain, even if they suffer trade diversion at the margin. One sector in which restrictive rules of origin could potentially encourage investment diversion is consumer electronics.

The NAFTA also includes some innovative provisions which, although of less immediate interest to Asian countries, could be important to the extent that they presage developments in GATT or APEC. The NAFTA text on trade-related investments measures (TRIMs) goes far beyond the provisions in the current Uruguay Round draft by banning export performance, domestic content, domestic sourcing, trade balancing and technology-transfer requirements. In the area of dispute settlement, the NAFTA establishes a trilateral trade commission to adjudicate trade disputes, including the vexing areas of anti-dumping and countervailing duties.[3] Investors are afforded the right to binding arbitration in established international fora rather than pursuit of remedies through the host country legal system. The treaty does not, however, break any new ground on subsidies.

Lastly, the NAFTA and accompanying side agreements are likely to address labor standards and environmental issues in greater depth than previous international trade agreements. The preamble makes explicit reference to sustainable development. It is likely that environmental issues and experts will be included in panels, and that derogation of environmental standards will be prohibited as an investment inducement. The NAFTA also specifies that certain existing international environmental treaties take precedence over GATT obligations.

These provisions and anticipated accompanying legislation are likely to greatly ease the treaty's passage in the US where criticism has focused on 'runaway plant' concerns related to lax labor standards and environmental laws in Mexico. Indeed, President Clinton is probably a more credible salesperson for the pact in the US than was President Bush, and with the leaderships in the three member countries solidly behind the agreement, its enactment is likely.

Hufbauer and Schott (1993a) predict that the industry-specific rules of origin and the dispute settlement mechanisms are likely to be challenged under GATT Article XXIV. As a result, 'the NAFTA will probably be consigned to GATT limbo, in which the pact is neither approved nor disapproved and in which other GATT members reserve their rights to contest the agreement at some future date if their GATT rights are impaired by

NAFTA preferences' (p.112).

Modeling trade diversion

The most obvious channel for impairment is through trade diversion, though under current GATT rules third parties could not ask for compensation unless the regional bloc raised external barriers.[4] This can occur when the preferential reduction in trade barriers within an FTA creates a price wedge between the goods produced in member states and goods originating outside the FTA, and import sourcing is switched from relatively more efficient non-member suppliers to relatively less efficient, though preferentially treated, member suppliers. Trade diversion is thus a function of the magnitude of the trade barrier being removed (the size of the preference) and the relative efficiencies of member and non-member suppliers.

To investigate the possible scope of trade diversion associated with NAFTA, a series of simple partial equilibrium models of competition between Korea and Mexico in the US market have been estimated. This approach has the advantages of being relatively straightforward to implement and permitting the identification of the sectors with greatest trade diversion. The approach has the disadvantage of ignoring general equilibrium effects, and being limited to Korea-Mexico competition in the US market. The model could be made comprehensive by expanding it to include all non-NAFTA suppliers and all intra-NAFTA trade.

The structural equations of the partial equilibrium model of US imports from Korea can be written

$$\ln M^d = \alpha_1 + \beta_1 \ln Y^{US} + \beta_2 \ln(PX_i^K/P_i^{US}) + \beta_3 \ln(PX_i^K/PX^M) + u_1,$$
$$\ln M^s = \alpha_2 + \beta_4 \ln C^{iK} + \beta_5 \ln(PX_i^K/P_i^K) + u_2,$$
$$\ln M^d = \ln M^s$$

where M is US imports from Korea, Y is US national income, P are indices of domestic traded goods prices, PX are an indices of export prices, C is a measure of supply capacity, the u are the error terms, the superscripts s and d indicate quantities supplied and demanded, the subscript i indicates industry, and the superscripts K, M, US, refer to Korea, Mexico, and the United States, respectively.[5] All nominal values are expressed in real terms, and all price indices are converted to a common currency. Trade volumes and prices are endogenous; the remaining variables are exogenous.

This model was estimated for a sample of 46 industries encompassing the whole traded goods sector. The sectors are defined in Appendix Table 5.1. The regressions were estimated using annual data for the period 1962-1991, dropping observations where Korean and/or Mexican exports to the US were less than $1 million. The regressions were estimated with and without lagged dependent variables. The regression results are listed in Appendix Table 5.2.

What is of most immediate interest are the estimates of the cross-price elasticity between Korean and Mexican exports (β_3, above). In only around half of the cases (22 out of 46) did the coefficient take the expected negative value. In the remaining cases the coefficients were positive, suggesting that Korean and Mexican exports to the US are complements rather than substitutes. The 22 negative cross-price elasticity estimates were then applied to the data on US tariff and non-tariff barriers on Mexican exports found in Roland-Holst, Reinert, and Shiells (1992), and those prepared by Peat Marwick and reported in Hufbauer and Schott (1992). Both data sets are based on actual tariff-collection rates and thus reflect the extensive duty-exemptions through the Generalized System of Preferences and the Offshore Assembly Provision of US trade law that Mexican exports to the US receive. (Statutory tariff rates overstate the true barriers that Mexican products face in the US market.) The estimated tariff-equivalents of the non-tariff barriers differ slightly across the two data sets, and calculations are presented using both of them.

The product of the cross-price elasticity and the trade barrier figure is the percentage reduction in Korean exports that would occur if Mexico were afforded unimpeded access to the US market. This calculation, applied to 1991 Korean exports to the US, using the Roland-Holst, Reinert, Shiells (RHRS) data is reported in Case A of Table 5.1; the same calculation using the Peat Marwick data is presented in Case B.

According to Case A, the NAFTA would result in a loss of $717 million of exports to the US, or 1 percent of Korea's global exports. The sector of greatest trade diversion would be textile spinning and weaving, where a combination of large trade preferences (17 percent) and a high cross-price elasticity (-6.99) would completely eliminate Korean exports to the US of $463 million. Other product categories of large trade diversion losses would include footwear ($152 million) and plastic products ($64 million).

The estimate of total trade diversion derived in Case B is somewhat larger, $909 million, or 1.27 percent of Korea's global exports. The larger figure is mainly due to higher estimates of trade diversion in plastic products ($191 million) and footwear ($216 million).

The NAFTA is to be phased in over time, however, so it is not totally appropriate to apply these trade diversion calculations to current trade flows. Rather, it would be better to apply them to the trade flows that could be expected to exist at the time of full implementation. To address this issue, a model of trade specialization was estimated and used to project Korean exports in 2000.

The model is essentially a reduced form model of export specialization in which exports are a function of eleven resource endowments (labor, physical capital, human capital, arable land, forest land, pasture land, coal, oil, minerals and transport costs. The model and its estimation are discussed in detail in the Appendix.) The model was estimated for a panel of 30 countries for the period 1968-1988. ARIMA models were then estimated to generate forecasts of Korean factor endowments for 2000. The factor endowment forecasts, combined with the coefficients from the cross-country model, and the actual data for 1991, were used to derive projections of the Korean export pattern in 2000. The projected export shares, along with the actual data for 1991 are reported in Table 5.2.

This approach has the advantage of being more consistent with the timing of the actual implementation of the NAFTA. It also has the advantage of allowing us to see if Korean export specialization is shifting into or away from sectors of possibly significant trade diversion. Its disadvantage is that the forecasts of exports undoubtedly contain forecast error.

The results of these computations are reported in Table 5.1 Cases C (RHRS) and D (Peat Marwick). The Case C calculation indicates that Korea could be expected to suffer a $1.2 billion loss in exports due to trade diversion in 2000, or 1.05 percent of projected global exports, a slight rise from the previous case. Again, the largest sector of export loss is spinning and weaving, followed by footwear, and plastic products.

The trade diversion estimates in Case D are somewhat higher, $1.6 billion, or 1.31 percent of Korea's global exports. The largest sector of export loss is again spinning and weaving; however, plastic products replaces footwear as the second largest sector of export loss in the Case D calculations.

These results, while interesting, are based on some non-robust estimates of the cross-price elasticity between Mexican and Korean exports to the US. Moreover, this model is a simple three-country model and the trade diversion estimates obtained specifically for Korea might decline if the model was embedded in a complete general equilibrium system in which other, non-Korean sources of supply were available. It would be desirable then to have some alternative method of computation. The export specialization projection model is quite useful in this regard, since it enables us to project Mexican exports and thus to see if it is likely that the two countries' export patterns are likely to converge or diverge, and thus increase or reduce the likelihood of trade diversion.

Mexican exports were projected under two scenarios. First, they were calculated using the factor endowment forecasts generated by the ARIMA models. Some, especially Hufbauer and Schott (1992), argue that implementation of the NAFTA would represent a fundamental regime change in Mexico (or at least make permanent the recent reforms). They claim that changes in investor expectations about the future policy regime would result in additional capital inflows of $12 billion annually. So the Mexican export pattern was projected under a second scenario, in which $12 billion in additional annual capital accumulation was factored into the capital stock projection. Projections of Mexican export specialization under these two scenarios (Mexico 2000A and 2000B, respectively) along with the actual Mexican export pattern in 1990 (the most recent year available) are reported in Table 5.2.

As one can see, the Mexican export pattern is projected to become more similar to the Korean trade pattern. The Finger-Kreinin index of export similarity varies between 0 and 100, with 0 indicating complete dissimilarity, and 100 indicating identical export composition.[6] The index for Korea-Mexican trade rises from 36 in 1990, to 47 in 2000 using the Mexico 2000A projection, and 48 using the Mexico 2000B alternative.

This suggests a thought experiment. Assume that US real imports grow at 3 percent annually in each category, and that any Mexican exports above this rate displaced the exports of all non-NAFTA suppliers equiproportionately. How would Korea be affected?

The results obtained using the Mexico 2000A and 2000B projections are reported in Table 5.3 Cases E and F, respectively. In Case E, in which Mexican exports are computed from the ARIMA model factor endowments, total trade diversion losses to Korea are estimated to be $2.9 billion or nearly 2.5 percent of Korean global exports. The bulk of the loss is in radio, television, and telecommunications equipment ($1.9 billion), followed by apparel ($405 million), and other electrical machinery (largely household appliances, $161 million).

The losses are even greater in Case F in which Mexico is assumed to receive additional capital inflows. In this case, Korean trade diversion losses are estimated to be $3.5 billion, or nearly 3 percent of projected global exports. Again, the sectors of greatest trade diversion loss are radio,

50

televisions and telecommunications ($2.4 billion), apparel ($332 million) and other electrical machinery ($189 million).

These estimates of possible trade diversion losses, while substantial, are similar in magnitude to other existing estimates. Kreinin and Plummer (1992) take statutory tariff rates (it is unclear whether they account for existing Mexican duty-exemptions), assume a two-thirds tariff 'passthrough,' and calculate that the NAFTA would divert $1 billion of trade from Korea, about 5 percent of Korean exports to North America, or just over 2 percent of Korea's global exports in 1987, their base year. They also estimate that the NAFTA would divert $484 million of ASEAN trade, about 4 percent of their exports to North America, or less than 1 percent of their global exports.

The Kreinin and Plummer estimates are subject to several qualifications, however. First, as mentioned above, it is unclear whether they properly take into account existing duty-exemptions on Mexican exports.[7] To the extent that they ignore these they will overstate the price wedge created by the NAFTA and concomitantly overestimate trade diversion. Second, and possibly more importantly, they do not appear to take non-tariff barriers into account. These are very important quantitatively, especially in the important textiles and apparel sector. This omission would downwardly bias their trade diversion estimates. Third, the basis of their two-thirds tariff passthrough calculation is unclear. Fourth, the Kreinin and Plummer calculations are based on 1987 trade patterns – not the trade pattern that will exist when the NAFTA changes actually are implemented.

Lower estimates of potential trade diversion losses are obtained by Primo Braga *et al* (undated). They apply two models. The first is a partial equilibrium model similar to the first model presented in this chapter. Unlike that model, however, the elasticities they use are selected from the existing literature, not estimated directly, and there is reason to question the applicability of the parameters they used.[8] In any event, Primo Braga *et al* obtain estimates of trade diversion of less than 1 percent of total exports for East Asian countries as a whole, and only $60 million for Korea from a base of $19.2 billion exports to the US. Trade diversion is highest for Hong Kong. Primo Braga *et al* report a second set of calculations based on a gravity model of trade. In this model Korea's losses are somewhat higher: $141 million on a base of $20.6 billion of exports to the US or 0.7 percent.

Lastly, the calculations presented in all of these models implicitly assume the external barriers of the NAFTA countries remain at their current height. The most obvious deviation from the assumption would be if tariff and non-tariff barriers were reduced through the Uruguay Round negotiations. If this were to occur, it would reduce the effective preference margin, and thus the extent of trade diversion. Primo Braga *et al* suggest that a successful conclusion of the Uruguay Round could cut the trade diversion estimates roughly in half. On the other hand, new protection, such as the reimposition of voluntary export restraints on the importation of autos into the US market, would raise the preference margin granted under the NAFTA.

The estimates of trade diversion reported by these studies may be overstated if the rules of origin effectively negate the trade liberalization. Strict rules of origin could undermine trade liberalization by undercutting the advantages of locating certain production activities within the region by binding those benefits to the location of other, less competitive, activities in the region as well. This possibility is most obvious in the case of textiles and apparel, where apparel liberalization could be offset by rules of origin which tie the benefits to backwards integration of upstream textiles activities through the 'triple transformation' test, and in the motor-vehicle sector, where liberalization of assembly activities is tied to stringent regional content standards. Models such as those reviewed here which do not take these conditionalities into account may overstate the extent of intra-regional trade liberalization, and hence the scope of diversion.

A final issue is possible investment diversion. This would be most likely occur in sectors in which the NAFTA creates large preference margins or rules of origin encourage regional production; and in which production by multinational firms is important. Kreinin and Plummer examined preference margins and foreign direct investment flows into Korea and ASEAN and concluded that for Korea the most likely candidates for investment diversion would be the chemicals, machinery, electronics and transport equipment sectors. For ASEAN they would be food, chemicals, textiles, metals and electronics. An interesting issue here is to pose the hypothetical question of how might the NAFTA affect the future composition of production in these countries. The export specialization model developed in this paper could be of obvious use in this regard.

McCleery and James (1993) put investment diversion at the center of their analysis of the possible effects of the NAFTA. Their model consists of a series of linked national macromodels, in which the main impact of the NAFTA is to alter rates of return on capital. They simulate their model using historical data for the period 1980-1986 and obtain some very interesting results: they find that the NAFTA reduces the global exports of the ASEAN countries from 0.19 percent in the case of the Philippines to just under one percent (Indonesia). With regard to GDP, the NAFTA reduces Indonesian

GDP by more than 1 percent, and reduces the GDPs of other Asian countries by lesser amounts: 0.49 percent (Singapore), 0.18 percent (Malaysia), 0.06 percent (the Philippines) and 0.04 percent (Thailand).

Conclusions

This chapter has presented a series of models to analyze prospective trade diversion effects due to the NAFTA. The calculations indicate that the NAFTA could result in export diversion losses to Korea in the US market on the order of 1 to 3 percent of Korean global exports. The total impact of the NAFTA would be somewhat higher, as these calculations do not account for possible trade diversion losses in the Canadian and Mexican markets. This paper computes these losses for Korea alone, but the models could be extended easily to other third countries. Indeed, it quite possible that trade diversion losses could be relatively larger for the more labor-abundant economies of Southeast Asia.

In light of these results, what should be the response of the Asian countries? Hufbauer and Schott (1993) suggest that in cases where there is significant trade diversion that the NAFTA members offer trade compensation under GATT auspices. This certainly warrants serious consideration.

Another possibility would be for Asian countries to join the NAFTA. The NAFTA has an accession clause which states that any 'country or group of countries may accede to this Agreement subject to such terms and conditions as may be agreed between such country or countries and the Commission and following approval in accordance with the applicable approval procedures in each country.' In practice, the 'customized' nature of the NAFTA would make accession problematic. Nonetheless, accession raises interesting possibilities.

Asian countries could use the NAFTA accession clause to call the US's bluff in bilateral negotiations. Asian countries which were truly willing to undertake reasonable measures to comply with an expanded NAFTA could publicly indicate their willingness to do so, and force the US to justify its recalcitrance to liberalize its own practices.

This could be particularly important if the Uruguay Round fails and the GATT system goes into decline. Indeed, in such circumstances the NAFTA and APEC could become the nuclei of a trans-Pacific economic space.

In public debate in the US, support for the NAFTA has become a litmus test to measure support for free trade. The results in this paper suggest otherwise. Yet, in one sense those who view the NAFTA as tantamount to free trade may have it right. Mexico is a large, labor-abundant country, and the NAFTA binds the US to something approximating free trade. While Asian countries may suffer losses due to trade diversion in the medium-run, in the long-run the NAFTA may actually be to their advantage, in that it makes the imposition of new protection against them ineffective. Precisely because trade and investment can be diverted to Mexico, trade restrictions become relatively less effective, and in a political sense, desirable. Ironically, with trade restrictions looking less effective, US policymakers would be forced toward economically more desirable, and politically less feasible, first-best solutions for sectoral competitiveness problems. The long-run effect of NAFTA may thus be to foreclose trade policy remedies to competitiveness problems to the benefit of both the US and Asia.

Notes

1 Comprehensive assessments of the pact are contained in Hufbauer and Schott (1992, 1993a). A compendium of formal economy-wide models of the NAFTA is contained in US International Trade Commission (1992). English and Smith (1993) is an evaluation of the NAFTA from an Asia-Pacific perspective.

2 The latter concern is revealing. With the US tariff on autos only 2.5 percent, the NAFTA's scope for enhancing Mexico's attractiveness as a production location would seem decidedly modest. The 'export platform' argument would only gain force if external barriers were higher. The negotiating position of the Big Three automakers could be best interpreted as a demand that future protection could not be circumvented through the use of Mexican production *by non-North American firms*.

3 The NAFTA negotiators also avoided the EC trap of common external anti-dumping and countervailing duties. Indeed, the Trade Commission may study reform of the existing laws.

4 See Hufbauer and Schott (1992b) for a proposal to make trade diversion in and of itself grounds for compensation.

5 Korean prices and production indices come from the Bank of Korea; US domestic prices were constructed from US Department of Commerce, *Producer Price Indices*; and the remaining data come form the International Monetary Fund, *International Financial Statistics*. The capacity variable is a step function of Korean industrial output of the form

$CAP_{it} = \max(Q_{it}, Q_{it-1})$ where Q is industrial output. It would have been desirable to use sector-specific export price indices for Mexico, but these were unobtainable.
6. The index is defined as:

$$S(a,b) = \sum_i \min(x_{ia}, x_{ib})*100,$$

where X_{ia} (X_{ib}) is the industry i export share in country a's (b's) exports. This measure was originally proposed by Finger and Kreinin (1979). See also Kellman and Schroeder (1983).
7. Their paper is odd in this respect. They appear to take the Generalized System of Preferences into account in calculating possible ASEAN, though not Korean, trade diversion.
8. The crucial cross-price elasticity are based on Cline (1978), who in turn relied on estimates published in the early 1970s. One questions the reliability of product-specific estimates from such dated sources when applied to prospective effects on today's East Asian countries.

References

English, H. Edward and Smith, Murray G. (1993), 'NAFTA and Pacific Partnership: Advancing Multilateralism?,' in Noland, Marcus (ed), *Pacific Dynamism and the International Economic System*. Institute for International Economics, Washington, DC.

Finger, J. M. and Kreinin, M. E. (1979), 'A Measure of "Export Similarity" and Its Possible Uses,' *Economic Journal*, vol. 89, pp. 905-12.

Hausman, Jerry A. and Taylor, William E. (1981). 'Panel Data and Unobservable Individual Effects,' *Econometrica*, vol. 49, no. 6, pp. 1377-1398.

Hufbauer, Gary Clyde and Schott, Jeffrey J. (1992), *North American Free Trade: Issues and Recommendations*. Institute for International Economics, Washington, DC.

_____ (1993a), *NAFTA: An Assessment*, Institute for International Economics, Washington, DC.

_____ (1993b), 'Regionalism in North America,' paper presented at the Conference on Regional Integration and its Impact on Developing Countries, Institute of Developing Economies, Tokyo, February 3-4.

Kellman, Mitchell and Schroeder, Tim (1983), 'The Export Similarity Index: Some Structural Tests,' *Economic Journal*, vol. 93 pp. 193-8.

Kreinin, Mordechai E. and Plummer, Michael G. (1992), 'Effects of Economic Integration in Industrial Countries on ASEAN and the Asian NIEs,' *World Development*, vol. 20, no. 9, pp. 1345-1366.

Leamer, Edward E. (1984), *Sources of International Comparative Advantage*, MIT Press, Cambridge, Massachusetts.

Lopez-de-Silanes, Florencio; Markusen, James R.; and Rutherford, Thomas (1992), 'The Auto Industry and the North American Free Trade Agreement: Employment, Production, and Welfare Effects,' paper presented at the American Economic Association Winter Meeting, Anaheim, California, January 5-7.

McCleery, Robert K. and James, William E. (1993), 'Implications of NAFTA for East Asia: Investment Diversion or Opportunity,' East-West Center, Honolulu, Hawaii, unpublished manuscript.

Primo Braga, C.A., Raed Sfadi and Yeats, Alexander (undated), 'Implications of NAFTA for East Asian Exports,' International Economics Department, World Bank, Washington, DC.

Roland-Holst, David; Reinert, Kenneth A.; and Shiells, Clinton R. (May 1992), 'North American Trade Liberalization and the Role of Non-tarifff Barriers,' in *Economy-wide Modeling of the Economic Implications of a FTA with Mexico and a NAFTA with Canada and Mexico*, USITC Publication 2508, Washington, DC.

US International Trade Commission (May 1992), *Economy-wide Modeling of the Economic Implications of a FTA with Mexico and a NAFTA with Canada and Mexico*, USITC Publication 2508, Washington, DC.

Table 5.1
Trade diversion estimates

	Case A	Case B	Case C	Case D
Animal & animal products	165	51	0	0
Fish and preparations	0	0	0	0
Food crops	0	0	0	0
Tobacco	0	0	0	0
Agricultural commodities	0	0	0	0
Beverages	0	0	0	0
Natural fibres	0	0	0	0
Natural rubber & gums	3311	0	5425	0
Wood and wood pulp	24	0	31	0
Crude materials	37	18	37	18
Coal, coke & briquettes	0	0	0	0
Petroleum & products	0	679	0	791
Non-ferrous metals	0	158	0	188
Spinning & weaving	463852	463852	889487	889487
Other textile products	0	0	0	0
Wearing apparel	0	0	0	0
Leather & products	0	0	0	0
Footwear	152024	215874	152758	216917
Wood products	218	36	246	41
Furniture & fixtures	0	0	0	0
Pulp & paper	0	0	0	0
Paper products	36	47	0	0
Printing and publishing	0	0	0	0
Basic chemicals	8716	5665	23325	15161

Table 5.1
Trade diversion estimates, *continued*

	Case A	Case B	Case C	Case D
Synthetic resins	0	0	0	0
Other chemicals	0	0	0	0
Drugs & medicine	0	0	0	0
Other chemical products	951	0	1609	0
Rubber products	5776	8520	10344	15257
Plastic products	64612	190605	124181	366335
Pottery, china, etc.	0	0	0	0
Glass & glass products	0	0	0	0
Other mineral products	0	0	0	0
Iron & steel	7832	12531	18256	29209
Fabricated metal products	0	0	0	0
Office & computing equipment	0	0	0	0
Other machinery	0	0	0	0
Radio, television	0	0	0	0
Other electrical machinery	0	0	0	0
Shipbuilding & repairing	0	0	0	0
Railroad equipment	169	236	486	680
Motor vehicles	0	0	0	0
Aircraft	0	0	0	0
Motorcycles & bicycles	0	0	0	0
Professional goods	0	0	0	0
Other industries	0	0	0	0
Total	707723	898273	1226184	1534084
Memorandum				
Aggregate exports	71870184	71870184	118869967	118869967
Trade diversion as a percentage of aggregate exports	0.98	1.25	1.03	1.29

Table 5.2

Exports Share	Korea 1991	Korea 2000	Mexico 1990	MexicoA 2000	MexicoB 2000
Animal & animal products	0.1	0	1.51	2.98	2.69
Fish and preparations	2.09	2.38	1.27	1.13	1.14
Food crops	0.75	0.39	7.44	2.81	2.75
Tobacco	0.1	0.06	0.11	0.09	0.09
Agricultural commodities	0.52	0.34	0.54	0.47	0.45
Beverages	0.06	0.05	1.02	0.59	0.62
Natural fibres	0.57	0.51	0.63	0.23	0.23
Natural rubber & gums	0.11	0.11	0.23	0.36	0.34
Wood and wood pulp	0.05	0.04	0.42	0.44	0.42
Crude materials	0.21	0.12	2.44	1.82	1.71
Coal, coke & briquettes	0	0	0	0	0
Petroleum & products	2.07	1.46	36.77	29.3	27.89
Non-ferrous metals	0.51	0.36	3.19	3.09	2.91
Spinning & weaving	8.35	9.68	1.02	1.29	1.34
Other textile products	3.51	2.17	0.44	0.66	0.62
Wearing apparel	9.16	5.34	0.32	1.1	0.9
Leather & products	2.2	1.38	0.21	0.23	0.23
Footwear	4.37	2.66	0.26	0.77	0.69
Wood products	0.3	0.2	0.52	1.1	0.99
Furniture & fixtures	0.23	0.17	0.17	0.43	0.4
Pulp & paper	0.43	0.14	0.41	1.1	0.93
Paper products	0.12	0	0.19	0.69	0.59
Printing and publishing	0.29	0.27	0.22	0.26	0.26
Basic chemicals	1.8	2.92	4.05	5.51	5.91
Synthetic resins	2.45	4.2	1.73	2.39	2.57

Table 5.2, *continued*

Exports Share	Korea 1991	Korea 2000	Mexico 1990	MexicoA 2000	MexicoB 2000
Other chemicals	0.25	0.22	0.47	0.31	0.33
Drugs & medicine	0.18	0.2	0.37	0.23	0.25
Other chemical products	0.28	0.29	0.69	0.57	0.6
Rubber products	1.68	1.82	0.15	0.19	0.2
Plastic products	1.89	2.2	0.43	0.56	0.58
Pottery, china, etc.	0.12	0.1	0.16	0.12	0.12
Glass & glass products	0.24	0.27	0.96	0.91	0.94
Other mineral products	0.6	0.51	0.72	0.22	0.28
Iron & steel	5.75	8.11	2.91	2.52	2.62
Fabricated metal products	2.39	2.86	1.77	2.58	2.67
Office & computing equipment	4.04	4.35	1.81	3.91	4.06
Other machinery	4.2	4.94	3.55	6.02	6.13
Radio, television	19.37	14.2	0.86	3.39	4.12
Other electrical machinery	3.1	2.48	1.77	2.33	2.41
Shipbuilding & repairing	5.9	11.37	2.53	3.23	3.52
Railroad equipment	0.9	1.56	0.07	0.03	0.03
Motor vehicles	4.19	4.98	13.67	11.73	11.96
Aircraft	0.56	0.66	0.54	0.17	0.18
Motorcycles & bicycles	0.29	0.52	0.11	0.12	0.13
Professional goods	1.17	1.6	0.91	1.02	1.13
Other industries	2.54	1.8	0.42	1	1.03

Table 5.3
Trade diversion estimates

	Case E	Case F
Animal & animal products	0	0
Fish and preparations	2354	3050
Food crops	0	0
Tobacco	2	2
Agricultural commodities	287	280
Beverages	0	0
Natural fibres	0	0
Natural rubber & gums	220	213
Wood and wood pulp	14	13
Crude materials	11	3
Coal, coke & briquettes	NA	NA
Petroleum & products	408	382
Non-ferrous metals	146	136
Spinning & weaving	16853	20228
Other textile products	18022	17587
Wearing apparel	404799	332390
Leather & products	7365	8391
Footwear	96266	89811
Wood products	12618	11534
Furniture & fixtures	20334	19749
Pulp & paper	2599	2218
Paper products	0	0
Printing and publishing	1884	2210
Basic chemicals	4229	5290
Synthetic resins	7626	9531

Table 5.3
Trade diversion estimates, *continued*

	Case E	Case F
Other chemicals	0	1
Drugs & medicine	0	0
Other chemical products	122	215
Rubber products	4458	5435
Plastic products	22038	26676
Pottery, china, etc.	39	219
Glass & glass products	3238	4443
Other mineral products	0	0
Iron & steel	5719	8917
Fabricated metal products	45346	52394
Office & computing equipment	78917	88505
Other machinery	53356	59157
Radio, television	1865663	2439987
Other electrical machinery	161065	188881
Shipbuilding & repairing	794	1043
Railroad equipment	0	0
Motor vehicles	27325	39227
Aircraft	0	0
Motorcycles & bicycles	811	1175
Professional goods	8657	12245
Other industries	46696	51755
Total	2920278	3503296
Memorandum		
Trade diversion	118869967	118869967
as a percentage of aggregate exports	2.46	2.95

62

Model specification and estimation

A model of export specialization is necessary to generate projections of Korean and Mexican exports in 2000. A conventional starting point for econometric analysis of international trade flows is the Heckscher-Ohlin-Vanek model. This approach employs the standard assumptions of microeconomic trade models (factor price equalization or endowment similarity, identical homothetic preferences, etc.) to generate a reduced form representation of a country's trade pattern based on available technology and its relative factor endowments.[1] A country's output (Q), is produced from a factor use matrix (A), and a set of endowments (V):

(1) $Q = A^{-1}V$.

World output can be described similarly:

(2) $Q_w = A^{-1}V_w$

Under the assumption of identical homothetic utility functions and factor price equalization, each country consumes each variety of the commodities in the same proportion:

(3) $C = sQ_w$,

where s is the country's share of world output, and s is defined as (4) $s = (Y_i - B_i)/Y_w$

where Y is income and B is the trade balance evaluated at the vector of common goods prices, p.[2]

Net exports (T) are simply the difference between production and consumption

(5) $T = Q-C$,

or, by back substituting,

$= A^{-1}V - A^{-1}sV_w$,

$= A^{-1}(V - sV_w)$.

Unfortunately, as Leamer (1984) notes it is 'wildly optimistic' to expect to be able to estimate this model directly. The excess factor supplies are correlated, and a regression of trade on a subset of them is bound to lead to biased and inconsistent estimates, a problem compounded by any errors in measurement of the endowments. Instead, researchers have estimated reduced forms where data on industry net exports are regressed on national factor endowment data:

(6) $T_{ij} = \Sigma_k \beta_{ik} V_{kj} + u_{ij}$

where

T_{ij} = net exports of commodity i by country j,

V_{kj} = endowments of resource k of country j,

β_{ik} = coefficients indicating the impact on net exports of commodity i of an increase in the kth endowment, and

u_{ij} = a disturbance term.

For some purposes it may be desirable to examine gross, rather than net, exports. The natural theoretical starting point for such an investigation would be through the specification of a differentiated products model, in which product varieties are differentiated by country of origin. Under the prior assumption of identical homothetic preferences, each country will consume identical proportions of each variety of each good, hence each country will export $(1-s)$ of its production:

$$(7) \qquad X = (1-s)Q$$

or, by back substituting,

$$X = (1-s)A^{-1}V.$$

Again, it is effectively impossible to estimate equation (7) directly, and instead a reduced form analogous to (6) is estimated:

$$(8) \quad X_{ij} = \Sigma_k \beta_{ik} V_{kj} + u_{ij}.$$

The model was estimated for a using a pooled time-series cross-section panel of 30 countries for the years 1968, 1972, 1976, 1980, 1984, and 1988.[3] The explanatory variables consisted of nine factor endowments (labor, physical capital, human capital, arable land, pasture land, forest land, coal, oil, and minerals), and the c.i.f./f.o.b. ratio which was used as a proxy for transport costs.[4]

The regressions were estimated using both random- and fixed-effects estimators; choice between the two estimators were made on the basis of the test outline in Hausman and Taylor (1981). In principle, since gross exports are truncated at zero, these regressions should be estimated using limited dependent variable techniques. In reality, less than 3 percent of the observation were zero-valued. Preliminary estimates on single year cross-sections indicated that with so few (and apparently random) zero-valued observations, the Tobit estimates were virtually identical to those obtained from OLS. The regressions have been estimated with the dependent and explanatory variables in both log and level form. Choice between these specifications was done on the basis of goodness-of-fit and the plausibility of the resulting projections. These regressions are summarized in Appendix Table 5.3.

Univariate ARIMA models were then used to generate forecasts of the exogenous variables for 2000. The estimated coefficients from the export specialization model were then combined with the ARIMA forecasts of the factor endowments to compute projections of export specialization in 2000.

Data sources

The trade data originate from the GATT tapes. The labor endowment was defined as the economically active population; the data come from International Labour Organisation (ILO), *Yearbook of Labour Statistics,* various issues. The capital stock was calculated by summing and depreciating the purchasing power adjusted gross fixed investment series in the diskette accompanying Robert Summers and Alan Heston, 'The Penn World Table (Mark 5)' *Quarterly Review of Economics*, May 1991. The asset life of capital was assumed to be 18 years and the depreciation rate 13 percent.

Human capital was calculated by multiplying the economically active labor force by the Psacharopoulos index of per capita educational capital. The Psacharopoulos index is defined as the average per capita expenditure on education embodied in the labor force calculated from data on the highest level of educational achievement, years duration of schooling at each level, and expenditures per year at each level normalized by the amount of expenditure for one year of primary school education. Data on educational achievement and schooling duration are found in the United Nations Educational Social and Cultural Organization (UNESCO), *Statistical Yearbook*. Expenditure weights come from George Psacharopoulos, 1973, *Returns to Education*, Jossey-Bass, San Francisco.

Data on land endowments come from the Food and Agricultural Organisation (FAO), *Production Yearbook*.

The coal endowment was measured by domestic production in thousands of metric tons and comes from US Bureau of Mines, *Minerals Yearbook*. (Data on coal mining capacity or reserves were unavailable for most countries.) The minerals index is the value of domestic production of thirteen minerals; the production data are from the *Minerals Yearbook*, the price data are from the IFS. (The composition of this index was determined by taking the top twenty minerals [excluding oil, natural gas, and coal] by value of world output in 1984 and then dropping whose for which price data could not be found.) The oil endowment in proven reserves was taken from the *Oil and Gas Yearbook*, published by the American Petroleum Institute.

Lastly, the c.i.f./f.o.b. data come from the IMF, *IFS Trade Supplement*.

In some cases, data for Taiwan were unavailable from these sources, and instead come from *Taiwan Statistical Data Book*, Council for Economic

Planning and Development, Executive Yuan, Republic of China.

Appendix notes

1 See Leamer (1984) for a discussion of these assumptions and how they can be relaxed while preserving the linear (or at least monotonic) relationship between trade and factor endowments.
2 The assumption of homothesticity can be replaced with that of a linear expenditure system without changing the ultimate reduced form of the regressions, though the interpretation of the coefficient on the labor endowment is different.
3 The countries are Argentina, Austria, Brazil, Canada, Denmark, Finland, France, Federal Republic of Germany, Greece, Hong Kong, Indonesia, Israel, Italy, Japan, Republic of Korea, Malaysia, Mexico, Norway, Pakistan, Peru, the Philippines, Singapore, Spain, Sweden, Taiwan, Thailand, Tunisia, Turkey, United Kingdom and the United States. This was the largest set of countries for which a complete set of the factor endowment variables could be constructed for the years 1968 and 1988.
4 Alternatively, one could think of locational proximity as an endowment. The regressions were also estimated with the length of coast included as an endowment; the coast variable was significant in neither the fish and preparations regressions nor any other regression in the sample.

Appendix Table 5.1 Industry Definitions

Sector:	SITC
Animals & animal products	00, 01, 02, 091, 21, 291, 41, 43
Fish and preparations	03
Food crops	04, 05, 06, 07
Tobacco and manufactures	12
Agricultural commodities	08, 099, 22, 292, 42
Beverages	11
Natural fibres	26
Natural rubber & gums	23
Wood & wood pulp	24, 25
Crude minerals	27, 28
Coal, coke, & briquettes	32
Petroleum & products	33, 34, 35
Non-ferrous metals	68

	ISIC
Spinning & weaving	3211
Other textile products	321-3211
Wearing apparel	322
Leather & products	323
Footwear	324
Wood products	331
Furniture & fixtures	332
Pulp & paper	3411
Paper products	341-3411
Printing & publishing	342
Basic chemicals	3511
Synthetic resins	3513
Other chemicals	351-3511-3513
Drugs & medicine	3522
Other chemical products	352-3522
Rubber products	355
Plastic products	356
Pottery, china, etc.	361
Glass & glass products	362
Non-metallic mineral products	369
Iron & steel	371

Appendix Table 5.1
Industry Definitions, *continued*

Fabricated metal products	381
Office & computing equipment	3825
Other machinery	382-3825
Radio, television	3832
Other electric machinery	383-3832
Shipbuilding & repairing	3841
Railroad equipment	3842
Motor vehicles	3843
Aircraft	3845
Motorcycles & bicycles	3844+3849
Professional goods	385
Other industries	390

Appendix Table 5.2
US-Korea trade equations

Industry	Sample period	IMPORT DEMAND							IMPORT SUPPLY					
		Constant	lnMt-1	lnYus	ln(Pxk/Pus)	ln(Pxk/Pxk)	R2	DW	Constant	lnMt-1	lnCap	ln(Pxk/Pxk)	R2	DW
Animals & products	1961-91	-61.21 (-1.08)	-	8.07 (1.19)	-1.47 (-0.47)	-0.86 (-0.66)	.80	2.88	6.32 (3.24)a	-	0.07 (0.16)	6.71 (1.20)	.77	2.50
National & synthetic rubber & gums	1983-91	34.12 (0.15)	-	-3.37 (-0.12)	13.56 (0.79)	-4.19 (-1.32)	.38	2.51	-16.56 (-1.76)	-	5.16 (2.62)c	-37.17 (-1.76)	.42	2.74
Raw wood	1969-91	31.23 (1.44)	0.06 (0.27)	-3.21 (-1.23)	-4.99 (-1.15)	-2.10 (-0.72)	.29	2.07	9.42 (3.73)a	-0.01 (-0.03)	-1.04 (-2.70)b	3.59 (0.89)	.35	2.07
Crude minerals	1961-91	-5.55 (-0.87)	0.24 (1.24)	1.42 (1.73)c	-0.92 (-0.69)	-1.23 (-0.68)	.09	2.02	5.13 (3.73)a	0.21 (1.12)	0.22 (1.63)	-1.31 (-0.59)	.11	1.94
Petroleum & products	1981-91	99.42 (0.62)	-	-10.88 (0.60)	4.07 (0.43)	-3.39 (0.69)	.29	1.50	21.42 (3.06)b	-	-2.40 (-1.63)	27.52 (2.86)b	.57	2.84
Nonferrous metals	1967-91	3.26 (0.77)	0.92 (5.90)a	-0.30 (-0.20)	-0.33 (-0.22)	-0.15 (-0.13)	.86	2.40	1.94 (2.14)b	0.70 (3.37)a	0.19 (0.70)	-2.73 (-1.29)	.87	2.21
Spinning & weaving	1961-91	3.09 (0.49)	0.94 (6.91)a	-0.27 (-0.29)	0.58 (0.94)	-0.42 (-0.94)	.96	2.15	1.36 (1.96)c	0.87 (10.47)a	0.08 (1.10)	-1.41 (-3.06)a	.97	2.64
Footwear	1963-91	-3.24 (-0.37)	0.87 (6.53)a	0.62 (0.49)	-0.63 (-0.60)	-0.24 (-0.36)	.97	2.47	2.58 (2.25)b	0.68 (3.57)a	0.42 (1.31)	0.51 (0.53)	.98	2.13
Wood products	1961-91	55.06 (3.72)a		-5.26 (-2.93)a	-1.96 (-1.61)	-0.15 (-0.20)	.90	1.25	16.32 (2.77)b		-1.01 (-0.95)	8.36 (1.33)	.76	0.88
Paper products	1965-91	-48.75 (14.70)a		6.98 (17.27)a	1.67 (1.86)c	-0.05 (-0.10)	.97	1.91	3.64 (17.48)a		1.21 (23.74)a	0.49 (0.63)	.98	2.11

Appendix Table 5.2
US-Korea trade equations

Industry	Sample Period	IMPORT DEMAND							IMPORT SUPPLY					
		Constant	lnMt-1	lnYus	ln(Pxk/Pus)	ln(Pxk/Pxk)	R2	DW	Constant	lnMt-1	lnCap	ln(Pxk/Pxk)	R2	DW
Basic chemicals	1965-91	-39.37 (-2.29)b	0.69 (3.78)a	5.18 (2.30)b	0.93 (0.39)	-1.26 (-0.53)	.86	1.59	-0.20 (-0.24)	0.56 (3.46)a	1.11 (2.73)b	0.91 (0.26)	.87	1.59
Other chemical products	1965-91	-21.21 (-2.42)b	0.76 (5.99)a	2.83 (2.40)b	1.67 (1.35)	-0.59 (-0.60)	.94	1.40	0.49 (1.17)	0.61 (4.57)a	0.68 (3.12)a	1.50 (1.06)	.95	1.41
Rubber products	1965-91	4.00 (0.52)	0.94 (10.37)a	-0.38 (-0.36)	0.48 (0.46)	-0.03 (-0.04)	.98	1.94	0.76 (1.37)	1.01 (6.62)a	-0.16 (-0.54)	0.92 (0.83)	.98	2.09
Plastic products	1963-91	1.94 (0.30)	0.97 (10.29)a	-0.16 (-0.17)	-1.36 (-1.34)	-0.16 (-0.25)	.98	2.21	1.28 (2.05)c	0.89 (7.25)a	0.04 (0.18)	0.82 (0.89)	.98	2.01
Iron & steel	1965-91	23.68 (0.55)	-	-1.16 (-0.23)	1.11 (0.44)	-0.38 (-0.28)	.93	1.69	18.39 (2.02)c	-	-0.75 (-0.43)	2.46 (0.68)	.93	2.00
Railroad equipment	1979-91	-103.18 (-3.47)b	-	13.20 (3.65)b	5.08 (1.36)	-0.41 (-0.17)	.71	1.80	-24.62 (-3.74)a	-	6.62 (4.82)a	-13.73 (-1.90)c	.85	2.50

Note: t - statistics in parentheses. The superscript [a] indicates significance at the 1 percent level, [b] at the 5 percent level, and [c] at the 10 percent level.

70

Appendix Table 5.3
Export Regressions for Year 2000 Projection

	Labor	K	HK	Arable	Pasture	Forest	Coal	Oil	Min	CIFFOB	F-Test	R^2
Animal & animal products	-a	-b	a								a	0.362
Fish & preparations		a	b		-a						a	0.420
Food crops	-a	b	c							a	a	0.215
Tobacco & Mfrs			b		c						a	0.212
Agricultural commodities	-b		b	a	-a		b			b	a	0.554
Beverages		a			a	-a				-b	a	0.35
Textile fibers				-b	-c				-a	a	b	0.156
Rubber, crude, synthetic			c			c			-b			0.107
Wood & wood pulp				-b		c					b	0.116
Crude materials			c	a	-c		c		-b		a	0.446
Coal, coke, briquettes		a									a	0.202
Petroleum & products								a			a	0.36
Non-ferrous metals			a					c	c	-b	a	0.371
Spinning, weaving, etc.		a	a	a					c		a	0.474
Other textile products											a	0.149
Wearing apparel			c									0.079

	Labor	K	HK	Arable	Pasture	Forest	Coal	Oil	Min	CIFFOB	F-Test	R^2
Manufacture of leather											c	0.1
Footwear												0.057
Wood products	c	-c	b	-a				-b	a		a	0.465
Furniture & fixtures			b								a	0.177
Pulp & paper	-a	-c	a	-b					a	-c	a	0.458
Paper products	-a	-a	a	c							a	0.574
Printing and publishing		b	b	c							a	0.208
Basic chemicals		a	a	c							a	0.487
Synthetic resins	c	a		c							a	0.369
Other industrial chemicals	-a	a	a	a		-a	c				a	0.436
Drugs & medicine	-b	a	b							-b	a	0.543
Other chemical products	-a	a	a			-a				-a	a	0.823
Rubber products		a	a	a					b		a	0.417
Plastic products		a	a	a			c		a		a	0.399
Pottery, china, etc.			c				-a				a	0.33
Glass & glass products		a	a								a	0.214
Other nonmetal mineral products		a								-c	a	0.217
Iron & steel	c	a		b			c				a	0.244

72

	Labor	K	HK	Arable	Pasture	Forest	Coal	Oil	Min	CIFFOB	F-Test	R^2
Fabricated metal products		a	a	a							a	0.443
Office computing equipment		b	a	-a	a				-c		a	0.596
Other machinery		b	a								a	0.247
Radio, television	-a	a	a	a			-a				a	0.776
Other electrical machinery	-a	b	a				-a				a	0.722
Shipbuilding & repairing		a									a	0.202
Railroad equipment		a		c							a	0.297
Motor vehicles	-a	b	a			-b	-a		a		a	0.747
Aircraft		b										0.087
Motorcycles & bicycles		a		b					c		a	0.352
Professional goods	-a	a	a			-a					a	0.746
Other industries							-b				a	0.272

Note: The letter a, b, and c stand for a significance level of a two-tailed t-test of 1, 5, and 10 percent respectively. Minus sign indicates a negative coefficient. The F-test is pertaining to the hypothesis that all of the coefficients except the constant are jointly equal to zero.

73

6 Imbalances in the Asia–Pacific economy and the role of Asian NIEs

Hong Yul Han

It is commonplace to say that the economies of the Asia-Pacific region are dynamic. The remarkable economic performances of Japan and the Asian newly industrializing economies (ANIEs) have positioned these countries at the crux of the world economy. This region's share of world GNP has risen from 41 percent in 1980 to 50 percent in 1990. Also, the share of exports has grown from 29 percent to 38 percent. Rapid economic growth over the last 20 years also reflect the dynamism of the Asia-Pacific economy. The ANIEs recorded 8.5-9.4 percent of real GDP growth in the 1970s and 6.3-9.6 percent in the 1980s, though this trend is expected to moderately decelerate in the 1990s due to worldwide recession and industrial structure adjustments.

The main impetus of such rapid economic growth can be attributed to the region's outward-looking, trade-oriented development policy. Korea and Taiwan have adopted strong government-led development strategies in contrast to the market-oriented policies of Singapore and Hong Kong. The developing countries of this region such as Malaysia and Thailand, also using outward-oriented policies, recorded high average growth rates. China seems to have successfully introduced market forces pursuing an export-led development strategy, which resulted in 9.5 percent growth rate in the 1980s.

The dynamism of the Pacific economy is represented not only by GDP and trade growth rate but also by rapid expansion of the manufacturing sector, rapid increase of R&D investment and foreign direct investment. Particularly, the manufacturing sector of countries like Korea, Indonesia, Malaysia and China recorded a higher growth rate than that of their respective GDPs. By intensifying the competition between the regional countries, rapid expansion of the manufacturing sector became one of the most important contributing factors to the rapid growth of this region.

The very dynamism of the region, however, has created a number of structural imbalances that could undermine regional economic cooperation.

Most of all, trade imbalances within the region have been a source of conflict, with the United States increasingly applying protectionist pressures on various Asian countries. The developed Pacific economies have also varied widely in performance. During 1990-1992, Japan recorded the highest average growth rate among all developed countries. The US generally showed a poor performance mainly as a result of twin deficits and erosion of its industrial competitiveness. Other developed countries, such as Australia, Canada and New Zealand, are expected to recover from their recessions of the late 1980s.

If the Pacific economy is to sustain its high level of activity and assume the role as 'locomotive' of the world economy, adequate international cooperation is necessary to resolve such imbalances. However, continuous attempts to remedy the problem have failed in the past. This is partly due to the lack of policy coordination or cooperation, compounded by the huge US investment and savings gap as well as closed Japanese markets. Attention must also be paid to the relatively new structural changes, particularly in Japan, ASEAN and ANIEs, because the rapid economic integration in this region reinforces the current alignment of trade imbalances.

Characteristics of the Asia-Pacific economy

Growing interdependence

With world trade expanding in the second half of the 1980s, regional economic interdependence further intensified. Increasing regional interdependence in this area is demonstrated by rapid growth of intra-regional trade. As seen in Table 6.1, the intra-regional export of Pacific economies as a whole, increased from 53.6 percent to 64.9 percent between 1980-90. By 1990, most of the intra-regional export shares of the Asia-Pacific economies exceeded 60 percent.

In general, ANIEs and less developed countries became more heavily dependent on regional trade than developed countries. For instance, in 1990 the export shares of ANIEs grew 7 percentage points reaching 69 percent while the ASEAN share was about 75 percent. For the past few decades, the importance of the US market increased as the export share of Asia-Pacific countries has continuously increased showing 21 percent in 1990 from 17.8 percent in 1980. Meanwhile, ANIEs' share of regional imports substantially increased from 9.6 percent in 1980 to 16.2 percent in 1990. Considering the slight decrease in Japan's import share, from 10.0 percent in 1980 to 9.5

Table 6.1
Asia-Pacific export/import matrix

	Asia-Pacific			NIEs			Asean 4			US			Japan			Korea		
	'80	'90	Δ	'80	'90	Δ	'80	'90	Δ	'80	'90	Δ	'80	'90	Δ	'80	'90	Δ
Export																		
World	30.9	40.7	9.8	3.9	8.98	5.08	2.5	3.2	0.7	11.6	14.7	3.1	6.9	6.8	-0.1	0.9	2.3	1.4
Asia-Pacific	53.6	64.9	11.3	9.6	16.2	6.6	4.7	5.2	0.5	17.8	21.0	3.2	10.0	9.5	-0.5	2.1	3.7	1.6
ANIE's	61.0	69.0	8.0	9.0	12.7	3.7	10.5	8.1	-2.4	24.6	24.6	0.0	10.0	10.4	0.4	1.0	1.5	0.5
ASEAN 4	77.2	74.7	-2.5	17.7	23.9	6.2	3.2	3.9	0.7	18.7	18.4	-0.3	34.5	23.0	-11.5	1.7	4.1	2.4
US	38.7	49.2	10.5	6.6	11.0	4.4	2.8	2.8	0.0	24.5	29.2	4.7	9.4	11.4	2.0	2.1	3.6	1.5
Japan	55.0	66.2	11.2	14.5	21.4	6.9	7.0	8.0	1.0	26.5	26.3	-0.2	-	-	-	4.1	6.3	2.2
Korea	59.7	67.1	7.4	7.3	12.6	5.3	5.0	5.9	0.9	-	-	-	17.4	17.5	0.1	-	-	-
Import																		
World	32.2	38.1	5.9	3.6	6.6	3.0	3.0	2.8	-0.2	12.5	11.8	-0.7	7.0	9.0	2.0	0.8	1.7	0.9
Asia-Pacific	53.8	63.5	9.5	6.6	11.8	5.2	7.5	5.6	-1.9	15.2	15.1	-0.1	11.8	15.1	3.3	1.6	3.3	1.7
ANIEs	68.1	75.7	7.6	7.0	10.4	3.4	11.2	8.2	-3.0	17.4	17.0	-0.4	23.0	23.0	0	1.4	2.3	0.9
ASEAN 4	67.8	99.5	31.7	13.7	20.0	6.3	4.8	32.6	27.8	17.0	13.8	-3.2	24.2	25.4	1.2	2.0	3.3	1.3
US	42.5	56.9	14.4	7.1	12.2	5.1	4.4	3.6	-0.8	-	-	-	12.8	18.0	5.2	1.7	3.7	2.0
Japan	50.9	59.2	8.3	5.2	11.1	5.9	16.3	10.9	-5.4	17.4	22.5	5.1	-	-	-	2.2	5.0	2.8
Korea	61.7	74.3	12.6	2.4	5.4	3.0	5.9	5.9	0	21.9	24.0	2.1	26.3	29.1	2.8	-	-	-

Note: World dld equals 100 for each import and export region category.
Source: Direction of Trade Statistics, Yearbook 1983 and 1991, IMF.

76

percent in 1990, the ANIEs became the second largest export market for the Asia-Pacific economies. As an exception, the US exported 49.2 percent. Though the US showed the least dependance on Asia-Pacific markets for exports, it recorded quite a remarkable increase since 1980 (38.7 percent in 1980). Note, however, that the exports of US to Canada increased for the last decade with a net increase of 7 percentage points in the region.

The ASEAN-4 countries posed the only remarkable exception. The regional dependence of exports from ASEAN-4 countries has decreased from 77.2 percent to 74.7 percent. The ANIEs became the largest export market for ASEAN-4 countries as the latter grew decreasingly dependent on the Japanese market, dropping from 34.5 percent to 23.0 percent, while the ANIEs' market grew from 17.7 percent to 23.9 percent. These changes seem to reflect the trade diversion effects caused by large-scale foreign direct investment in the ASEAN countries. For example, exports from ASEAN-4 countries to Korea increased substantially from 1.7 percent to 4.1 percent.

While Japan and the US remain the two most important capital suppliers for the Asia-Pacific economies, Japan has been surpassing the US since 1980 (see Table 6.2). Particularly, Japanese foreign direct investment in ANIEs has accelerated faster than that of the US, except in Korea. As far as ASEAN countries are concerned, the Japanese shares of total stock exceed that of the US except in the Philippines. Similarly, FDI from regional developing countries makes up the lion's share of the inward FDI from all developing countries. Finally, Japanese FDI to the US increased so rapidly that it surpassed the European Community's FDI in the US. In a bilateral sense, the increase in regional FDI greatly intensified interdependence.

Changes in industrial structure

In the 1980s, ANIEs and ASEAN experienced rapid changes in their industrial structures. Table 6.3 shows the change in shares of total value added by five sectors: natural resource processing, food processing, labor-intensive industries, capital-intensive industries and machinery industries.

During this time, Japan and the US produced over 60 percent of total value added from the machinery industry and capital-intensive industries with their ratios increasing during the 1980s. However, the industrial structure of such regional developed countries did not undergo major changes. On the other hand, the ANIEs appear to have experienced substantial structural change.

77

Table 6.2
Foreign direct investment in Asia

(Stock, %)

	Year	Developed Countries	North America	EC	Japan	Developing Countries Asia Pacific
Hong Kong	1989	83.1	38.6	20.0	36.0	16.9	88.2
	1984	92.0	58.8	16.2	22.9	8.0	76.5
Korea	1988	92.8	29.9	13.8	56.1	5.8	66.5
	1980	89.9	21.9	10.7	67.3	8.2	26.1
Singapore	1989	94.6	35.1	32.4	32.5	5.4	..
	1980	88.5	33.4	47.7	18.9	11.5	..
Taiwan	1988	72.3	44.4	18.5	37.1	27.7	61.9
	1980	63.2	55.4	15.3	29.4	36.8	71.6
Indonesia	1988	72.8	12.2	34.4	38.4	27.9	82.8
	1980	77.1	06.3	14.0	48.6	22.9	70.6
Malaysia	1987	59.2	12.4	46.1	33.9	40.8	93.0
	1981	58.6	11.5	49.4	30.0	41.4	92.2
Philippines	1987	90.6	65.0	17.2	14.7	9.4	78.4
	1980	92.0	63.7	13.7	18.3	8.0	64.6
Thailand	1988	77.3	31.7	19.9	47.5	22.8	98.4
	1980	80.2	40.5	22.5	36.2	20.3	99.9
China	1987	35.0	48.8	27.2	20.5	65.0	98.3
	1982	41.8	45.1	34.9	13.9	58.2	96.6

Source: UN World Investment Directory, 1992, Vol.1.

In Korea, the food-processing industry lost its significance, falling from 23.7 percent to 19.6 percent of total manufacturing. At the same time, the machinery industry gained a remarkable portion of the manufacturing pie, rising from 19.0 percent in 1980 to 30.8 percent in 1988. Taiwan and Singapore also showed similar changes, while Hong Kong suffered a lack of investment which largely stemmed from apprehension about its return to China. Malaysia and Thailand are most conspicuous among ASEAN countries. Malaysia increased its share of capital-intensive industries, rising from 11.5 percent to 21.4 percent, while Thailand increased share of labor-intensive industries from 12.0 percent to 24.0 percent. Malaysia notably had a resource-based industrial structure while Thailand had a tremendous share of food-processing industries in 1980.

Overall, the industrial structures of Asia-Pacific developing economies have been enhanced. Such structural changes coincided with the region's rapid economic expansion. Most of all, structural enhancement fulfilled the prerequisite of furthering economic development by improving competitiveness in international markets.

Another important characteristic of the Asia-Pacific economy is that it is the only region where catching-up process is taking place. Though 'catching up' originally referred to the typical development pattern of modern industries in Japan, a similar pattern can be observed in the Asia-Pacific countries. For example, Asian NIEs seem to have acquired competitiveness comparable to Japan's in many consumer products. Leading countries of ASEAN are also catching up with ANIEs, followed by China. Taiwan and Korea are advancing beyond the level of developing countries and are establishing their own ODA. Thailand and Malaysia are described as 'quasi-NIEs' and rely on less ODA. As NIEs like Korea move into more technologically sophisticated industries, they are expected to compete with Japanese and US industries in the near future. Moreover, the quasi-NIEs not only have begun to accelerate their exports of labor-intensive goods and processed materials, but have also become legitimate competitors with NIEs for more skill-intensive products.

Basic differences persist, however, between ANIEs and ASEAN countries in the catching-up process. That is, Korea and Taiwan are attaining a competitive status comparable to Japan through the efforts of their own firms, which are engaged in vigorous capital borrowings and technology imports. Meanwhile countries of ASEAN are catching up with ANIEs based on their reliance on foreign subsidiaries established mostly by Japanese FDI. This process of catching up has undoubtedly contributed to the sustained dynamism of the Asia-Pacific economy. Nevertheless, it is not yet clear how such basic differences in development strategies will affect the structure of this region's economies. Though foreign subsidiaries invited local firms and entrepreneurship, instability in the host countries could result from their mobility under the globalization strategy of parent firms.

Challenging issues in the Pacific economy

Economic cooperation between the regional economies is widely stressed as essential to boosting the Pacific economy's dynamism. Yet, limiting factors also exist, threatening to undermine international economic relations within the regions. Among the most significant threats are the problem of macroeconomic imbalances between regional economies and Japanese dominance in western Pacific countries, which could both reinforce trade imbalances as well as bring about instability in this region.

Trade imbalances

The patterns of trade imbalances in the Pacific economic region can be examined from several perspectives: the US trade deficit with other Asia-Pacific countries, particularly with Japan; Japan's surplus with other regional economies; and the remaining countries' trade surplus with the US and deficit with Japan.

The US trade deficits with most Asia-Pacific countries has been intensified during the 1980s. In 1991, the US trade deficit with Japan recorded $47 billion, an almost fourfold increase since 1980. On the contrary, Japan showed trade surpluses with most Asia-Pacific countries. For example Japan's trade surplus with ANIEs reached $40 billion in 1991, a stark contrast to its trade deficit in 1980. Among the countries of ASEAN, only Indonesia and Brunei, whose exports are natural resources, have recorded trade surpluses with Japan.

The current US account deficit can be attributed not only to the large gap between domestic savings and investments but also to the weakening competitiveness of US industries. Because of the huge trade deficit, however, administrative protection such as Anti-Dumping Super 301 measures have frequently been applied. Such actions have been supported by the public perception in the US that Japan's and other Asian countries' unfair trading practices are the major culprits of the US deficits. Considering the importance of the US market in the Asia-Pacific region, the US's protectionist sentiment at home is one of the most difficult barriers to building effective regional economic cooperation.

Still, the US holds a comparative advantage in high-technology sectors such as aerospace, supercomputers and genetics research. Moreover, the US is believed to have the most competitive service industries. If service markets of partner countries are sufficiently liberalized after the successful conclusion of the Uruguay Round, US service exports could compensate for the trade deficits in the goods market. Nevertheless, until such expectations are realized in the future, the serious trade imbalance will remain a major factor undermining regional cooperation and a stable economic environment.

Another aspect of regional trade imbalances is trilateral trade and industrial relationships among the US, Japan and other Asian countries. That is, a large share of exports from NIEs to the US is produced by using intermediate goods imported from Japan. Thus, increased exports from ANIEs to the US usually aggravates the former's trade balance with Japan. In other words, the more NIEs export to the US, the larger the US trade deficit with Japan becomes. Therefore, even if economic cooperation is intended to complete trade liberalization, it will only result in aggravating Asian countries' trade deficits with Japan, without improving US trade performance. While trade imbalances need to be corrected through economic cooperation, a trade imbalance, itself, is a major factor undermining economic cooperation. Therefore, trade imbalances in the Asia-Pacific region have been prolonged over a period of time, and will remain a major factor exacerbating instability in this region.

Table 6.3
Change in shares of industries of Asia-Pacific countries

(%)

	Resource processing			Food processing			Labor intensive			Capital intensive			Machine		
	'80	'88	Δ	'80	'88	Δ	'80	'88	Δ	'80	'88	Δ	'80	'88	Δ
Japan	17.2	15.2	-2.0	9.7	10.0	0.3	12.5	9.8	-2.7	24.4	23.6	-0.8	36.2	41.4	5.2
US	16.0	14.9	-1.1	11.2	11.7	0.5	11.4	10.6	-0.8	21.8	26.4	4.6	39.5	36.3	-3.2
Canada	23.3	23.0	-0.3	14.5	15.2	0.7	16.3	15.5	-0.8	20.5	19.8	-0.7	25.3	26.5	1.2
Australia	19.1	19.5	0.4	18.6	20.4	1.8	14.4	15.8	1.4	23.9	23.0	-0.9	24.0	21.4	-2.6
New Zealand	17.4	22.3	4.9	27.7	26.9	-0.8	20.3	18.6	-1.7	16.2	14.9	-1.3	18.4	17.3	-1.1
Singapore	24.7	11.6	-13.1	5.1	5.8	0.7	10.3	5.9	-4.4	11.6	20.2	8.6	48.3	56.4	8.1
Hong Kong	11.7	11.7	0.0	5.3	6.4	1.1	47.0	47.6	0.6	11.3	8.9	-2.4	24.7	25.4	0.7
Taiwan	24.5	24.1	-0.4	12.5	10.3	-2.2	26.9	16.0	-10.9	21.4	22.9	1.5	20.6	26.6	6.0
Korea	19.9	17.1	-2.8	17.3	11.8	-5.5	23.3	21.0	-2.3	20.5	19.3	-1.2	19.0	30.8	11.8
Malaysia	23.6	19.4	-4.2	23.7	19.6	-4.1	18.0	16.5	-1.5	11.5	21.4	9.9	23.2	23.0	-0.2
Thailand	16.3	15.6	-0.7	54.1	39.6	-14.5	12.0	24.0	12.0	8.3	8.6	0.3	9.3	7.2	-2.1
Philippine	17.8	19.8	2.0	31.0	43.5	12.5	17.1	13.6	-3.5	22.9	15.4	-7.5	11.1	8.6	-2.5
Indonesia	14.4	14.6	0.2	30.3	26.5	-3.8	23.5	26.8	3.3	18.3	21.9	3.6	13.5	10.1	-3.4
China	12.3	20.7	8.4	12.4	11.9	-0.5	22.2	18.4	-3.8	25.1	22.2	-2.9	27.9	26.9	-1.0

Source: Pacific Economic Development Report 1992-1993, PECC.

Table 6.4
Trade balance of the US and Japan with APEC

(Millions of US$)

	1980 USA	1980 Japan	1985 USA	1985 Japan	1991 USA	1991 Japan
USA	—	7,343	—	40,585	—	38,566
Japan	-12,183	—	49,749	—	-46,863	—
Developing Nations	-5,399	-914	-28,894	7,962	-35,575	31,972
ANIEs	-3,128	12,157	-21,010	13,179	-13,438	40,458
Korea	252	2,353	-9,907	3,015	-2,224	7,707
Singapore	1,048	2,413	-2,484	2,286	-1,408	8,811
Hong Kong	-2,341	4,211	-5,159	5,790	-1,599	14,271
Taiwan	-2,087	3,180	-10,460	2,088	-8,207	9,669
ASEAN	-4,862	-13,834	-6,645	-11,273	-8,119	-2,843
Indonesia	-3,994	-9,754	-2,437	-8,001	-1,675	-7,165
Thailand	397	800	-1,528	1,012	-2,693	4,188
Malaysia	-1,351	-1,434	-1,707	-2,163	-2,445	1,191
Philippines	86	-272	-1,021	-306	-1,439	315
Brunei	0	-3,174	48	-1,815	133	-1,372
China	2,591	763	-4,244	6,056	-14,018	-5,643

Source: IMF, Direction of Trade, Council for Economic Planning and Developed, China Taiwan Statistical Data Book, 1991.

Japanese dominance in ASEAN: Another source of instability and trade imbalances

The second half of the 1980s saw a rapid increase in FDI activities. This was triggered by substantial appreciation of the Japanese yen following the Plaza Agreement, so as to compensate for the weakened price competitiveness of Japanese products, to avoid protectionism in major export markets of developed countries, and to circumvent regionalism. However, the huge influx of FDI by Japan in ANIEs and ASEAN later resulted in substantial changes of the regional industrial structure and trade relationships.

Since launching their development plan in the 1960s, ANIEs accomplished

Table 6.5
Japanese FDI by area and industry

(Shares of manufacturing, %)

	World			NIEs			ASEAN			China		
	'85	'87	'90	'85	'87	'90	'85	'87	'90	'85	'87	'90
Total	83.7	139.3	310.8	7.6	11.7	23.3	11.2	12.8	20.8	0.3	1.7	2.8
Manufactures	24.4	36.0	81.6	3.3	4.8	7.7	4.0	4.9	9.9	0.05	1.0	2.8
Food	4.5	4.3	5.0	2.4	3.4	9.5	3.8	4.7	3.7	26.7	15.0	8.4
Textiles	8.5	6.5	4.9	10.7	7.9	7.1	20.4	17.1	11.8	4.4	4.8	7.7
Wood	4.6	4.1	3.6	0.9	0.7	0.9	3.9	3.5	4.4	5.1	2.8	1.5
Chemicals	16.3	14.6	13.4	25.4	22.4	18.5	10.7	9.8	11.3	22.3	15.1	1.75
Metals	21.3	17.5	12.6	5.8	6.2	6.9	36.8	35.3	22.4	8.3	9.5	6.1
Machinery	8.1	9.1	9.7	14.4	13.0	10.9	2.3	3.0	7.0	6.0	5.3	15.6
Elec. Machinery	15.4	19.9	24.9	19.0	23.2	24.0	4.9	7.7	20.6	10.1	36.3	35.8
Trans. Machinery	13.8	15.7	13.3	8.6	9.9	8.7	9.2	10.2	9.5	1.1	0.4	1.1
Others	7.5	8.3	12.4	12.9	13.3	13.4	8.2	8.8	9.3	6.0	10.7	16.2

Source: Ministry of Finance, Japan.

a higher-than-average growth rate through export promotion, industrial adjustment and technology imports. During this period, Japan provided Asian countries with capital goods and technologies, rather than raising its FDI. Therefore, the relationship between Japan and ANIEs economies was characterized by specialized production processes. For instance, Asian developing countries specialized in production processes requiring an intensive labor force, while Japan specialized in capital- and technology-intensive processes. However, increased FDI began to change this structure. FDI was intended to take advantage of low production costs, so it was concentrated on durable consumption goods, such as those produced by electric and electronics industries.

Since 1987, Japanese firms began shifting their FDI from ANIEs to ASEAN countries, as ANIEs lost their low cost advantage because of rising wages and appreciation of their currencies. Table 6.5 clearly shows the aforementioned changes. For instance, Japanese manufacturing to the NIEs between 1985-87 was valued at $1.5 billion, which was far greater than the $0.9 billion of ASEAN countries. However, between 1987-1990, the situation reversed such that ANIEs received $2.9 billion while ASEAN received $5 billion. Of course, the shift of FDI from ANIEs to ASEAN was driven by market forces, including the appreciation of currencies or changes in production costs. The development of telecommunications and transportation technologies also made it easier to implement globalization strategies through shifting FDI. This type of trend will continue for as long as the economic environment changes.

Already, Japanese FDI again seems to be floating from ASEAN countries to other regions. Though not represented in the table, Japanese FDI in ASEAN-4 countries reportedly has been declining since 1991. The reasons for such decreases in FDI are believed to include increasing labor costs, insufficient infrastructures and other factors. For example, Thailand's labor costs increased 60 percent over the past five years, Indonesia's labor costs doubled in three years, and Malaysia has been experiencing a 15 percent annual increase in its labor costs. Also, as these economies expand, managerial- supply bottlenecks accelerate such trends.

The most important reason for decreasing FDI in ASEAN countries may be the emergence of China and Vietnam, which are accelerating liberalization and expanding preferences on FDI. Moreover, labor costs in China and Vietnam are far below that of ASEAN. Although it is not clearly summarized in Table 6.5 due to lack of data, investments seem to have been diverted in the textile sector; ASEAN's investment share has decreased by 5.3 percent, while that of China increased by 2.9 percent between 1987-1990. Concerning machinery, ASEAN's share recorded a 4 percent increase, while China tripled investments to 15.6 percent up from 5.3 percent. A similar situation has been observed in transportation machinery as well.

If this change actually reflects the diversion of investments, it could harm ASEAN substantially, at least in the long run. First of all, Japanese firms have assumed extremely large shares of total ASEAN exports. In 1990, total exports of ASEAN-5 countries (Thailand, Indonesia, Singapore, Malaysia and the Philippines) recorded $141.6 billion, with the share of Japanese firms reaching 26.2 percent of total exports. In the case of Thailand and Indonesia, Japanese firms exported 33.9 percent and 33 percent, respectively, out of total exports. Also, the ratio of FDI to domestic capital formation for Singapore and Malaysia, recorded 36.6 percent and 21.2 percent respectively. Therefore, if Japan's FDI continues to decrease — or, even worse, if existing firms move to China and Vietnam — the growing and heavily export-dependent ASEAN economy will feel the negative effects.

Table 6.6
Shares of Japanese firms' exports in ASEAN

(Billions of US $, 1990)

	Thailand	Indonesia	Singapore	Malaysia	Philippines
Total Exports	23.7	25.7	54.6	29.5	8.2
Japanese firms	8.1	8.5	14.6	4.9	1.0
Exports Share	33.9%	33%	26.8%	17%	12.7%

Source: KOTRA.

Though this may be regarded as the same phenomenon experienced by ANIEs in the second half of the 1980s, some basic differences between them exist. First, Japanese FDI activity, particularly in Korea, was initiated within a limited scope. Most activities were isolated to certain areas of Korea. The main objective of Japan's FDI was to exploit low production costs and to export to third markets. The economic significance of FDI activity was to keep final goods exported by Japanese firms competitive in the world market. Therefore, ebbing Japanese FDI in the late 1980s has a limited impact on the Korean economy in several ways. Korean firms could cover export losses; though other benefits are lost, the initial benefits themselves were small. Also, Korea limited in some senses FDI and relied on other means for its economic growth, such as foreign borrowing and technology imports.

Japanese FDI in ASEAN is clearly an important means of achieving its globalization strategy. Globalization not only results in increased trade of components, parts, semifinished goods and business, but also leads to increased foreign direct investment and international specialization of particular types of production activities. Asia's pattern of production, which is realized by relocating production facilities through FDI, appears to be consistent with the pattern of changes in countries with comparative advantages.

The adaptability of the globalization strategy has become quick to respond to changes in the economic environment, thanks to advances in data processing and telecommunications. From the perspective of host countries, instability increases particularly when their economies become heavily dependent on foreign capital. It is not clear whether or not those Japanese firms actually remain in ASEAN countries even when their competitor succeeds in FDI activities in other areas, such as China and Vietnam. Korea experienced a similar situation. That is, Korean exports have decreased in the US and Japan, while exports from ASEAN increased. Considering the case of consumer electronics exports (see Table 6.7), total consumer electronics exported by ANIEs decreased by 31 percent between 1989-1991. In contrast, ASEAN increased their exports of these products eightfold during the same period. Until Korea or other ANIEs gain sufficient competitiveness in both capital-intensive and higher technology-intensive sectors, this trend will inevitably continue.

Of course, such competition between ANIEs and other developing countries may be an important source of dynamism in Pacific economies. Suppose, however, that the decreasing trends of Japanese FDI in ASEAN countries reflects true investment diversion, then in the long-term the future of ASEAN economies will rely on the direction of Japanese firms' globalization strategy. As a globalization strategy is directed mostly by market forces, the dominant power of Japanese firms in the western Pacific area may be generating regional instability.

Table 6.7
Trade in consumer electronic products between
Japan and Asian NIEs/ASEAN countries

(Unit : ¥ mil.)

Destination		World	Asian NIEs + ASEAN Countries		Asian NIEs		ASEAN Countries	
Type of Products		Imports from	Imports from	Export to	Imports from	Exports to	Imports from	Exports to
Total of Consumer electronic products	1989	214,452	145,272	389,502	134,983	351,886	10,289	37,616
	1991	238,246	177,164	690,670	93,627	494,445	83,537	196,225
	91/89	1.11	1.22	1.77	0.69	1.41	8.12	5.22
Audio-Visual Products	1989	145,399	111,342	288,974	106,612	272,620	4,730	16,354
	1991	135,680	118,373	554,095	70,778	390,589	47,595	163,506
	91/89	0.93	1.06	1.92	0.66	1.43	10.06	10.00
Other electronic products	1989	69,053	33,930	100,528	28,371	79,226	5,559	21,262
	1991	102,566	58,791	136,575	22,849	103,856	35,942	32,719
	91/89	1.49	1.73	1.36	0.81	1.31	6.47	1.54

Regarding regional trade imbalances, Japanese dominance in ASEAN could negatively affect efforts to remedy trade imbalances between Pacific economies and Japan. FDI usually accompanies an increase in bilateral trade between investing and host countries. In the case of Japan's FDI in western Pacific economies, two sources of such seem to exist. One is through intra-firm trade of components. Another source is the so-called 'reverse imports,' which refers to importing Japan's final goods produced by subsidiaries. This implies substantial 'trade diversion' from the perspective of third countries. Because of limited access to the Japanese market due to the closed distribution system, firms from third countries must compete with the remaining portion of the market and without the favorable distribution channels of domestic firms.

The role of Korea as a balancing economic power

Clearly, trade imbalances have been a source of regional friction and disputes. The dominance of Japanese capital in ASEAN could also create instability in these economies. Trade imbalance, of course, must be resolved to enhance regional cooperation and economic development. Regional imbalances have included the US-Japan trade imbalance — attributed to well-known causes US macroeconomic imbalances — and the weak competitiveness of US industries and closed Japanese markets. Also, the dominance of Japanese capital in west Pacific Asian countries have reinforced current patterns of trade deficits, making traditional macroeconomic alignment ineffective and bilateral trade talks to open markets. The approach to solving the problem of trade imbalances should therefore consider both of the following sources.

First, the US should direct its policies towards correcting macroeconomic imbalances and enhancing industrial competitiveness at the micro-level. Such familiar policy directions are still valid. Japan needs to make an effort to open domestic markets by reducing secondary trade barriers, such as easing its closed distribution channels, by stimulating domestic demand. Though shares of Japanese imports from the US and Asia-Pacific developing countries have grown, more must be achieved to encourage Japan to contribute to reduced trade imbalances and to support the growth of developing countries in the region, since its contributions are still less than those of the US.

Second, closer economic integration between Japan and ASEAN could strengthen the current pattern of trade imbalances and make the situation more difficult to resolve. This is one reason why trade negotiations focusing on bilateral trade proved to be ineffective. Also, Japan's dominance in ASEAN could potentially undermine the stability of the regional economies. Because the FDI activities are conducted under globalization strategy of Japanese firms, which makes the capital very mobile in response of changes in both economic and non-economic environments.

Both trade imbalances and instability must be corrected through proper industrial adjustment among the Asian countries. Industrial adjustment can be coordinated either through international cooperation or market forces. At present, the latter prevails in the Asian economies, integrating the ASEAN economies into the Japanese production networks, from which ANIE countries like Korea have been isolated.

This type of market-driven integration bears a certain degree of volatility in host countries for several reasons. First, the ASEAN economies will be forced into direct competition with ANIEs in more capital-intensive and higher skill-intensive industries in the near future. If Korea succeeds in its attempt to reach a higher stage of industrial structure comparable to those of developed countries, Japan's globalization strategy must change in response.

Its FDI activities in ASEAN must accelerate, enabling ASEAN to catch up with ANIEs. Also, Japanese parents must look toward other host countries substituting ASEAN countries.

In the former case, competition between ANIEs and ASEAN (actually Japanese subsidiaries located in ASEAN) economies would become fierce. If ASEAN succeeds in catching up with ANIEs, the trilateral trade imbalances among Japan, ANIEs and ASEAN will become further aggravated. This will force the host countries to cope with the dominance of Japanese capital. The latter case would occur if ANIEs were to adjust successfully their industrial structures and catch up with Japanese advanced industries' competitiveness. The resulting substantial amount of investment diversion would cause the existing firms to leave, which means that ASEAN would suffer from serious capital deformation. Excessive dominance by Japanese capitals would therefore result in either intensified trade imbalances or instability in the ASEAN region.

Though market-driven industrial structural change may create instability, it is hardly conceivable to coordinate international industrial adjustment. In this context, it would be desirable to find balancing powers to avoid potential instability and to mitigate the current trade structure of the Asia-Pacific economy. The ANIEs, particularly Korea and Taiwan, are regarded as having the greatest potential for assuming such roles for a number of reasons.

First, the ANIEs can provide fairly well-developed export markets for both unskilled labor-intensive products from developing countries and more skill- and technology-intensive products from regional developed countries. In fact, NIEs, as a group, have become a significant economic power in the region. As observed in Table 6.1, ANIEs have became the second largest export market for the Asia-Pacific economy, absorbing more than 15 percent of all intra-regional exports, and also becoming the largest export market for ASEAN. It is worthwhile to note that Korea and Taiwan almost completely opened their manufacturing markets by 1990. Some observers also project that ANIEs will be able to continue relatively rapid economic growth and enter into a higher stage of industrialization. As the income level of ANIEs rises, the import demand for advanced products will expand, which in turn, will contribute to the mitigation of regional trade imbalances. It is of utmost importance for ANIEs to provide market access for other developing countries, as well as to achieve mature industrial economies.

Second, ANIEs may be able to play the role of tempering Japan's dominance in capital in ASEAN. In fact, this region emerged as Korea's most important FDI recipient. In most of the host countries except for Indonesia, Korea's FDI is concentrated in both labor-intensive and high-technology sectors such as electric and electronic appliances, as shown in Table 6.8. Also, it was surveyed that the majority of Korean firms investing in ASEAN appear to be optimistic about their investments and future prospects for business. Therefore, by mitigating Japan's dominance, Korean FDI in these countries may function as a balancing power, together with Taiwan, when Japan diverts investments to other parts of Asia.

One important aspect of FDI is that it should not be regarded simply as a transferral of financial resources but as a package consisting of technology and managerial know-how. Therefore, increased FDI by ANIEs in western Pacific countries will also involve the same function. While some advanced Japanese technology is being transferred to these areas — resulting in diminishing importance of technology for ANIEs FDI — the ability of ANIEs to make use of existing technologies through diffusion and adaptation should not be underestimated. That is, ANIEs' role in the so-called 'two stage flow in the transfer of technology,' is significant in that technologies developed in industrialized countries may first be transferred to and modified in the ANIEs before they are passed on to less-developed countries.

Thus far, this chapter has brought attention to the roles of ANIEs and Korea, the provision of larger markets for exports from both developing and developed countries, and balancing power to ease the dominance of Japan in ASEAN countries through increased FDI. It is also important to suggest some policy implications for ANIEs so that they may perform such roles more effectively.

First of all, the desired role for Korea requires fairly sophisticated international specialization. However, as was mentioned earlier, the coordination of international industrial adjustment is inconceivable and the cycle of 'catching up' grows shorter between ANIEs and ASEAN. In this context, the role of government in facilitating FDI flows is emphasized, although the ultimate decision to invest is up to individual firms. For example, providing information about host countries' economic environments is essential. Also, both the investing and host countries' governments may take cooperative initiatives to promote investments.

To sustain Korea's FDI activities, it must be supported by the successful industrial restructuring of the Korean economy. As Japan pursued a full industrial structure by integrating countries of ASEAN minus Korea, it may be desirable for Korea to consider strategic alliances with other developed countries like the US to obtain advanced technologies to enhance its industrial structure. For instance, Korea is attempting to build technological alliances by establishing techno-marts and systems that provide US technological information, though the US has not yet shown a clear response to this idea. Korea and the US or Canada are also cooperating by combining their comparative advantages. For example, advanced US defense technology could easily be commercialized by using Korea's relatively competitive manufacturing ability and by producing internationally competitive products.

Table 6.8
Korea's FDI in Southeast Asia by factor intensity and technology

(%)

Classification	Indonesia	Malaysia	Philippines	Thailand	China	S. Asia
Labor-intensive,						
Low-technology	63.3	12.0	23.9	37.6	61.8	78.9
Foods	21.3	0.0	0.1	4.5	10.2	7.1
Textile & apparel	19.4	0.8	16.1	4.7	10.8	56.3
Footwear & leather	10.2	0.0	4.7	8.2	18.0	2.5
Wood & furniture	2.8	10.9	0.4	0.0	0.3	0.0
Other manufactured goods	9.6	0.3	2.6	20.2	22.5	13.0
Labor-intensive,						
High-technology	16.3	50.1	46.0	46.3	23.3	3.1
Paper & printing	0.6	1.7	0.0	4.3	0.0	0.0
Fabricated metals	12.6	48.4	46.0	38.4	19.7	3.1
Machine & equipment	3.1	0.0	0.0	3.6	3.6	0.0
Capital-intensive,						
Low-technology	3.7	23.3	1.3	10.7	3.5	11.5
Nonmetallic minerals	2.8	23.3	1.3	10.7	3.5	10.3
Basic metals	0.9	0.0	0.0	0.0	0.0	1.2
Capital-intensive,						
High technology	16.7	14.7	28.8	5.4	11.4	6.5
Chemicals & petroleum	16.7	14.7	28.8	5.4	11.4	6.5

The above numbers are based on the total existing investments in 1991.
Sources: Ryou & Song (1993).

Overhauling defense technology industries is, however, just one illustration of potential opportunities for cooperation. Sub-regional cooperation on an ad hoc basis may effectively ease the current regional trade imbalances strengthened by Japan-ASEAN integration, without stirring up resistance from other countries in the Asia-Pacific area. Regional initiatives formed through close economic cooperation among Asia-Pacific countries to resolve the imbalances faced by the region have turned out to be rather unproductive thus far. Though the initiation of APEC in 1989 was regarded as an important step toward regional economic cooperation, no official mechanism has yet been determined. Moreover, the recent call for the APEC summit meeting by President Clinton faces resistance from ASEAN. It still seems implausible for APEC to harmonize and coordinate its trade and industrial policies toward other regional economies to resolve the problem of regional imbalances.

References

Drysdale, Peter (1990), 'Asia-Pacific Economic Cooperation in the Changing Global Environment: Issues and Prospects' in Suh, Jang-Won and Ro, Jae-Bong (eds), *Asia-Pacific Economic Cooperation: The Way Ahead*, KIEP, Seoul.

Ichimura, Shinichi (1993), 'Role of the US and Japan in a Newly Emerging Asia-Pacific Era' in Suh, Jang-Won (ed), *Korea's New International Economic Diplomacy Globalization Policy,* KIEP, Seoul.

James, William (1990) 'Basic Directions and Areas for Cooperation: Structural Issues of the Asia-Pacific Economies' in Suh, Jang-Won and Ro, Jae-Bong (eds), *Asia-Pacific Economic Cooperation: TheWay Ahead*, KIEP, Seoul.

Korea Institute for International Economic Policy and Korea National Committee for Pacific Economic Cooperation (March 1993), *Asia-Pacific Economic Cooperation in the Era of Economic Blocs: Korea's Role and Choice* , KIEP Policy Research No. 93-06, Seoul.

Ryou, Jai-Won and Song, Byung-Nak (March 1993), 'Korea's Foreign Direct Investment in Southeast Asia,' KIEP Working Paper No. 93-02, Seoul.

Scalapino, Robert A. (1993), 'New World Economic Order and Korea's International Role' in Suh, Jang-Won (ed), *Korea's New International Diplomacy and Globalization Policy*, KIEP, Seoul.

Sekiguchi, Sueo (1991), 'Japanese Economy and Its Roles in the Northeast Asian Cooperation,' Regional Forum on Northeast Asian Economic Cooperation, KIEP, Seoul, September.

Suh, Jang-Won (September 1992), 'Trade Imbalances and Regional Initiatives in Asia-Pacific Economic Cooperation,' Asian Forum 1992 Conference.

Yamazawa, Ippei (November 1990), 'Flying Wild-Geese in the Pacific:

Patterns of Industrial Development Among Asian Countries,' Asian Development Bank.

Yoo, Jang-Hee (July 1991), 'The ANIEs — An Intermediate Absorber of Intraregional Exports?,' KIEP Working Paper No. 91-04, Seoul.

World Bank (April 1992), *World Bank and CEPR Conference on New Dimensions in Regional Integration.*

7 The Republic of Korea and the US: Trade and trade policy issues

James M. Devault

Since the end of World War II, the Republic of Korea and the United States have maintained a special relationship. At first, this relationship was dominated by their common military and foreign policy interests, but more recently, economic ties between the two nations have strengthened. The US has been Korea's most important trading partner for some time while Korea has become an important trading partner of the US as well.

In this chapter, I examine the economic relationship between the US and Korea. The purpose of this examination is in part to determine the direction of the relationship and in part to consider how the relationship can be improved for both countries. To assess the future course of this relationship, it is important to understand the transformation which has occurred in Korea over the last three decades. Since 1960, Korea has been transformed from a poor, agriculturally based economy to an industrialized economy that is on the verge of full membership in the OECD. As the Korean economy has undertaken this remarkable transformation, the pattern of trade between the US and Korea has changed, and the structural reforms now taking place in Korea suggest that this change is likely to continue.

Improving economic ties between Korea and the US can be most readily accomplished through the mutual relaxation of trade barriers. While this is an obvious point, this does not mean that implementing mutually beneficial reductions will be easy. The ease with which the trade barriers of both nations can be dismantled depends on the nature and size of these barriers as well as the industries protected by them. The extent of trade liberalization also depends on other factors, such as the current account position of each country, the nature of each country's exports and imports, and the forum fornegotiating the removal of trade barriers. All of these factors are assessed in what follows.

The chapter begins by providing an overview of each country's external position and then focuses on the nature of trade between the two countries. The trade barriers of the US and Korea which have the most adverse consequences for bilateral trade are then examined. Finally, future prospects for the relationship are discussed.

International trade, Korea and the US

This section examines the external positions of both Korea and the US and discusses the bilateral trading relationship between the two countries. The current account positions of both countries, summarized in Table 7.1. Starting with Korea's current account position, Korea's merchandise exports grew during the period at an average annual rate of 9.3 percent while its merchandise imports grew at an even faster rate of 12.4 percent. As a result, Korea's merchandise trade balance slipped from $7.7 billion surplus in 1987 to a surplus of $0.9 billion in 1993. A similar pattern is evident with trade in services. Overall, the current account balance of Korea declined during the period, falling from a surplus of $9.9 billion in 1987 to a deficit of $0.7 billion in 1993.

Table 7.1
Korean and American current account positions (US$ billions)

Year	1987	1989	1991	1993*
Korea				
Merchandise exports	46.2	61.4	69.6	78.9
Merchandise imports	38.6	56.8	76.6	78.0
Merchandise trade balance	7.7	4.6	-7.0	0.9
Service credits	8.8	10.3	12.2	14.7
Service debits	-5.4	-9.4	-13.3	-16.2
Service balance	3.4	0.9	-1.1	-1.5
Current account balance	9.9	5.1	-8.7	-0.7

Table 7.1 *(continued)*
Korean and American current account positions (US$ billions)

Year	1987	1989	1991	1993*
	US			
Merchandise exports	250.2	361.7	416.0	447.9
Merchandise imports	409.8	477.4	489.4	576.9
Merchandise trade balance	-159.6	-115.7	-73.8	-129.1
Service credits	88.4	113.9	145.7	167.9
Service debits	-87.5	-97.7	-113.2	-124.7
Service balance	0.9	16.2	32.5	43.2
Current account balance	-163.4	-101.2	-8.3	-66.4

* Estimate based on data for first three quarters
Source: International Financial Statistics, IMF

In contrast, the US current account balance improved significantly during the period as its current account deficit fell by about 60 percent. The US current account improvement is due in part to more rapid growth in merchandise exports, which expanded at an annual rate of 10.2 percent. Merchandise imports grew at an annual rate of only 5.9 percent and because of this, the US merchandise trade deficit fell by some 19 percent. The improvement is even more dramatic in services as the service 'balance' increased from $0.9 billion in 1987 to $43.2 billion in 1993. The large surplus in service trade helps to explain why the US has been very persistent in its efforts to reduce trade barriers in this area.

Table 7.2 summarizes the direction of trade for both countries between 1987 and 1993. The table shows clearly the declining importance of the US as an export market for Korea. Exports to the US accounted for some 40 percent of Korea's exports in 1987 but this figure was cut in half by 1993. While the Japanese and EC shares of Korea's exports remained about the same, the fraction of Korea's exports going to Asian nations other than Japan nearly tripled as trade with China and the ASEAN nations expanded rapidly. The share of Korea's imports from the US and Japan dropped 25 percent during the period while the share of Korea's imports from other Asian nations rose by over 85 percent. Overall, there is a clear shift in the direction of Korea's trade away from the Western nations and Japan and towards the developing nations of East Asia.

The direction of US trade did not change significantly between 1987 and 1993, but trade with Korea did decline, at least in percentage terms. The fraction of US exports going to Korea fell by 25 percent during this period while the share of US imports from Korea dropped by an even larger percentage. The one country with which the US has experienced a noticeable increase in trade is Mexico, and it is quite likely that some of the trade lost by Korea has been diverted to Mexico. Trade with Canada, Japan and the EC remained almost unchanged between 1987 and 1993.

Table 7.2
Direction of trade statistics for Korea and the US

Year	1987	1989	1991	1993*
Korean exports (expressed as a percent of total exports)				
US	38.9	32.4	25.5	17.5
Japan	17.8	21.1	17.0	14.4
EC	14.0	11.5	13.7	13.2
Other Asia	12.2	15.9	22.1	34.5
Other	17.1	19.1	21.8	20.5
Korean imports (expressed as a percent of total imports)				
US	21.4	25.1	23.5	15.6
Japan	33.3	27.9	26.2	25.6
EC	11.2	10.6	15.1	10.3
Other Asia	11.1	11.0	12.4	20.7
Other	23.0	25.4	22.8	27.8
US exports (expressed as a percent of total trade)				
Korea	3.2	3.7	3.7	2.5
Canada	23.5	21.5	20.2	21.8

98

Table 7.2 *(continued)*
Direction of trade statistics for Korea and the US

Year	1987	1989	1991	1993*
US exports (expressed as a percent of total trade)				
Japan	11.1	12.3	11.4	10.5
EC	23.7	23.8	24.4	20.8
Mexico	5.7	6.9	7.9	9.0
Other	32.7	31.9	32.4	35.4
US imports (expressed as a percent of total trade)				
Korea	4.2	4.2	3.5	2.4
Canada	16.8	18.2	18.4	18.9
Japan	20.8	19.7	18.7	18.1
EC	20.0	18.0	17.6	16.6
Mexico	4.8	5.6	6.3	6.7
Other	33.3	34.4	35.6	37.3

*Estimate based on data for first three quarters
Source: Direction of Trade Statistics, IMF

Table 7.3 contains a summary of bilateral merchandise trade between Korea and the US. The table shows that the large trade deficits experienced by the US between 1986 and 1988 fell sharply thereafter. The reduction of the trade imbalance is due primarily to a significant decline in Korea's exports to the US, a decline largely attributable to increased competition from countries such as Indonesia, Malaysia, Thailand and China. Exports of products such as textiles, apparel, and footwear from these countries compete directly with Korean exports and have become more competitive in recent years because of rapid increases in Korean wages. Korea's graduation from the US Generalized System of Preferences in 1989 has also hurt its export growth because graduation eliminated preferential tariff treatment for many Korean products. While Korea lost this preferential treatment, many of its competitors in East Asia still retain it.

Table 7.3
Korean merchandise trade with the US (in US$ millions)

Year	Korean exports to the US	US exports to Korea	Difference
1986	13920	6355	7565
1987	18382	8099	10283
1988	21478	11257	10221
1989	20203	13478	6725
1990	19446	14399	5047
1991	18311	15518	2793
1992	15785	15099	686
1993*	12652	11337	1315

*Estimate based on data for first three quarters
Source: Direction of Trade Statistics, IMF

Table 7.4 lists the 10 most important exports of each country to the other from 1989 until 1992 at the six-digit level of the Harmonized Tariff Schedule (HTS). Table 7.4 shows that integrated circuits are Korea's leading export to the US at this level of disaggregation, followed by data processing machines, leather apparel, and VCRs. Other key Korean exports to the US include footwear, passenger cars, microwave ovens and machine parts or accessories.

Table 7.4 also illustrates the changing nature of Korea's US exports. A decade ago, Korea's exports were dominated by products such as footwear, textile and apparel. As Korea's industrialization has progressed and its wages have increased, exports of these products have declined and been replaced by less traditional products. For example, Table 7.4 indicates that Korean footwear exports to the US fell by 52 percent between 1989 and 1992. Exports of integrated circuits, on the other hand, increased from virtually nothing in 1985 to over 10 percent of Korea's US exports in 1992.

Table 7.4
Leading Korean and American bilateral exports

HTS #	Product	Value of shipments			
		1989	1990	1991	1992
Leading Korean exports to the US (millions of $US)					
8542.11	Integrated circuits	1531	1430	1493	1721
8471.92	Data processing machines	534	706	623	754
4203.10	Articles of leather apparel	839	851	705	639
8521.10	Video recording or reproducing apparatus	552	384	511	618
6403.91	Leather footwear, covering the ankles	725	1040	741	480
6403.99	Leather footwear, not covering ankles	834	935	724	465
8703.22	Passenger cars with IC engines over 1000 but n/o 1500 cc	608	813	698	452
8473.30	Machine parts and accessories	183	197	185	383
8703.23	Passenger cars with IC engines over 1500 but n/o 3000 cc	974	280	351	301
8516.50	Microwave ovens	376	288	227	257
Leading US exports to Korea (in millions of $US)					
8802.40	Aircraft exceeding 15,000kg	708	406	790	932
8542.11	Integrated circuits	394	512	466	540
4101.21	Whole raw hides	613	624	529	535
2710.00	Petroleum oils	90	454	446	487
5201.00	Cotton, not carded or combed	428	481	356	347
8803.30	Parts of airplanes or helicopters	315	298	233	299
1201.00	Soybeans	220	194	240	247
1001.90	Wheat and muslin	298	216	209	236
1005.90	Corn	640	604	179	205
4403.20	Coniferous wood	258	272	230	185

Source: Operation of the Trade Agreements Program, USITC, various years.

Leading US exports to Korea in 1992 include aircraft, raw hides and integrated circuits. Other important exports include petroleum products, aircraft parts, cotton, soybeans, wheat, corn and wood. The concentration of US exports in the areas of heavy manufactures, raw materials and agricultural products reflects the comparative advantage of the US in these areas. The US exports few consumer goods to Korea because this is an area in which Korea has a comparative advantage.

I now review the most significant barriers to trade between the two nations. Removal of some or all of these barriers is an important objective if the economic relationship between the two countries is to be improved. I proceed by examining US barriers to Korean exports and then consider Korean barriers to US exports.

Significant US trade barriers to Korean exports

While the US has one of the most open economies in the world, it continues to impede trade in several industries through high tariffs and/or quantitative restrictions. In addition to this more traditional protection, the US has also begun to use its 'unfair trade' laws more frequently and with greater impact over the last 10 years.

The impact of these trade barriers on Korea's exports has been extensive. While the average US tariff rate is quite low and now stands at about five percent, tariffs remain high in a number of industries. These industries typically involve goods whose production is relatively labor intensive, such as textiles, apparel, footwear and leather products. Thus weighted-average US tariff rates on textiles and apparel are 14 and 22 percent, respectively. Tariff rates on footwear range between 10 and 40 percent while rates on leather goods such as gloves, handbags and luggage, range from 12 to 16 percent (US International Trade Commission, 1989, pp. 2-7). Unfortunately for Korea, its comparative advantage lies at least in part in the production of these goods. Thus Korea's exports of apparel, textiles, footwear, and leather products accounted for nearly 25 percent of its total US exports in 1992. Based on this information, it appears that high US tariffs are a significant barrier to Korean exports.

In addition to high tariffs, the US also employs quantitative restrictions to limit imports of certain products. Two of these quantitative restraints are of particular importance to Korea. The first is the Multifiber Arrangement or MFA. The MFA is a system of bilateral quantitative restraints employed by the developed countries to limit textile and apparel imports from developing countries. The US has negotiated several bilateral agreements with Korea since the inception of the MFA in 1974. These agreements have become more and more restrictive over time. There are two reasons for this: first, the coverage of US agreements with Korea has been expanded to include more fabrics and products; second, textile and apparel imports from Korea have been allowed to grow at an annual rate of only 1 percent. Since imports from other countries have been allowed to grow more rapidly, Korea's share of total US textile and apparel imports has been declining. Between 1989 and 1992, Korea's share of all US imports subject to the MFA fell from 11 percent to 7.1 percent (USITC, 1990, p. 81, and USITC, 1993, pp. 102-3).

The second quantitative restriction of importance to Korea involves steel, which accounts for a significant portion of Korea's global exports, including about 5 percent of its US exports. During the mid-1980s, the US negotiated 'voluntary' restraint agreements (VRAs) with most of the major steel exporters, including Korea. Before the expiration of these VRAs in 1992, negotiations began on a multilateral steel agreement (MSA) that would apportion global steel trade after the VRAs expired. As of this writing, negotiations involving the MSA have been unsuccessful and it is likely that without an agreement, more restrictive measures will eventually be taken. Because of this, the Korean government has been pressing for the successful completion of the MSA.

Quantitative restrictions are only one of the non-tariff barriers (NTBs) used by the US to restrict imports. Of the remaining NTBs, antidumping (AD) duties are undoubtedly the most important. These duties are imposed against imports which are dumped or sold at 'less than fair value.' While the GATT allows countries to penalize foreign exporters who engage in dumping, there is broad agreement among international economists that most AD laws are protectionist (Boltuck and Litan, 1991). It is now widely recognized that dumping is rarely 'predatory,' and because of this, AD duties provide protection which lacks any real justification.

Table 7.5 provides a summary of the US AD duties now being levied against Korean exports. The table shows that Korean exports are now subject to 17 different AD duties, making Korea one of the countries most frequently subject to US AD duties. In addition, the value of Korean exports subject to US AD duties is now about $2.5 billion, roughly 18 percent of all Korea's US exports in 1993. These facts suggest that Korea has been hard hit by the US unfair trade laws, but it is worth noting that when the individual duty rates are

Table 7.5
Current US AD orders against Korean products

Product	Original punitive duty	Value of imports prior to imposition of duty (millions of $US)	Year duty imposed
Television receivers	14.6%	241.6	1984
Photo albums	64.8%	38.0	1985
Pipe fittings	12.5%	3.2	1986
Brass sheet and strip	7.2%	6.6	1986
Stainless steel cookware	8.1%	47.2	1987
Color picture tubes	1.9%	65.1	1987
Business telephones	13.9	130.5	1990
Nitrocellulose	66.3%	0.3	1990
Sweaters of manmade fibers	1.3%	453.9	1990
PET film	4.9%	41.4	1991
Circular welded steel pipes and tubes	6.0%	172.6	1992
Stainless steel pipes and tubes	6.8%	15.2	1992
Steel wire rope	1.5%	64.2	1993
DRAMs of one megabit or more	3.9%	1082.6	1993
Stainless steel butt-weld pipe fittings	21.2%	1.5	1993
Cold-rolled steel products	15.0%	49.3	1993
Corrosion-resistant steel products	18.0%	80.2	1993

Source: Anti-dumping reports of the USITC

weighted by the value of imports in each case, the average rate is only 6.8 percent. While this average is significant, it is not so high as to dramatically reduce Korean exports in most cases. Indeed, in the single most important US AD case involving Korea, imports of Korean DRAMs valued at $1.1 billion were subject to an AD duty of only 3.9 percent. Despite these relatively low rates, Koreans are certainly justified in their concern about the growing use of AD duties, particularly because they have so often been the target of these duties.

In addition to the AD cases just described, US imports of certain Korean products are also being penalized for violating US patent, copyright, or trademark laws. At present, 10 exclusion orders are in effect against a number of Korean products including certain types of memory chips (USITC, 1992, pp. 211-216). These orders prevent the subject Korean products from entering the US, but their impact is difficult to measure because information on the value of the Korean exports denied entry is not available. Furthermore, the justification for these orders is stronger because the US penalizes domestic producers who infringe on US patents, copyrights, or trademarks. Nevertheless, several US trading partners have complained that the treatment of foreign defendants in these cases is more adverse than the treatment accorded domestic defendants, and a GATT ruling against the US supports this complaint (USITC, 1992, p. 39).

Significant Korean trade barriers to US exports

Korea is still emerging as an industrialized nation and its trade policy reflects this. On the one hand, its trade barriers are lower than those of most developing countries and those of other newly industrialized nations such as Brazil. On the other hand, its trade barriers are still greater than those of the major industrialized nations. Because of this, the major industrialized nations and the US in particular have pressed Korea to liberalize trade. Korea has responded by engaging in several trade policy reforms, the most recent of which were initiated in 1988 and 1992.

Prior to these reforms, average tariff rates were about 21 percent, and had fallen only slightly from about 25 percent at the time of the last major liberalization in 1979 (Young, 1992, p. 179). These rates are very high in comparison to the rates of the industrialized nations, which typically average about 5 percent. The reforms enacted in 1988 brought the average tariff rate down to 11.4 percent in 1991, and when the reforms are completed in 1994, the average tariff rate will have dropped even further to 7.9 percent (USTR, 1992, p. 1). Even after these reforms, however, tariff rates on many goods exported by the US will remain high. Thus the average tariff on agricultural products will be 16.6 percent and tariffs on products such as potatoes, nuts, fresh fruit, and fruit juices will be even higher, ranging between 30 and 50 percent (USTR, 1992, p. 1).

In addition to tariffs, Korea also uses import licenses to restrict imports. All imports must be licensed, but most licenses are granted automatically. Products that are not granted automatic licenses are subject to quotas or banned altogether. Successive liberalizations have increased the percentage of products for which licenses are automatically granted from 69.1 percent in 1979 (Young, 1992, p. 180) to over 95 percent in 1992 (USTR, 1992, p. 2), and Korea has pledged to eliminate all quantitative restrictions which are inconsistent with the GATT by 1997. Agricultural goods account for most of the imported products subject to quotas or bans and among these goods are a number of particular interest to the US, such as beef, apples, oranges and rice. Nonetheless, Korea has increased the number of agricultural products granted automatic licenses by 243 since 1988 (USTR, 1992, p. 2).

Despite the reforms made by the Korean government and the reduction in formal trade barriers, the US has complained recently that informal trade barriers still exist. For example, the US claims that clearance of customs often takes far too long and that Korean health and safety standards are used to restrict US exports of agricultural products. Discussion of these issues produced an agreement in 1992 known as the Presidents' Economic Initiative. In 1993, a second, more comprehensive initiative known as the Dialogue for Economic Cooperation was undertaken. The purpose of both initiatives (in the eyes of US negotiators) is the reduction or removal of Korea's informal trade barriers.

In addition to the barriers that limit US exports of goods, Korea also has a number of barriers that restrict US exports of services. These barriers have become the focus of greater US attention as the importance of service exports in the US current account has increased. Two areas that are of particular importance are insurance and banking. Liberalization of the Korean insurance market has become an important goal of US insurers because Korea has the sixth largest insurance market in the world. Not only is the market large, but it is expected to grow at an annual rate of some 15 to 20 percent in the near future. The Korean insurance market is dominated by a small number of Korean firms that underwrite 85 percent of domestic life insurance policies.

These firms effectively control the insurance market because life insurance accounts for about 82 percent of the overall market (Clifford, July 1993, pp. 62-63).

Insurance has been a point of dispute between Korea and the US since 1979, when an American insurance company filed a complaint against Korea. As a result of this case, Korea agreed to open its markets to greater competition, but the US insurance industry was not satisfied and the US Trade Representative filed a second case in 1985. In 1986, the case was resolved when Korea agreed to let US firms underwrite both life and non-life insurance. Even though these measures increased foreign market access, they did not end the dispute. Many US firms still complain that they are discriminated against by regulations that benefit the major Korean insurers and help to limit foreign competition.

Banking is another important service sector in which US and foreign participation remains limited. The major problem according to US banks is the dominance of credit markets by the Korean government. The government originally took control of the credit market to fuel Korea's industrialization but now appears reluctant to relinquish this control. The government still controls interest rates and continues to be very influential in the allocation of credit. While reforms are underway, US and foreign banks still complain about discrimination that makes it difficult to raise capital. They point to the very limited foreign share of total bank deposits (around 1 percent in 1989) as evidence of this discrimination (Clifford, November 1990, pp. 59-60).

Korean officials defend the regulation of the service sector on the grounds that regulation is necessary to maintain the competitiveness of domestic firms. The main argument is that the service sector requires protection from foreign competition to mature and become globally competitive. This argument is also used to justify gradual liberalization of the service sector, much to the frustration of the US and other foreigners, who have insisted on more immediate access. Despite these problems, progress is being made in reducing barriers to US providers in these and other important service sectors, such as telecommunications and transportation.

Greater liberalization by Korea is also likely in the treatment of inward foreign direct investment (FDI), which until recently has been tightly controlled through a system of onerous restrictions. These restrictions have greatly reduced the attractiveness of FDI in Korea, and when combined with the increasingly liberal treatment of FDI in other East Asian countries, the result has been a substantial decline in the flow of FDI into Korea. Increasing liberalization has already begun under the Kim government and is likely to accelerate because FDI represents an important source of technology for Korean manufacturers. Without access to foreign technology, Korea's movement towards a technologically advanced industrial base will be jeopardized. This is one important area in which progress can be mutually beneficially to both the United States and Korea.

A final complaint that the US has is the absence in Korea of any strong protection for intellectual property rights (IPRs). IPRs have become an important concern of the US as counterfeiting of products produced by US firms has grown worldwide and as infringement of US-held patents, trademarks and copyrights has increased. Estimated global losses for US firms from copyright infringement alone exceeded $2 billion in 1992 according to the International Intellectual Property Alliance, an industry trade group (*The Asian Wall Street Journal Weekly*, April 1993, p. 4). According to this group, Korea was responsible for about 20 percent of this loss, or about $400 million.

To combat foreign violations of US-held IPRs, Congress passed the so-called 'special' 301 provision of the Omnibus Trade and Competitiveness Act of 1988. This provision allows the US Trade Representative to target particular countries who provide inadequate protection for US-held IPRs. The most serious offenders are referred to as 'priority foreign countries' and are subject to accelerated 301 investigations. Less serious offenders are placed on the 'priority watch list' or just the 'watch list' and are subject to periodic investigations designed to determine whether progress is being made in protecting IPRs.

In 1989, Korea was placed on the priority watch list, and this triggered some serious reforms that strengthened Korea's IPR laws. These improvements were viewed as significant by the US Trade Representative, and Korea was removed from the priority watch list and placed on the watch list. Nonetheless, US officials complain that while Korea's IPR laws are now stronger, enforcement of these laws has not been strict enough to prevent serious violations, which continue. In May 1993, Korea was again placed on the priority watch list, but it now appears that the Korean government has begun serious enforcement of its laws. One reason for this is that inadequate enforcement of Korean IPR laws has discouraged foreign firms from transferring technology to their Korean operations.

Future prospects

What are the prospects for the economic relationship between Korea and the US? The future of the relationship depends on several factors, including the impact of several recently completed trade agreements, the nature of bilateral negotiations between the two countries, and the increasing integration of Korea with the rest of the East Asian economy. I now address each of these factors.

Two recently completed trade agreements have the potential to significantly alter the relationship between the US and Korea. The first of these is the North American Free Trade Agreement (NAFTA), which liberalizes trade between the United States, Canada and Mexico. NAFTA is likely to reduce the flow of trade and investment between the US and Korea for two reasons. First, by providing preferential treatment to trade among its members, NAFTA is likely to divert trade away from non-members such as Korea. Second, NAFTA is likely to divert FDI from Korea and other East Asian economies to Mexico. Estimates of Korea's losses from NAFTA vary, but a recent study by Noland (1993) suggests that these losses will be in the neighborhood of one to three percent of Korea's global exports.

This is a substantial figure, but it is likely to overestimate the damage produced by NAFTA for two reasons. First, Noland's study uses partial equilibrium analysis and ignores the beneficial impact that increased growth within NAFTA will have on Korea's exports. Korea's losses due to NAFTA are also likely to be reduced by the passage of the second recently completed trade agreement, the so-called Uruguay Agreement. This agreement reduces tariff and non-tariff trade barriers globally, and thus will reduce the preferential treatment provided by NAFTA while at the same time stimulating additional exports from non-members. The Uruguay agreement should help to increase trade between the United States and Korea not only because it reduces tariffs but also because it phases out the Multifiber Agreement over a ten year period. The Uruguay Agreement also restricts the use of antidumping laws, something which may help Korea. On net, it seems likely that the combination of the Uruguay Agreement and NAFTA will produce at worst a very modest decline in Korea's US exports.

US exports to Korea will be boosted by the Uruguay Agreement as well. This agreement strengthens the protection of IPRs while at the same time freeing up trade in agriculture. Both of these areas have been points of contention between the United States and Korea. Korea may also be forced to accelerate the liberalization of financial services, something which should

109

help US banks and other US financial service providers.

In addition to NAFTA and the Uruguay Agreement, future trade and investment flows between the US and Korea will depend on bilateral negotiations between the two countries. Future prospects are not very encouraging here even though the Clinton administration has recently sought to negotiate with Korea. This is because the US has traditionally relied on more aggressive policies (or the threat of more aggressive policies) in its efforts to extract unilateral trade concessions from Korea. This approach has produced some success for the US in terms of opening markets, but it has also produced an acrimonious atmosphere that undermines negotiations and may ultimately limit progress. This approach has also failed to produce a mutual reduction of trade barriers because the US has offered little in exchange for the concessions it has extracted from Korea.

A more constructive approach would rely less on the threat of trade restrictions and focus more on areas of mutual benefit, such as Korea's treatment of FDI. Such an approach, however, requires a sincere commitment on the part of both governments to further liberalization. This commitment seems to have been made by the Kim government, which has undertaken a number of substantial reforms. Nonetheless, some of the most troubling areas for the US have not yet been addressed, including automobile trade.

The final factor that will influence future economic ties between the US and Korea is Korea's accelerating integration with the East Asian economy. This integration has become increasingly apparent as the focus of Korean exports has begun to shift away from the US market and towards East Asian markets. The trend towards integration is bolstered by the pattern of Korean FDI in other East Asian economies, particularly the lower wage ASEAN countries. For Korea, this increased integration is healthy as it reduces Korea's dependence on the US market and allows Korean producers to remain competitive in world markets. Korea's increasing involvement in East Asia is also important in that this region is now the most economically vibrant in the world.

The shift in the Korean economy towards East Asia reflects a trend that the US is also engaged in, albeit to a lesser degree. Given the increasing reliance of both countries on East Asia, it would be wise for Korea and the US to recognize their common interest and work together in ways which would foster further economic integration in the region. The natural forum for this cooperation is the APEC group, which has begun to establish and implement an agenda that should ultimately produce freer trade and investment flows and greater economic growth throughout the region.

References

Boltuck, Richard and Litan, Robert E. (1991), *Down in the Dumps: Administration of the Unfair Trade Laws*. The Brookings Institute, Washington, DC.

Clifford, Mark (1 November 1990), 'Fear of the Foreigner,' *Far Eastern Economic Review*, pp. 59-60.

_____ (1 July 1993), 'No Assurance,' *Far Eastern Economic Review*, pp. 62-63.

Destler, I.M. (1992), *American Trade Politics*, 2nd edition, Institute for International Economics, Washington DC, and The Twentieth Century Fund, New York.

Noland, Marcus (1993), 'Asia and the NAFTA,' KAEA Conference on US-Korea Economic Partnership, Philadelphia, July 29-30.

The Asian Wall Street Journal Weekly (26 April 1993), 'Asian Nations Face US Listing of Intellectual-Property Offenders,' p. 4.

United States International Trade Commission (1989), *The Economic Effects of Significant US Import Restraints, Phase 1: Manufacturing*. USITC No. 2222.

_____ (1990), *Operation of the Trade Agreements Program, 41st Report*. USITC No. 2317.

_____ (1992), *Operation of the Trade Agreements Program, 43rd Report*. USITC No. 2554.

_____ (1993), *Operation of the Trade Agreements Program, 44th Report*. USITC No. 2640.

United States Trade Representative (1992), *National Trade Estimates Report on Foreign Trade Barriers: Korea*, Washington, DC.

Young, Soo-Gil (1992), 'Import Liberalization and Industrial Adjustment,' in Corbo, Vittorio and Suh, Sang-Mok (eds), *Structural Adjustment in a Newly Industrialized Country: The Korean Experience*, John Hopkins Press: Baltimore and London.

111

Discussion

John W. Kendrick

I agree with the other speakers who believe that further liberalization of foreign trade and investment by South Korea will be beneficial not only to its trading partners but also to the Korean economy. As an owner of the Korea Fund, like Professor Klein, I am glad that I can now buy shares in selected individual companies! More importantly, the access by Korean firms to world financial markets should reduce their cost of capital and promote new investment.

If the Korean economy is to continue its splendid record in coming years, it is important that a substantial proportion of gross domestic product (GDP) continue to be devoted to saving and investment. I am referring not just to tangible nonhuman capital outlays − structures, producers' durable equipment and inventory accumulation − but to all outlays that increase output and income-producing capacity for future periods. This would include nontangible investments in research and development (R&D), and human investments in rearing, education and training, health and safety, and mobility. And it would include tangible as well as nontangible investments of all sectors − personal and governmental as well as business.

In my study, *The Formation and Stocks of Total Capital* (1976), I found that in the United States the rate of economic growth is closely related to the rate of total capital formation. For my Presidential Address to the Atlantic Economic Society, published in the *Atlantic Economic Journal* (March 1994), I have updated through 1990 the estimates of total investment and capital, by type. They show that the rate of growth of total factor productivity 1929-1990 is explained by the rate of growth in the ratio of nontangible to tangible capital, human and nonhuman. This is to be expected since nontangible investments are designed to increase the quality and efficiency of the tangible factors. I feel sure that my findings would also hold for other countries, as the research of Hak K. Pyo suggest they do for Korea.

Certainly, the expansion of educational opportunities indicated by the increase in enrollments in higher education from 319,000 in 1975 to almost 1.6 million in 1990 was an important factor in the country's strong economic growth. Particularly important for raising productivity have been the activities of the Ministry of Science and Technology, the Korean Advanced Institute of S&T, which has strengthened postgraduate training locally, and the Korean Science and Engineering Foundation that is expanding scholarship programs to send S&E students abroad.

It is noteworthy that in South Korea almost one-third of the degrees in natural sciences have been earned by women, a much higher proportion than in Japan. It is also encouraging that expatriate scientists and engineers are returning from abroad as salaries and living and working conditions improve in South Korea.

With respect to R&D, as a percentage of GDP, it increased from 0.5 in latter 1976 to 1.0 in 1983 and to around 2.0 percent in the early 1990s (NSF, 1993, p. 97). Industrially funded R&D has grown faster than the total, rising from one-quarter of the total in 1976 to almost three-quarters in 1990. This has greatly enhanced the ability of Korean firms to adapt foreign technologies to their production requirements. Since 1966, the Korea Institute of Science and Technology has supported applied Research. The Korean Science and Engineering Foundation, modeled after the US National Science Foundation, supports basic research. Science and Engineering Research centers have been established at universities around the country for the common utilization of advanced R&D facilities together with industry and government.

Since the US, Japan and Germany all spend close to 3 percent of GDP on R&D, this would seem to be a reasonable target for the Korean Ministry of Science and Technology to set for attainment by the early years of the 21st century. Also important in fostering invention and technology transfer are licensing of foreign patents or cross-licensing; exchange of information through journals, international meetings, etc; and joint ventures with foreign multi-national companies both in Korea and abroad.

It is inevitable that the trend rate of growth of productivity and real GDP per capita in South Korea will eventually slow down. But I expect the gap with the industrialized nations to narrow further until it is no longer significant if pro-growth policies are continued.

113

Timothy J. O'Brien

As an attorney representing Korean businesses doing business abroad and in some cases representing US and other foreign businesses doing business in Korea, I would like to address some of the problems which I have helped my clients to deal with, commenting very much on a micro- and not on a macroeconomic level. These remarks and observations come purely from a practical and a business viewpoint not from an academic or a policy viewpoint. I will be reporting on what sort of things the businesspeople identify as the problems they are facing, rather than arguing to support any policy positions .

President Clinton's 1993 visit to Korea was, I think, quite successful. Judging from press reports, it focused mostly on security issues, which should not be surprising, given the recent 40th anniversary of the signing of the truce that ended the Korean conflict. Mr. Clinton seems to have satisfied the Koreans on the key security issues, and I think he probably left them happier than they expected to be on some of the economic issues as well. The resolution of issues with the Japanese − or at least the beginnings of a resolution or framework agreement − has taken some of the pressure off the Koreans, and perhaps the lowering of tensions with Japan will result in facilitating relations between the US and Korea. The New Economic Plan announced by President Kim and the Dialogue for Economic Cooperation announced by Presidents Kim and Clinton all should contribute to this.

At the same time, it is important to acknowledge the distinction between the situation in Korea and the situation in Japan. Too often Koreans have the unhappy experience of finding that when foreign critics aim their slings and arrows at Japan they tend to hit Korea, too. And I think everybody welcomes the idea that Korea has to be judged on its own merits and not as another Japan.

Granted, it may be fair to say that Korea still has a perhaps exaggerated sense of itself as a weak country, a poor country, a country that needs to protect itself from the outside. That perception has not yet caught up with the reality. We all know the proverb about the shrimp between two whales that Koreans like to use to emphasize their vulnerability. But I really think that Korea has now become at least a dolphin − perhaps a shark, some would say, but not a shrimp anymore.

Many Korean governmental policies and attitudes (and, indeed, popular attitudes) appear to be relics of the time when the Korean GNP was small, when Korea had a chronic foreign exchange deficit, when it was perhaps

114

closer to Malawi in economic development than Japan, and when it was indeed a shrimp. Notwithstanding, a case can be made that the Korean business sector certainly, and probably a broad swath of the Korean government too, really believe in – and accept the necessity of – market opening, far more so than their counterparts in Japan. It is in this context that some of the US trade initiatives, in the past, appear to have been heavy-handed and even counterproductive, notably in the case of the beef controversy, still ongoing to some extent. I recall some years ago we had terrible demonstrations – farmers cutting their pinkies off in front of the US embassy – and an incredible amount of bad feeling generated over what was really not a very strategic market and probably one the Australians and others will get more benefit out of it than the US. The Koreans now think – perhaps it's wishful thinking on their part – that given all this, there is now a possibility that trade and economic issues can be handled at a lower volume and that we can work toward a balanced trade with a results-oriented focus.

Again, I think President Kim's New Economic Plan will happily facilitate many of these developments. In particular, Korea has a production capability that may offer strategic advantages to US industry; and US industry has the technology which is the key need for Korean industry. That is something which Korean government leaders and industry leaders really sense at this point and they are anxious to realize the possibilities through strategic alliances and other forms of cooperation. One question is how receptive the US businesses and investors are going to be to those overtures.

Judging from my conversations with Korean businessmen when they speak about their experiences here in the United States, the challenges are numerous. My comments are much more personal than might be the case if I were talking about the American side, because the Americans already have articulate spokespeople through the American Chamber of Commerce in Seoul, who put out position papers every month to summarize all the issues. Koreans, to my knowledge, don't have quite the same ability to put their case.

Beginning with anti-dumping, legitimate questions can be raised as to whether the anti-dumping system accomplishes enough good for the US industries that they're aimed at helping so as to justify the harm they do to US consumers, to say nothing of the ill effects on producers in Korea. But I will leave that question to economists. Even if anti-dumping is taken on its own terms, Koreans find much to be unhappy about with the way in which dumping duties impose an anti-competitive burden on them and other producers through somewhat unrealistic and artificial rules and procedures. To give a couple of examples, in calculating dumping margins it is required

115

that a company show 10 percent selling and general expenses. This means that if you're more efficient than that you won't get any benefit from it. You'll be assumed to have those expenses. Likewise, you'll be assumed to have a profit margin of 8 percent no matter what your industry. All of this goes into the calculation of the margin.

We also have had a lot of emphasis on cost of production rather than home country prices for determining duties. Now this puts a great administrative burden in terms of showing what the cost of production was in the first place and, in the second, is quite a burden on a start-up industry which is having heavy initial expenses which all go into the mix for the calculation of duties. The enormous cost of anti-dumping proceedings is another serious problem for the Koreans, both administrative and in terms of out-of-pocket expenses. That brings us to lawyers and the legal system.

Koreans generally find themselves somewhat baffled by the American legal system, particularly when they first approach it. Koreans are developing a lot more sophistication but nonetheless I think Koreans find it rather strange that there are so many lawyers in the United States – by some statistics 800,000 – which compares to less than 10,000 in Korea, and so Koreans find they are in a radically different society over here. They have a hard time understanding the role of lawyers in the negotiation process of business deals. They are surprised to find so many misunderstandings developing into huge litigations with mountains of discovery and certainly mountainous legal fees. They are understandably nervous about the jury system – they have a hard time understanding how the jury system is applicable to civil cases, and are concerned in that regard also with possibilities of racial prejudice or other parochial prejudices, and I could not say that those fears are without basis.

Koreans are baffled by the complexity of US law – the very fact that we can cover an entire library wall with the volumes of the US legal codes whereas with Korea we could probably fit the corresponding Korean codes on the top of a small desk – the fact that when you ask a lawyer a question you don't really get much of an answer. One of my friends was complaining about 'octopus' lawyers – 'on the one hand, on the other hand, on the other hand.' Koreans often find themselves – particularly the trading companies whom I represent – in the position of being lenders to less than blue-chip companies. They therefore often find themselves in the throes of bankruptcy litigation because our system is based on rehabilitating and even blessing the debtor rather than to help the creditor – whereas for Koreans usually the deadbeat will spend some time in jail. The unavailability of criminal sanctions for failure to pay debt is another thing to which Koreans must take some adjusting. At the same time their lawyer will be telling them you better be careful with this guy because if you don't watch out he'll sue you because you didn't lend him even more money. The legal theories of lender liability, which fortunately seem to be subsiding somewhat, are another source of concern for Koreans.

Another area of increasing concern is with respect to tax issues. Transfer pricing issues under 482 are a source of great problems for many Korean corporations. At least one was given a huge assessment which I think is still under litigation and new changes in other tax rules relating to thin capitalization and so-called earnings stripping also will put on Koreans what they perceive as an unfair burden of having to pay tax on income that they never earned. Again, I am not putting these forward as value judgments or even necessarily as trade issues. In fact the Koreans have just started their own 482 equivalent, and they're out there hammering away at the foreigners with the same gusto as the IRS. My point is, as one considers the implications of changing bilateral economic policies, these are some of the things that the Koreans talk about when they discuss doing business in the US.

E. Djimopoulos

Myung-Gun Choo proposes the expansion of NAFTA into a World Free Trade Area (WORFTA), by the near term expansion of NAFTA through the inclusion of South Korea, Taiwan, Australia and New Zealand into a trans-Pacific organization. This is seen as the first step towards a US-led free world trade regime following the free-trade principles of the GATT.

The paper raises several important issues. The first issue open for consideration is that concerning the formation of regional trading groups. Are FTAs in general and NAFTA in particular, avenues towards freer, more liberal world trade? Does the formation of NAFTA move the whole world towards the ideal of universal free trade or is it simply the US reaction to the formation of the European Union and the increasing economic expansion of Japan into Southeast Asia? Is NAFTA a way for the US to carve out and preserve the markets of the Americas against perceived competition from the Japanese, the Europeans and the Southeast Asian countries? If NAFTA is only a defensive reaction on the part of the US, it may simply result in a Fort America, where foreign intrusions will be fought by the collective application of member-country measures against the assaults of European and Asian economic invaders and therefore be against a world free-trade regime.

117

Even assuming that universal free trade is desired by the US and the other major economic powers, a second issue is raised in the readers' minds. Is the piecemeal, ad hoc assemblage of regional FTA groupings the best way to achieve this goal, or should the countries' efforts be devoted to the pursuit of liberalized trade arrangements through the GATT and the eventual furthering of the achievements of the Uruguay Round?

Underlying the whole paper and motivating the proposal for a WORFTA is the third issue that can be perceived throughout the paper and is mentioned explicitly by Choo. This is the fear felt by many Asian countries towards being relegated to the growing Japanese economic sphere of influence in the Pacific. In addition these countries fear that domestic political pressures in the US may lead to an apparent abdication of the American economic interests and an indifference toward the fate of US political allies in the region (primarily South Korea and Taiwan). These considerations seem to be major factors motivating the conciliatory approach of Korea and Taiwan towards the bilateral pressure exerted by the US on issues of trade and international finance.

It will be a major error if the US government, and following it US business, concede East and Southeast Asia to the Japanese and do not try to counteract by using their influence. Many of the residents of these countries would welcome increased US economic involvement as it would provide a counterbalance to Japanese economic might. The US still has a large pool of goodwill in many of these countries. The worldview of rival European and American trading blocs and an Asian trading bloc under Japanese influence does not seem a desirable one from the Asian or the US perspective. The US should expand its contacts to the East and Southeast Asian countries in order to maintain its position as a world economic leader. While an expansion of NAFTA, which has several non-trade-related aspects, into a WORFTA may not be the preferred option of the US or the other parties involved in the potential agreement, a more tolerant and accommodating attitude towards the East and Southeast Asian countries may prove highly profitable for the US. These countries have not only been collectively the fastest growing economies during the past two decades, but they can help in the maintenance and expansion of the US economic presence in Asia. The big prize gradually making its entrance onto the world economic stage is China. An active US presence in the East and Southeast Asia countries provides a close contact with developments in this vastly populous part of the world. Instead of US businesses trying to go it alone in China, they could approach this potentially very important market through joint ventures or intermediary enterprises in

South Korea, for example, whose businesses have been active during the past few years in various investment and trade arrangements with the Chinese. This cooperation could provide benefits to all parties involved. The Chinese could get the technological assistance they need without seeming inordinately dependent on the US, while the US and Korean businesses could contribute their varied expertise and improve their chances for success in their ventures into the Chinese market.

Jae Won Lee

Marcus Noland's paper is very timely and helpful. The potential trade diversion effect of NAFTA has been a serious concern to outsiders, especially Asians who do not have a free-trade area of their own. Mexico's membership in NAFTA would certainly strengthen Mexico's position as their competitor in supplying products to the vast US and Canadian markets. NAFTA would also provide the US a sizable market protected from outsiders.

Noland skillfully navigates through the complex problems of trade diversions, trade deflections and investment diversion. He then produces tangible projections of the anticipated magnitude of the trade diversion effects on Korean export industries by combining regression estimations and ARIMA extrapolations. Noland continues on to discuss a few possible responses by Asian nations. Finally, he provides them with some cold comfort by concluding that Asian nations' suffering from the trade diversion will end in the long run and that the NAFTA will actually be to the advantage of Asian countries as well as to the United States.

Regarding cross-price elasticity regression estimations, (Appendix Table 2) Noland states that, out of 46 industries under study, only 22 industries show the correct sign for the estimated cross-price elasticity between Korean and Mexican relative prices. The other 24 industries have positive cross elasticity, which led to Noland's statement, 'Korean and Mexican exports to the US are *complements* rather than *substitutes*.' Such a literal interpretation does not seem to be appropriate, especially when the data used in this set of estimations are inadequate. As the industry-wise export price index data are not available for Mexico, Noland has used for Mexican industries the country's aggregate export price index data instead, whereas for Korean industries the corresponding industry-wise export price index data have been used. Furthermore, the presence of multicollinearity and the lagged dependent

119

variable as an explanatory variable compound the estimation problem.

Noland proceeds with his estimation of the diversion impacts by using the cross-elasticity estimates with the correct sign and assigning zero value to those with the wrong sign. Such an asymmetric treatment of the cross-elasticity estimation is an arbitrary and questionable procedure.

Noland later states that the Asian concern over the trade and investment centers on *motor vehicles,* and *textiles* and *apparels.* But the estimated cross elasticities for motor vehicles, wearing apparels and other textiles industries must have had a wrong sign, because those industries are excluded from Appendix Table 5.2. Spinning and Weaving industry is the only textile related industry that is included in Appendix Table 5.2.

Besides the data problem, a conceptual problem may arise in using the Mexican historical data in projecting the future impact of the NAFTA. The sample period for the regression estimation is from 1962 to 1991. During this period, Korea and Mexico have not exactly exported the products that directly compete with each other. In fact, Noland's estimated Finger-Kreinin Index of export similarity between Korea and Mexico even in 1990 is 36 out of the maximum possible value of 100. The index must have been significantly lower during the earlier segment of the sample period. Once NAFTA is in effect, Mexico will start producing and exporting the products that will be in more direct competition with Korean exports to the US as indicated by Noland's estimated Korea-Mexican export similarity index value of 47 for the year 2000. If so, the pre-NAFTA cross elasticities between Korean and Mexican products can be considerably different from the post-NAFTA cross-elasticities, casting more doubt on the wisdom of using the Mexican historical data for such regression-based projections. A possible way to get around the problems may be to estimate the cross elasticities by using the industry-wise data set for a country like Taiwan as a proxy for that of Mexico. Since Korea and Taiwan have had a greater degree of export similarity for the sample period, this would more closely approximate the expected post-NAFTA trade competition between Korea and Mexico.

To comment on the estimation of the NAFTA's Reduction of the Tariff and Nontariff Trade Barriers, Noland uses the estimated trade barriers based on actual tariffs rather than the statutory ones, thereby incorporating the GSP and Maquiladora provisions in his set of the estimated trade barriers. This is certainly very appropriate approach.

The pending Uruguay Round results will somewhat reduce the Mexico's NAFTA advantage in trade barriers. But it is of course premature to fully incorporate this aspect in the projection models.

To make the projections more relevant, Noland uses ARIMA to project the Korean export pattern for the year 2000. [Table 5.1: Cases C and D] Just a word of caution is warranted here, because such a mechanical projection cannot fully incorporate any post-NAFTA trade adjustments that Korea will undoubtedly undertake. Furthermore, ARIMA projections based on such a small sample size as 21 annual observations (1968-88) are inadequate.

Admitting that the regression-model projections are based on somewhat *non-robust* estimates of the cross elasticity, Noland presents another set of the trade diversion projections based on ARIMA extrapolations of Mexican exports with and without $12 billion annual investment diversion to Mexico. The results then are used to make projections of the trade diversions under a set of simple assumptions.

This ARIMA projection is free from the troubles associated with the regression estimation of the cross elasticities. But ARIMA merely carries out a mechanical projection of the Mexico's past export behavior before NAFTA. When we realize that NAFTA will result in enormous trade readjustments among both the member nations and outsiders, one can question the effectiveness of using the Mexico's *pre*-NAFTA export behavior along with a set of simple assumptions to project *post*-NAFTA export pattern.

In spite of those data and estimation problems, which are to the large extent beyond his control, Noland has presented a lucid analysis of the complex and urgent issue. His insight and methodology are certainly valuable and educational to many.

Young Back Choi

James M. Devault's paper presents an overview of the nature of the existing trade relationships between the US and Korea, including the trade barriers on both sides, and makes some interesting observations along the way.

The much-publicized US trade imbalance against Korea in the late 1980s is largely eliminated, as of 1993, between an almost 20 percent decline in Korean exports to the US and an almost 30 percent increase in the US exports to Korea since 1989. Devault explains that the decline in the Korean exports to the US may have come about because Korea has become less competitive vis-a-vis Indonesia, Malaysia, Thailand and China in its major export goods— textiles, apparel, and footwear. The increase in the US exports to Korea is explained partly by the elimination of trade impediments and partly by the demand-led growth in Korea.

Devault rightly observes that, while the average US tariff is around 5 percent, tariffs are much higher on many labor-intensive goods such as textiles, apparels, footwear and leather products which, incidentally, account for almost 40 percent of Korean exports to the US. Korean products, in other words, are subject to a much higher average tariff than the average as a whole suggests. Devault observes that it is the problem of the Korean industrial structure that happens to have comparative advantage in areas where the US is 'import sensitive,' implying that if Korea became competitive in less labor-intensive products the problem might be lessened. But judging by the punitive anti-dumping duties imposed on DRAM, I am not sure whether the implication is warranted.

Regarding anti-dumping (AD) and anti-subsidy (AS) duties, Devault observes that 'the duties now being levied are significant but are not so large as to dramatically reduce Korean exports.' But the words such as 'significant', or 'not so large,' or 'dramatically,' are not precise and tend to understate the real impacts of the US non-tariff barriers. For instance, Devault fails to mention the uncertainty and hardship caused by the arbitrariness of AD and AS duties and exclusion orders. Moreover, the real harm of the arbitrary measures such as AD and AS duties is that protectionists and special-interest groups in other countries will come to realize the effectiveness with which various US industries can erect trade barriers, and imitate their American counterparts, thereby severely limiting international trade.

Devault rightly points out that the trade barriers in Korea, though still higher than those of the major industrialized nations, are lower than most other LDCs – the average tariff standing at some 11 percent in 1991 and scheduled to be lowered to some 8 percent in 1994, from some 25 percent in 1979. From the point of view of the US government, Korea may be regarded as a showcase, not only from political and foreign policy points of view – given the record of Korea's economic development and democratization – but also from trade policy point of view. Here, Section 301 and other forceful measures of bilateral trade negotiation, such as AD and AS duties, have been singularly effective. Flush with success, US trade officials may be tempted to eliminate the remaining vestiges of trade barriers in Korea.

Despite enormous satisfaction their accomplishments must bring to the US trade officials, (especially after frustrating and futile negotiations with Japan), the US government should realize that its trade policy is not necessarily effective where it is successful. The main reason why the heavy-handed approach of the US to trade negotiations has been successful against Korea, but not against Japan, is that the expected result of playing tough will be much more damaging to Korea than to the US. The US exports to Korea is only some 3 percent of its total exports while Korean exports to the US is over 20 percent of its total, albeit down from some 40 percent a decade ago. In a game of chicken between a Cadillac and a Hyundai, as it were, the Hyundai inevitably plays chicken. For if both refused to play chicken, the Cadillac could end up with some dents, but the Hyundai might be totally wrecked. But the point is that precisely because Korea is relatively insignificant to the US, the attainment of a complete bilateral trade balance with Korea will not significantly alter the overall US trade balance. Hence, success is not necessarily effective.

This will be even more so if the settlement is made not in the form of special concessions to the US, as in the past, but in the opening of the market to all, as it ought to be. This point should be borne in mind when US trade officials push for further liberalization of financial markets and agricultural markets. I am not arguing against the liberalization of trade. I am merely observing that the gain for the US would be relatively small.

Devault ends his paper with an optimistic note: 'the prospects for freer trade between Korea and the US are good.' I hope he is right, but I am not sure how. Yes, Korea is committed to further liberalization – we can be assured of this because the majority of Koreans, both policymakers and citizens, seem to be convinced that liberalization would be good for them. But I am not sure whether the same can be said about the US policymakers or citizenry. I fail to see sufficiently strong forces that have interest in preventing the trade barriers in the US from rising, and Devault does not provide any in the paper. What can prevent the US from using more frequently non-tariff barriers such as AD and AS duties and exclusionary orders, as Korean exporters move out of textiles and apparel and into other industrial products?

Part II

FINANCIAL LIBERALIZATION

8 Financial liberalization and reform in Korea

Soon Cho

Financial liberalization and reform in Korea has been undertaken as a part of a structural adjustment policy since the early 1980s. In this chapter, I hope to give a review of these reforms and to discuss related policy tasks to be tackled in the years ahead.

In discussing financial liberalization and reform in Korea, it may be useful first to look at a general picture of development which has been accompanied by financial repression. In carrying out the Korea's first Five-Year Development Plan started in 1962, and the subsequent development plans, the Korean government intervened extensively in financial matters.

The insufficient level of domestic savings in the economy was compensated for by an inducement of foreign capital and an expansion of the monetary base, while interest rates were regulated at levels well below market rates to provide funds at low costs to strategic industries. At the early stage of economic development, this government-led development strategy seemed to be effective in channeling financial resources into priority sectors of the economy, thus supporting high economic growth.

As a result of the accommodating monetary stance, that is to say, the rapidly increasing quantity of money and low-interest rates, chronic inflation was generated and the development of the financial sector become seriously retarded, weakening the long-term growth potential of the economy.

Owing to the across-the-border regulation of interest rates coupled with a high rate of inflation, the Korean people showed very low propensity to bank deposits and other financial assets. This in turn caused shortages in the assets amount of funds intermediated through financial institutions to the real sector. As a consequence, a curb market flourished, providing funds to companies unable to tap the organized market.

Commercial banks meanwhile became very lax in their business discipline, looking to a government safety-net because of wide-ranging government intervention in credit allocation. This was a major factor in the under-development of banks' ability and willingness to investigate the credit worthiness of the low applicant. The banks just distributed loanable funds to aid uses on collateral. Thus, small and medium-sized firms without sufficient collateral had great difficulties in obtaining funds intermediated through financial institutions.

In addition, commercial banks came to be burdened with an overhang of bad loans, mainly reflecting the inefficient allocation of funds that resulted from their handling of substantial volume of policy-based loans. A good example of this was the overlapping and excessive investment in heavy and chemical industries in the latter half of the 1970s.

All these problems in the financial industry were not explicitly exposed until the second oil crisis in the late 1970s. It then became evident that, as the economy grew larger and more complex, a government-led development strategy was no longer viable. With the recognition of the inefficiency of government intervention, a series of economic reforms to achieve structural adjustment was undertaken in early 1980s, and these extended to the financial sector as well.

Among the main financial liberalization and reform measures taken since the early 1980s, the government first privatized commercial banks by selling the shares of the commercial banks owned by the government. It thereby reduced regulations governing their internal management and operations in order to enhance their autonomy and to promote competition in the financial market. In addition, entry barriers to the financial sector were lowered, thus allowing the establishment of new financial institutions. Also, some preferentially low interest rates were abolished, and a few money market rates were liberalized.

It must be admitted, however, that this financial liberalization and reform of the early 1980s was rather limited. The banks were privatized, but they were not completely liberalized. The bank ownership was privatized, but their operation was still effectively under government control. The reasons why financial liberalization was not done very extensively was because people were worried that there would be possible adverse effects of financial liberalization and reform. Certain strategic industries or large exporters were afraid to stand on their own feet and do without government protection because they had long grown accustomed to government subsidies in obtaining low-cost bank loans.

In the latter half of the 1980s, Korea was able to reverse fundamentals in the form of price stability, a high rate of growth and a current account surplus. Hence favorable development gave the Korean economy another chance to proceed further along the road to financial liberalization and reform.

A wide-ranging deregulation of interest rates of banks and non-banks was attempted in December 1988. However, the timing of this move proved unfortunate: there appeared great inflationary pressure beginning early 1989, and this led to the reintroduction of the de facto controls on liberalized interest rates.

The country in 1989 and in 1990 faced a great deal of difficulties with the eruption of widespread labor disputes, intense speculative activities and mounting inflationary pressure, compounded by a slower rate of growth. Among the various tasks that await us in the future, the most crucial is to implement the program of deregulation of interest rates, through which the allocation efficiency of funds can be promoted and the competitiveness of the financial industry strengthened.

Interest-rate deregulation will help restore competitive equality between banking institutions and non-bank financial institutions. This would contribute to the improvement of overall financial efficiency, and the effectiveness of monetary policy could be raised by the full-scale use of open market operations, the most important policy instrument. In this context, it is very important for Korea to successfully achieve the second phase of interest-rate deregulation which is to be introduced this year under the announced draft plan.

Next, government intervention in the internal management of commercial banks should be phased out. Recently, the government introduced a new method of selecting the presidents of commercial banks to enable the banks to have managerial autonomy.

Other tasks to be tackled are a practically inspired adjustment of entry barriers as well as a rational realignment of business boundaries among financial institutions. The Korean government already announced a comprehensive plan to deal with this task last June.

We also need to develop an effective foreign exchange market in which the price mechanism can function efficiently in the determination of exchange rates. This means abolishing the remaining foreign exchange controls including those on capital transactions. In the meantime, attention should be paid to improving the skills and professional acumen of market participants.

Ongoing financial liberalization and reform, however, may well bring about increased competition and greater volatility of interest rates and exchange rates, entailing various risks that could weaken the soundness of the management of financial institutions and threaten the stability of the financial system as a whole. To cope with such side effects, appropriate and active preparations on the part of financial institutions are called for.

Needless to say, none of these tasks can be carried out overnight. The financial practice of each country is the product of its own history and customs, and the deep-rooted practices engendered by financial repression for nearly 30 years cannot be reformed without sufficient time. It is obvious that the Korean financial market and system in their present state are not capable of countering the adverse effects of rapid financial liberalization and reform including capital market opening with its increased capital mobility. Financial liberalization does involve cost, the cost of instability. You need to reduce the cost as much as possible, but you certainly should not over-deregulate. At the same time, you should not over-delay it either. The longer you delay the process of liberalization, it is likely that you end up paying the higher cost for that.

In this respect, price stability should be emphasized more than ever to satisfy the preconditions for financial liberalization and reform. Having said this, Korean people and the government are nonetheless convinced that financial liberalization and reform will continue to progress and that this will greatly contribute to the sustained development of the Korean economy into the 21st century through enhancing its overall efficiency.

While there will doubtless be numerous unexpected obstacles to be overcome in this process, the fresh challenges that these financial reforms pose are not to be avoided but should be faced with resolution and prudence.

9 Financial structures in industrialized countries: Lessons for reform in Korea

Thomas Chiang, Bang Nam Jeon and Kap-Soo Oh

Financial systems differ from country to country. The difference stems from different history, traditions, commercial practices, consumer needs and cultures, evolving over time. The national financial system, however, fulfills a number of common basic functions, such as bridging the credit supply process with the savings collection process, regulating and smoothing the national payments system, managing various debts and investments, and providing a number of financial services. The financial system also serves as a vehicle for the implementation of monetary policy in each country. During the last decade, in the financial industry, there has been an increasing trend toward greater deregulation, liberalization, despecialization and internationalization. The globalization of world financial markets has been one of the most profound changes in international finance during the same period.

These new trends have created and enhanced the commonalities in the different national financial structures and generated categorically similar country groups in their financial systems. The Korean financial system, which may be characterized as rather strictly defined and closely regulated banking and securities sectors, along with relatively less strictly regulated non-bank financial institutions and curb market, is currently under the process of restructuring. The most important issues facing Korea under the current environment are: (1) ownership linkages between the banking and commerce sector, (2) the scope of services provided by banks and nonbank financial institutions, and (3) the abolishment of various price regulations maintained in the financial sector. The purpose of this chapter is to conduct a critical survey of financial system structures in major industrial countries focusing on the above three issues and derive policy implications for the currently ongoing financial reform in Korea. There are three essential questions to address. First, should the cross-ownership between banking and commerce be allowed in Korea? Second, should Korea adopt a separated (specialized) banking system or a universal banking system? Finally, what would be the macroeconomic implications of price deregulations in the current Korean financial system?

Banking and commerce:
Integration versus separation of ownership linkages

One of the most important determinants of the structure of the national financial system is the extent of ownership linkages between the financial and nonfinancial (commercial and/or industrial) sectors. The ownership linkages can take place by allowing commercial ownership and control of banks and/or through bank ownership and control of commercial firms. Allowance or restrictions on such ownership linkages expose national views on competition policies in industrial and financial sectors and on the supervision of financial services. According to our survey, in most industrial countries, banking and commerce are generally separated. Banking-commercial ties are found to be the exception rather than the rule in industrial countries.

In the United States, for example, banking and commerce are generally kept apart. First, banks are generally prohibited from holding participations in non-financial enterprises. Although the US Bank Holding Company Act allows bank holding companies to maintain up to five percent shares of any individual commercial enterprise, such holdings are not widespread. However, several large corporate conglomerates have been observed to own 'non-bank' banks, utilizing a strict interpretation of the legal definition of a 'bank' as an institution that accepts deposits and makes commercial loans. The Competitive Equality Banking Act of 1987 was aimed at correcting these loopholes. Second, Industrial and Commercial companies are generally prohibited from controlling a bank. Non-financial companies may acquire up to a maximum of 25 percent of shares in a bank. A bank holding company that controls a bank is strictly restricted in its activities to banking-related business.[1]

In Canada, commercial control of banks has been prevented by establishing a 10 percent limit on a single shareholder's ownership of a chartered bank's stock. Under the ongoing deregulation process, however, the Canadian government has proposed to limit further the commercial links with financial institutions. In Japan, banks may hold participations in non-financial enterprises within the limits of five percent of such enterprises' capital. Larger participations require prior authorization by the Fair Trade Commission. There is no restriction on non-bank participations in banks. Links between banks and commercial firms in Japan are usually not based on majority stock ownership or holding company affiliations. Rather, a group of companies, which can include a bank, may be loosely affiliated through shared directors, long-term financial and management relationships, and small ownership interests in each other. The existence of commercial financial groupings through informal affiliations, known as Keiretsu, has been a subject of controversy with the United States in the context of the Structural Impediment Initiative.

Additional examples of separation between banks and commercial firms can be found in several European Countries, including the United Kingdom, Italy, the Netherlands, Sweden and Switzerland. The Europe 1992 program, just started, continues barrier between banking and commerce.

In terms of regulations of ownership linkages in industrial countries, banks' participations in commercial firms are most strictly regulated. On the other hand, regulations concerning commercial firms' ownership of banks seem to be less strictly regulated. This is partly due to the fact that the attention of regulators is more focused on bank behavior than industry behavior.[2]

One of the most conspicuous counter-examples for the ownership linkages is Germany. German banks can exert significant ownership control over industrial firms. The only limit is that a bank's investments including shares in banks and commercial firms (if the shares exceed 10 percent of a commercial firm's capital) may not exceed the bank's capital. Additional evidences of German banks' significant influence over commercial firms are the proxy votes by banks of their clients' shares and the presence of bankers on most of the largest corporations' management. On the other hand, nonbank ownership of banks are not widespread, although it is permitted. Commercial ownership of banks is reported to only account for approximately five percent of German banking assets.

The recent decision by the Bank of Italy allowing banks to become shareholders in Italian firms is expected to change the Italian financial system's structure. The decision marks a reversal of a policy of strict separation between banking and industry introduced in 1936.[3]

An interesting form of indirect ownership linkages between banking and commerce through a common holding company can be found in a couple of European countries. In Belgium and France, bank participations in non-financial firms and vice versa are in principle prohibited or very limited. Common holding companies are found to own banks and control commercial firms.

The separation of banking and commerce dates as far back as 1694 when the act that established the Bank of England prohibited the Bank from dealing in merchandise. The earliest US banks followed English tradition. As we surveyed, in most industrial countries, banking and commerce are generally kept apart. Why not allow banks to own commercial firms, or even commercial firms to own banks? We list a number of arguments that have led many industrial countries to strictly control ownership linkages between banks and commercial enterprises.[4]

The first consideration is the concentration of power in the financial system or in the economy as a whole. The prevention of undue power concentration has often been a motive for merger controls in financial sector and for restrictions on ownership linkages between banking and commerce in industrial countries. Mergers, concentration and close ties between banking and commerce have been considered to be an obstacle to promoting market competition. The second argument in favor of restrictions on ownership linkages between banking and commerce is related to ensuring the safety and soundness of financial institutions and of providing adequate investor protection. The risk of problems spreading from commercial owner to bank (and vice versa) and an unwanted extension of the banking safety net are major concerns. If commercial ownership of banks resulted in a further increase in overall leverage, the fragility of both the financial and nonfinancial sectors could increase further.

The third argument is the potential for conflicts of interest. It is feared that banks having close ties with industry may give their affiliated clients preferential treatment in their business operations. Furthermore, when a commercial firm has substantial control over a bank's investment policy, the firm may have incentives to shift risks to unformed, naive bank clients by choosing excessively risky investment projects.[5]

The essential question about allowing ownership linkages between the financial and non-financial sectors in Korea is that of permitting corporate conglomerates to acquire financial (banks and/or nonbank banks) institutions. Great economic power of conglomerates (*chaebols*), relatively large risks in non-financial businesses, heavy reliance on bank loans for funding by the corporate sector, and potential conflicts of interest and self-dealing seem to provide rationales for a limited form of ownership linkages in between banking and commerce in the ongoing process of financial structure reforms in Korea.

Under these current circumstances, permitting commercial firms to controls banks should not be pursued at least in the near future. The risks associated with commercial ownership and control of banks seem to be considerable. A commercial firm that owns a bank would be more apt to make its banks' credits available to its affiliated customers rather than to unaffiliated customers or its competitors. Those risks of the impartiality of lending decisions would rise more with commercial ownership of banks. If commercial firms control banks on a wide scale, the resulting economic power base may undermine the nation's will to control inflation, creating serious implications for monetary policy in Korea.

Scope of services: Banking versus nonbank financial services

'Banking' describes deposit-based lending in a single entity, while 'nonbank' financial services include securities activities and insurance business. Today, with the advent of entities such as nonbank banks, the lines of separation between the two have blurred.

One of the most significant features of recent developments in financial and banking industry structures in industrial countries has been a move by banks into the securities business. This process of fading barriers between banking and nonbank financial services as well as despecialization in the banking industry provides opportunities to banks for a wide range of activities such as the new issuing, broker/dealer activities in the secondary market for securities and related derivatives, portfolio management, investment advisory services, and the dissemination of market information.

Our observation indicates that only a few industrial countries separate banking and securities activities fairly rigidly. The so-called universal banking system, which are predominant in many European Countries such as France, Germany, the Netherlands and Switzerland, allows banks to provide a wide range of both banking and securities services directly or 'in-house.' Insurance underwriting is still generally limited to separate insurance companies in these countries. Especially in the German

Universal banking system, banks are free to decide about specialization, and securities houses are legally regarded as banks.

A milder form of integration between banking and nonbank financial services can be found in the so-called blended system countries, including the United States, Japan, Canada, the United Kingdom, Belgium and Sweden. These countries advanced integration either by allowing banks to own nonbank financial subsidiaries (Belgium, Canada, Japan, Sweden, United Kingdom) or by permitting a common holding company to have significant ownership interests in both banks and nonbank financial firms (the United States).

The United States and Japan have long had strict separations between the banking and securities industry. The Glass-Steagall Act of 1933 in the United States prohibits commercial banks from underwriting, holding or dealing in corporate securities, either directly or through securities affiliates.[6] The Act also stipulates that securities firms cannot accept deposits and make uncollateralized commercial loans.

A driving force behind the Act was the serious concern that direct commercial bank involvement in the securities business would be detrimental to the stability of the US financial system due to the conflict of interest and increased riskiness of banks. The conflict-of-interest issue has been central again in the recent Congressional debates on financial regulation reform.[7]

In Japan, separation between the banking and securities industry has been maintained by not permitting banks and securities firms to own controlling interests in each other or to be owned by the same company. (Article 65 of the Securities and Exchange Law) The common ownership of banks and insurance companies is also restricted.

The separation of the banking and securities sector has, however, become less strict lately in the United States and in Japan. In the United States, securities activities by non-bank affiliates of banks have been allowed since 1987 if revenues therefrom do not exceed five percent of the subsidiary's total. (In 1989, the limit increased to 10 percent.) In 1989, several US bank holding companies were authorized to underwrite and deal in securities, subject to revenue limits and maintaining so-called 'firewalls' between banking and securities activities of one holding company. Financial Institutions Reform, Recovery, and Enforcement Act of 1989 removed legal impediments for M & A with savings and loans institutions by banks. In 1991, Financial Institutions Safety and Consumer Choice Bill aiming at abolishing legal restrictions on affiliations of securities firms by banks was introduced but rejected by Congress.

In Japan, the segmentation of the financial system including separation of long and short-term financing, trust activities and of banking and securities activities is under review. Although the complete removal of the separation line of banking and securities is not expected, an expansion of the business scope of both banks and securities firms by allowing mutual entry into the other sector through subsidiaries may be permitted. During the 1980s, banks had already been permitted to deal with government bonds and government bond futures, while securities firms were permitted to deal in CDs and CPs.

Gradual movement toward a universal banking system can be found in many other industrial countries including the United Kingdom, Canada and Italy. The separation of the banking and securities sectors became less strict in the United Kingdom since the so-called 'Big Bang' measures were taken on October 27, 1986. The Big Bang ended fixed commission on securities trading, abolished barriers between brokers and market makers, and admitted global banks and securities firms to the London Stock Exchange for the first time. Since then, UK banks have started to merge with securities brokerage and jobbing firms. The process of eroding the separation in Canada has accelerated during the 1980s. The removal of cross-ownership restrictions in 1987 and currently proposed additional ownership links between all types of financial institutions through either subsidiaries or a holding company implies that the Canadian financial structure approaches the universal banking system.

Recently Italy also transformed to a limited form of universal banking from 'polyfunctional' banking system. Under the previous system, which took shape in the 1980s, commercial-bank holding companies were forbidden from, for instance, doing factoring or leasing. Such business could be handled only by separate subsidiaries. Switching to a universal-banking structure makes banks' holding companies to engage in almost everything directly leasing, factoring, and long-term loans with the notable exception of trading securities yet.

The survey, reported so far, conveys a convincing message that the separation between banking and securities activities has been abolished or significantly reduced in most industrial countries. Recent legislation in some of those countries, either passed or proposed, tries to expand the integration of banking and securities-related activities through an expansion of 'banking powers' (the range of permitted activities) or ownership affiliations.[8]

Main arguments for separation between the banking and securities sectors include: (1) ensuring competitive fairness by preventing undue concentration of power, (2) avoiding conflicts of interest between the bank and its nonbank affiliates or between the bank and its clients, (3) inhibiting resource drains by securities affiliates from the bank, and preventing the extension of the bank safety net to nonbanking activities. Among the above, two of the most powerful arguments have been the riskiness argument (preventing risk contagion and protecting clients) and the conflict-of-interest argument.

The relatively illiquid and volatile nature of equity holdings can lead to heavy losses and may create a serious threat to the bank's solvency. A fear of spill-over effects of financial difficulties from non-bank affiliates to banks has been one of the main concerns. The conflicts of interests between the bank and its securities affiliates/its clients may lead the bank into temptation to underwrite poor securities to pay off its own loans and commercial banks may systematically fool the public into investing in low-quality securities.[9]

On the other hand, main arguments for integration between the banking and securities include the 'all-finance' argument and the economies of scale and scope argument. The all-finance argument emphasizes that German-type universal banking creates convenient and customer-oriented one-shop (supermarket-type) financial services. The existence of economies of scale and scope as a result of conglomeration in the financial industry may be a merit to enhance effective, cost-conscious banking and survive in the tough world financial market competition.

The strict separation of the banking and securities sector is expected to be gradually relaxed in Korea, extending the commercial banks' securities powers. Although maintaining the proper balance between progressive change toward the universal banking and caution for expected consequential negative side effects is not easy, the balance will be essential not only for the stability of the Korean financial system over time but also for the health and vitality of the economy at large. The increased sensitivity of the Korean securities markets to political or other unpredictable events and the potential conflict-of-interest issue are considered to be two of the most significant obstacles, among others, to the road toward the universal banking system in Korea.

Price regulation: Fixing vs market determination

In Korea, the authorities have exercised strong control over interest rates and the allocation of credit as well as the instruments of monetary policy. The behavior of banks has been closely monitored and controlled, and profit maximization based on the cost-conscious efficient banking has not been enthusiastically encouraged.

Intervention in the price mechanism of the financial sector by the authorities in industrial countries have also been often observed, but with different rationales. The most widely accepted rationale for market restrictions has been the argument that competition, if unchecked, can aggravate the solvency of financial failures. Interest rates have constantly been kept below the market equilibrium level, and fees and commissions for financial services have been fixed either by regulations or industry cartels in many industrial countries.

Government regulations of the financial sector in industrial countries have shifted from the restriction of market forces to more market-oriented systems since the 1960s, most conspicuously, during the past decade. A recent OECD report (1992) reveals that by the end of 1990, interest rate regulation virtually disappeared from the OECD member countries. Fees and commissions for financial services have also been deregulated further, along with the dismantling of an industry cartel to fix commissions for securities dealing activities. Additionally, restrictions on cross-border capital flows and the entry by foreign banks into domestic markets have been gradually relieved or reduced during the 1980s in industrial countries.

Domestic and external financial deregulation have largely been aimed at improving the efficiency of national financial systems by nurturing the competitive environment and stimulating market mechanisms in pricing financial assets. More harmonious and stable macroeconomic systems are expected to evolve when competition is promoted and the pricing mechanism is not distorted under domestic and external financial deregulation. Market risks are, however, expected to increase as the financial sector become more vulnerable to shifts in price developments. We test the validity of the above arguments about macroeconomic implications of financial liberalization using macroeconomic data in the major industrial countries (the US, UK, Germany and Japan) during the past two decades. Empirical results on the evolution of the system of macroeconomic variables are reported in Tables 9.1, 9.2 and 9.3.

139

First, we test multivariate cointegration in the system of key macroeconomic variables, including money, income, price, financial asset price and interest rates. The tests provide information about the existence of stability in the macroeconomy in the long-run context. A rejection of cointegration would indicate that the system of macroeconomic variables have not been harmoniously related in a stable fashion. The test results as reported in Table 9.1, confirming the existence of at least one cointegrating vector, suggest that in the four major industrial countries, the system of key macroeconomic variables has been related systematically in a stable fashion over the long run.[10] The estimation results using subsample period data indicate that the stability of the long-run economy has not changed significantly through the subsample periods of the 1970s and the 1980s.

This property of time-series data (i.e., the existence of cointegration) can be used to estimate the vector error correction model (VECM) to derive inferences about the short-run adjustment mechanism toward a long-run equilibrium path. Financial liberalization may render error correction mechanisms in which disequilibrium of any variable in the system during one period is corrected in the next period, moving toward the long-run equilibrium path with the help of the equilibrium error-adjustment mechanism. As reported in Table 9.2, evolution toward the error-correction mechanism in the 1980s for the system of macroeconomic variables can be found, especially in interest rates (by variable) and in the United States (by country). Tests for variance equality, reported in Table 9.3, reveal statistical evidence of a general increase in volatility of macroeconomic variables during the 1980s.[11]

Conclusion: Viable options

The current Korean financial system may be characterized as central regulation and control. The formal sector which includes the banking system and the securities market is highly regulated and segmented. Institutional functions are set by statute, and the authorities headed by the Ministry of Finance (MOF) control activity very closely. The non-bank financial institutions (NBFIs), which are a part of the formal sector, are generally not subject to as many controls from the MOF as banks. Several commercial banks have been privatized since 1981 and the scope of business activities allowed for banks and NBFIs has been expanded. The current legal framework implicitly assumes that banking and securities-related activities should be separate institutionally.

This chapter surveyed the financial system structure in industrial countries, focusing on three issues, including ownership linkages between banking and commerce, the scope of banking services, and macroeconomic environment under financial liberalization. The Korean financial system has various options from which to choose. Under current circumstances, permitting commercial firms to control banks is not considered to be a viable option at least in the near future. The further expansion of the business scope of both banking and securities institutions seems to be unavoidable by allowing mutual entry into the other sector via separate subsidiaries or common holding companies.

However, moving toward the universal banking system in Korea should take into account increasing needs and demand for financial services by the personal sector and the sector of small and medium-sized enterprises. Nurturing the fundamental macroeconomic environment as well as enhancing the efficiency of financial institutions by encouraging fair competition and by improving profit/cost-conscious management are essential preconditions for the successful institutional restructuring in the Korean financial system.

Table 9.1
Tests for multivariate cointegration
in the system of macroeconomic variables

	Number of cointegrating vectors		
Country	74:1-80:12	74:1-80-12	81:1-90:12
Germany	1	1	2
Japan	4	3	2
UK	3	3	2
US	2	2	2

Note: Test results are based on the trace test proposed by Johansen (1988). The number of cointegrating vectors reported are significant at 5 percent; length of lag is set to 4.
Source: International Financial Statistics tape, IMF.

Table 9.2
Estimated vector error correction model

$$\Delta X_t = \gamma Z_{t-1} + \Gamma(L)\Delta X_t + U_t$$
$$X = \{ m, y, p, s, i \}$$
$$Z = \{EC(1), \ldots, EC(k)\}\backslash$$

A. Germany

DV	EC(1)	EC(2)	R^2	DW	Q
74:1-80:12					
ΔM	-0.00198*		0.38	2.1	40*
ΔY	0.000298		0.25	2.0	19
ΔP	-0.00023*		0.37	2.0	20
ΔS	0.000104		0.3	2.0	24
ΔI	0.12		0.45	2.0	19
81:1-90:12					
ΔM	0.00179	0.00209	0.32	1.8	54*
ΔY	0.00496	-0.000502	0.35	2.0	26
ΔP	-0.00068	0.00019	0.46	1.9	45*
ΔS	0.0113	-0.00337	0.3	2.0	28
ΔI	0.1206*	-0.0336	0.36	1.9	21*

B. Japan

DV	EC(1)	EC(2)	EC(3)	R^2	DW	Q
74:1-80:12						
DM	-0.0068	0.0362	0.0106*	0.61	2.0	28
DY	-0.0017	-0.0088	-0.0012	0.49	2.0	19
DP	0.005*	0.022*	0.018	0.48	1.9	34*
DS	0.00013	-0.00033	-0.00014	0.29	2	16
DI	-0.033	-0.092	0.078	0.26	2.0	11

142

Table 9.2
Estimated vector error correction model, *continued*

B. Japan

DV	EC(1)	EC(2)	EC(3)	R^2	DW	Q
81:1-90:12						
DM	-0.00004	0.0026		0.69	2.2	58*
DY	-0.001	0.0002		0.41	1.9	57*
DP	-0.00005	0.00028		0.43	1.9	54*
DS	-0.0008	-0.0046		0.42	2.0	25
DI	0.0069*	-0.047*		0.20	2.0	35

C. UK

DV	EC(1)	EC(2)	EC(3)	R^2	DW	Q
74:1-80:12						
ΔM	-0.0026	-0.00222	0.00339	0.2	2	68*
ΔY	0.00318*	0.00183	-0.00131	0.25	2	24
ΔP	-0.00124*	-0.0051*	0.00656*	0.49	2	17
ΔS	-0.00673	-0.0103	0.0154	0.44	2	19
ΔI	-0.1455	0.3537	-0.4063	0.29	2	12
81:1-90:12						
ΔM	0.00235*	0.00478		0.28	2	49
ΔY	0.00097*	0.00302*		0.24	1.9	17
ΔP	0.000089	-0.00176*		0.34	2	62*
ΔS	0.00176	0.00195		0.17	2	17
ΔI	-0.0396	-0.359		0.29	2	26

D. US

DV	EC(1)	EC(2)	R²	DW	Q
74:1-80:12					
ΔM	0.0004	-0.00033	0.44	2.1	48*
ΔY	0.0005	0.00015	0.55	2.0	9
ΔP	-0.00017	-0.00057*	1.8	0.63	24
ΔS	-0.00178	-0.00309	0.4	2	16
ΔI	-0.0211	-0.0096	0.62	1.8	15
81:1-90:12					
ΔM	-0.00399	0.00605	0.37	1.9	95*
ΔY	-0.00081	0.00115	0.43	2.0	20
ΔP	0.00112	-0.00142*	0.54	1.8	33
ΔS	-0.0121*	0.017*	0.34	2.0	16
ΔI	0.1539*	-0.214*	0.40	1.9	20

Note: All variables except interest rates are in the logarithm.
* indicates significance at five percent. EC(i) gives the estimated coefficient on the ith error correction term. Length of lag is set to 4. DV indicates dependent variable.

Table 9.3
Tests for the variance equality between the 1970s and 1980s in four major industrial countries

Country	Univariate test ($H0 : s2I = \sigma2II$)					Multivariate test ($H0 : \Sigma I = \Sigma II$)
	m	y	p	s	i	
Germany	0.419	0.122	0.006*	0.000*	0.665	0.0001*
Japan	0.461	0.145	0.000*	0.000*	0.004	0.0001*
UK	0.001*	0.013*	0.000*	0.08	0.000*	0.0001*
US	0.001*	0.472*	0.003*	0.000*	0.933	0.0001*

Note: * indicates significance at five percent. Univariate tests are based on F statistics, and multivariate tests are based on $\chi2$ statistics.

Notes

1   There are, however, more than 40 non-bank companies that are permitted to own 'non-bank banks' acquired before the Competitive Equality Banking Act of 1987.
2   For the detailed information on regulations concerning ownership linkages in the financial sector, see OECD (1992).
3   *The Economist,* June 5, 1993.
4   Oppositions to close associations between banks and commercial firms have been from time to time expressed by chiefs of monetary authorities in industrial countries, for instance by the Governor of the Bank of England, the Governor of the Bank of Italy and the President of the Federal Reserve Bank of New York. A statement by E. Gerald Corrigan, President of the FRB of New York, before the US Senate Committee on Banking, Housing, and Urban Affairs, May 15, 1991, contains the most rigorous arguments against commercial ownership of banking organizations.
5   Results of a recent study, on the other hand, suggest that a policy of allowing banks to hold a limited share of borrowing firms' equity may actually improve the overall investment efficiency of US firms. (Berlin et al. 1993)
6   The Act applies only to national banks and state chartered banks that are members of the Federal Reserve System and permits limited holdings of corporate bonds and equity under certain conditions.
7   An example of the conflict-of-interest case is when banks lend money to a corporate client and underwrite that client's securities at the same time.
8   OECD (1992) reports that prohibitions or restrictions on the acquisition of securities companies by banks have been lifted in various OECD member countries including France (1985 & 1987), the United Kingdom (1986), Denmark (1986), Canada (1987), Greece (1987), Italy (1991) and Belgium (1991).
9   A recent empirical test, comparing the underwriting activities of the bank securities affiliates with the activities of independent investment banks during the 1920s in the United States, reports no evidence that commercial bank securities affiliates systematically fooled the (naive) public investors. Instead, some evidence was found in the study that the markets have rationally discounted for potential conflicts among the bank affiliates. (Kroszner and Rajan, 1993)

10 According to Johansen (1988) and others, the existence of cointegrating relationships is synonymous with the existence of a long-run equilibrium relationship between the economic variables.

11 Of course, the differences in statistical inferences between the subsample periods of the 1970s and the 1980s reported in this study cannot necessary be attributed only to financial liberalization/deregulation.

References

Berlin, Mitchell, Kose, John, and Saunders, Anthony (1993), 'Should Banks Hold Equity in Borrowing Firms?' working paper.

Cumming, Christine M. and Sweet, Lawrence M. (Winter 1987-88), 'Financial Structure of the G-10 Countries: How Does the United States Compare?' *Quarterly Review,* FRB of New York .

Corrigan, E. Gerald (Summer 1991), 'Balancing Progressive Change and Caution in Reforming the Financial System,' *Quarterly Review,* FRB of New York, pp. 1-12.

England, Catherine (1991), *Governing Banking's Future: Markets vs. Regulation,* Norwell, MA.

Granger, C. and Engle, Robert (1987), 'Dynamic Model Specification with Equilibrium Constraints: Co-integration and Error Correction,' *Econometrica,* 55:251-276.

Johansen, S. (1988), 'Statistical Analysis of Cointegrating Vectors,' *Journal of Economic Dynamics and Control,* 12:231-254.

Kroszner, Randall S. and Rajan, Raghuram G. (April 1993), 'Is the Glass-Stegall Act Justified? A Study of the US Experience with Universal Banking before 1933,' working paper.

The Ministry of Finance (1993), *The Five-Year Foreign Investment Liberalization Plan,* Seoul, Korea.

OECD (1992), *Banks Under Stress.*

OECD, (October 1990), *Financial Market Trends: Financial Systems and Financial Regulation in Dynamic Asian Economies.*

The Economist (June 5, 1993), 'Universal Banking: Italian Style.'

Tseng, Wanda and Corker, Robert (1991), 'Financial Liberalization, Money Demand, and Monetary Policy in Asian Countries,' occasional paper, International Monetary Fund, Washington, DC.

10 Effects of capital market liberalization in Korea

Kwang W. Jun

In the past 30 years, Korea's securities markets have developed largely as a result of the government measures designed to stimulate domestic investment and the economy. In turn, Korea's capital market facilitated economic growth by providing long-term debt and equity finance for both the public sector and private enterprises.

The early development of the Korean securities market in the 1960s was supported by the Korean Securities and Exchange Commission, the Securities Supervisory Board, and (partial) deregulation of the domestic financial sector.

In the 1980s, the Korean stock market became one of the world's fastest growing bourses. In the second half of the last decade, stock market development was especially strong in Korea, propelled by extraordinary export performance and huge current-account surpluses. In the early 1990s, however, markets turned sluggish as investor confidence was eroded by deteriorating economic fundamentals, including rising inflation and growing trade deficits. Stock market performance has picked up strength since late 1992, along with improved prospects for trade and growth. At the end of 1992, the Korean stock market ranked fourteenth in the world in market capitalization, and was the third largest in Asia after Japan and Hong Kong.

Traditionally, the Korean market has been tightly regulated, and, until 1991, access to the domestic stock market for foreign investors was limited to indirect investment (for example, country funds). At the start of 1992, the Korean government took an important step towards opening up the market when it allowed direct foreign portfolio investment which has, so far, brought some $5 billion in foreign investment into the domestic stock market. There are, however, several rules and regulations that still limit foreign entry into the market.

This chapter[1] assesses the impact of stock market openings in Korea and sets forth some policy implications for further liberalization. It then reviews recent developments in the liberalization of Korea's capital markets. Quantitative analyses of the consequences of opening up the stock market in 1992 are also presented. Related policy issues in financial market liberalization are addressed, and the chapter closes with a short summary and conclusion.

Korean stock market and its internationalization

An overview of the Korean stock market[2]

The Korea Stock Exchange (KSE), the only formal securities exchange in Korea, was established on February 11, 1956. Initial trading on the KSE was dominated by bonds, as interest payments were exempt from taxation. The perceived need to develop a broader securities market led to a series of reforms and incentives designed to expand the market. By 1968 a wide range of tax benefits and preferential dividend treatment for shareholders had been introduced, encouraging more companies to seek a listing. In the following year, the first Korean investment fund was set up to enable local investors to make portfolio investment in equities.

The Exchange, which has been a non-profit organization since March 1988 is currently owned by 32 member securities companies, including two subsidiary firms − Korea Securities Settlement Corporation and the Korea Securities Computer Corporation. Transactions on the KSE, whose only trading floor is located in Seoul, may only be executed through securities companies that are members of the exchange.

Aside from the KSE, there is an organized over-the-counter (OTC) market to trade unlisted equity securities in Korea, comprising 66 companies (as at end of 1990) registered on the Korea Securities Dealers Association (KSDA). The OTC market was introduced in April 1987 to provide a market for small- and medium-sized companies as well as venture businesses not eligible for listing on the KSE. To be eligible for admission to the OTC market, a company is required to meet certain criteria which are less stringent than the listing requirements of the KSE. Shares traded on the OTC market are not subject to daily price fluctuation limits.

A total of 692 companies were listed on the KSE as of late June 1993. The increase in the number of listed companies was attributed mostly to a rapid expansion of the KSE during the second half of the 1980s, which saw a near doubling of the total number of listed companies. The listing of securities is regulated by the Listing Regulation of the Exchange, which classifies four different types of securities: equity securities, warrants, beneficial securities and debt securities.

All Korean shares have a nominal value, and shares may be either bearer or registered. The equity instruments most commonly traded in the securities markets in Korea are common shares and non-cumulative and participating preferred shares. Convertible bonds, convertible shares, and bonds with warrants may also be listed on the KSE. The 1984 amendments to the Commercial Code permit issuance of transferable warrants evidencing preemptive rights to acquire shares at specified prices for a stipulated period. Warrants with long-term options to buy shares at predetermined exercise prices are not currently available.

The Exchange has two separate market sections within which equity securities are traded. The main difference between the two sections is that margin requirements are permitted only in the first trading section, with the exception of securities issued by brokerage firms and companies with the capital stock of less than W1 billion. A newly listed equity security must be traded in the second trading section for at least one year after its initial listing. Additional listing criteria must be met for an equity security to be traded in the first trading section. By the end of June 1993, nearly three quarters of all companies listed on the Exchange were trading in the first trading section.

The Korean stock market has grown steadily, with the exception of the 1990-1991 period. Market capitalization of the KSE-listed stocks increased substantially from about W2.5 trillion (US$3.1 billion equivalent) in 1980 to a record high of approximately W95.5 trillion (US$120 billion equivalent) at the end of 1989. After a sluggish performance for 1990-1991, the total market capitalization had recovered to W95.1 trillion by June 1993.

The total trading volume (in market value) of equity securities listed on the Exchange has fluctuated widely, but generally with an upward trend. Substantial increases in trading volume were recorded in the second half of the 1980s when Korea experienced a strong bull market. The annual trading volume reached a record high of W81.2 trillion (US$102 billion equivalent) in 1989, more than 22 times the total volume during 1985. The increase in trading volume was prompted by the introduction of the Stock Market Automated Trading System (SMATS) in March 1988. The SMATS currently deals with almost all of the daily trading volume on the KSE. In 1990, the total trading volume declined to W53.5 trillion (US$67 billion equivalent), but rebounded to W62.6 trillion (US$78 billion equivalent) in 1991, and to a new high of W90.6 trillion (US$113 billion equivalent) in 1992.

149

The Korean securities market encompasses a broad spectrum of participants: more than six million individual investors, a host of institutional investors, 32 securities companies, and 692 listed companies. The number of individual beneficiaries of investment trusts have increased steadily to five million by the end of 1991, after passing the one million mark in 1985.

Because of the lack of natural resources and available capital, the Korean economy has relied heavily on foreign trade and external financing for growth. The government has pursued an open-door policy since the early 1960s and has gradually reduced barriers to international trade and capital movement. As part of its liberalization policy, the Korean government embarked upon a long-term plan for opening up the domestic securities market in January 1981. The internationalization of the securities markets, however, has been slower than planned. The opening of the Korean market for foreign investment has evolved in three major steps. Indirect portfolio investment (through the International Investment Trust) was first allowed in 1981, followed in 1984 by the Korea Fund, the first Korean country fund listed on international stock exchanges. In November 1985, the government allowed domestic corporations to issue equity-related securities overseas. And, in January 1992, as part of the government's revised plan for internationalization, direct purchase of Korean shares by foreign investors was permitted for the first time, though subject to certain limits.

Investment trusts, country funds and overseas equity offering

In October 1981, the government approved the first investment trusts exclusively for foreign investors. In the following month, the Korea International Trust (KIT) managed by the Korea Investment Trust Company, and the Korea Trust (KT), managed by the Daehan Investment Trust Company, were launched with an initial capital of $25 million each. These trusts, contractual and open-ended, were well-received by international investors. As a result, other similar investment trusts have since been introduced, attracting investments from Europe, the United States and East Asia.[3]

In May 1984, the Korea Fund was launched. It is a diversified closed-end investment company under the U.S. Investment Act of 1940, established for international portfolio investment in Korean securities. Its initial public offering in August 1984 of five million shares raised $60 million; the shares were then listed on the New York Stock Exchange. Reflecting strong investor

150

demand, the Korea Fund later issued two additional branches, totaling $90 million. Since then, seven different Korean country funds have been established raising more than $400 million. Some regional funds, moreover, have also invested in Korean equities. Despite the weakness of Seoul's stock market, five new Korean country funds were launched in 1991-92: Korea Asia which raised $110 million; Drayton Korea Trust, $42 million; First Korea Smaller Company, $20 million; The Korean Investment, $50 million; and Schroder Korea $50 million.

Korean country funds have performed exceptionally well. The Korea Fund has consistently traded at a premium over its Net Asset Value (unusual for a closed-end fund). By the end of 1992, that premium was 30 percent, the highest among country funds targeted at Asian markets. Korea Trust also traded at a premium, five percent. It is useful to note that the premium on Korea Fund declined substantially after the market opening as expected, and recorded a discount in March 1992 for the first time. Since then, the premium has recovered, thanks largely to improved prospects for market performance.

In November 1985, the Korean government took the first step towards allowing foreigners to invest directly in Korean securities.[3] It allowed domestic listed companies to issue convertible bonds, bonds with warrants, and depository receipts overseas. Under existing rules of the Korean SEC, a company is required to have net assets of, at least, W50 billion (US$62.5 million equivalent) to be eligible for international security issuance, although this requirement could be waived for a listed company that has obtained a high rating from an internationally accredited rating agency. Moreover, the base share price of the company must be above the weighted average price of all listed companies. To issue depository, a company's earnings per share must be 20 percent or more of par value for the previous two years and issue is restricted to no more than 15 percent of the outstanding shares of the company. A single foreign investor may exercise the conversion or subscription rights to acquire not more than three percent of a company's outstanding shares.

More recently, the Korean government relaxed foreign exchange controls to enable domestic institutional investors to hold foreign securities. Securities companies generally can invest up to $30 million in foreign securities, while companies licensed to manage overseas securities business may invest up to $50 million (on their own accounts). Investment trust companies and insurance companies can hold up to $10 million in foreign securities. A higher investment limit is applied to securities companies, partly because the government encourages the expansion of their international investment business. Where investment trust companies issue international trust units, they can hold up to US$30 million in foreign securities. For insurance companies with total assets exceeding W500 billion (US$625 million) for the preceding fiscal year, the foreign investment limit is $30 million.

Under the revised internationalization plan which began in 1989, a single foreign securities company could hold no more than 10 percent of all voting shares of domestic securities firms, up from five percent previously. The government plan further provided for the establishment of additional branch offices by foreign securities firms in Korea and domestic securities houses abroad.[4]

Experience of direct foreign investment since 1992

The Korean stock market was finally opened to direct foreign purchase on 3 January 1992. On that day, foreign investors' buying orders totalled W105 billion (US$138 million equivalent). By the end of March 1993, according to the Securities Supervisory Board (SSB), roughly 1,800 foreign investors from 38 countries had invested funds (the equivalent of $4.2 billion). In the first few months immediatedly following the opening of the Korean market, foreign investment inflows averaged more than $220 million a month (see Annex Table 10.1). There was a sharp reduction of this figure through October 1992 to a monthly average of less than $100 million. Since then, a market recovery has increased the monthly average to around $500 million. Of those 1,800 or so foreign investors, 1,200 were non-residents, including 1,044 foreign institutional investors.

Investors from the United Kingdom accounted for the largest share (38.5 percent) of equity investment flows at the end of March 1993, followed by the United States (30.7 percent), and New Zealand (5.5 percent). Cumulative purchases of Korean shares by all foreign investors were W3,725 billion with cumulative sales at W1,432 billion, net foreign purchases were W2,303 billion, or 2.08 percent of the capitalization of the KSE. Turnover ratios (by sales over total equity holdings) for foreign investors through the end of 1992 were 79.7 percent, compared to 133.3 percent for all investors in the Korean market. U.K. investors remained the most active traders compared to other major foreign investors.[5]

Through March 1993, foreign investors held W156 million Korean equity securities with a market value of almost W3 trillion. This translates as 3.0 percent in number of shares and 4.1 percent in market value of all Korean equity securities traded. Thus, the foreign share of the market value was relatively higher than that of the number of shares, which probably reflects their preference for high-quality – and, generally, high nominal value – equities.

The initial market reaction to direct foreign investment was positive, with the KSPI rising 2.2 percent on the first day of the market opening and 11.4 percent in January 1992, although a modest decline in interest rates also helped the market. Foreign investment appears to have raised liquidity in the domestic market, resulting in a roughly 40 percent increase in daily trading volume on the KSE in the first quarter of 1992. Higher volumes were accompanied by a shift in investment strategy. Local investors adopted a fundamental stock selection approach with special emphasis on high-growth, low P/E stocks – the strategy that foreign investors have pursued in the Korean stock market.

Because there were no clear distortionary effects of the market opening during the early phase, the Korean government loosened some of the rules that had restricted direct foreign investment. The ownership ceiling was raised on 1 July 1992 to 25 percent from an existing 10 percent on listed stocks – but only in those companies that had already issued convertible bonds overseas or were joint ventures with foreign companies. During late 1992, foreign investment was also allowed in previously restricted companies, such as POSCO, the world's third largest steel-maker, and KEPCO, the electric power monopoly.

Impact of stock market opening on domestic market and economy

Effects on market performance

i) Data The data on price index, dividend yield, price-earnings ratio, market capitalization, exchange rate, return on individual companies are from the emerging market database (EMDB) monthly files of the International Finance Corporation (IFC). In the absence of a better proxy, the short-term money market rate from the IMF's International Financial Statistics is used as a proxy for Korea's risk-free rate.

Data on incoming and outgoing foreign investment is obtained from the Korea Securities Supervisory Board (SSB). Global price indices, such as the Morgan Stanley Capital International (MSCI) and the International Finance Corporation Global (IFCG) indices, are provided by the IFC database. The S&P 500 composite, the FT 100 UK composite, and Japan's Nikkei indices are from IFC. To obtain the monthly volatility of Korean market return and IFC portfolio return, the Schwert (1989) procedure has been used, which is as follows:

Estimate a 12th order autoregression for the returns, including the dummy variables to allow for different monthly mean returns using all data available for the series:

$$R_t = \sum_{j=1}^{12} a_j D_{jt} + \sum_{i=1}^{12} b_i R_{t-i} + e_t$$

The absolute value of the residuals $|e_t|$ is the required estimate for the standard deviation for the month t.

The IFC price index includes 134 stocks, while the Korean stock price index (KSPI) has 694. The return on the KSPI has been used as a proxy for the market return, since it is a bigger sample of the market. Most of the variables are available from January 1986 to April 1993, except the data on risk-free returns, which is available only after November 1986.

ii) Descriptive statistic The descriptive statistic for the overall period is shown in Annex Table 10.2, while the period before the equity market was opened up to foreign investors is shown in Table 10.3; after the opening, Table 10.4. The mean return on the IFC index and the KSPI has clearly fallen after liberalization. The expected volatility of return also has fallen which is consistent with the normal risk-return equilibrium condition.

The return distribution of both the IFC index and the KSPI is a little more positively skewed after liberalization. The kurtosis of return on the IFC index rose from 2.46 to 3.40 after liberalization. Given the optimal kurtosis value of 3, the tails of return distribution became slightly thicker, implying more frequent observations with small absolute returns and occasionally large absolute returns after liberalization.

The autocorrelation using 12 lags of all the variables before and after the liberalization is shown respectively, in Tables 10.6 and 10.7. Returns on the IFC and KSPI are stationary before and after the opening of the market, which is generally consistent with market efficiency (at least in a 'weak form' sense) for both periods. Prior to January 1992, autocorrelations of price/earnings ratio and dividend yield die out gradually. This arouses suspicion about the presence of an integrated component. The *Augmented Dickey Fuller* (ADF) test done on both price/earnings and dividend yield indeed confirms a unit root in both the variables. Nevertheless, after January 1992, both

154

price/earnings ratio and dividend yield became stationary, indicating that the mean and variance of these variables are not a function of time anymore.[7]

iii) Changes in risk-return relationship Table 10.8 shows the *ex post* market price of risk for different periods. Market price of risk measures how much excess return should be paid *ex ante* to one investor for every unit of risk taken. It increased from -0.62 to 0.17 after the opening of the market. The bull period in Korean equity markets was from 1987 to 1989, with the KSPI composite breaking through the 1000 level in April 1989 from a rebased 100 on January 4, 1980.[8] The average market price of risk for that period was 0.19, the highest so far. The negative market price of risk, or the negative risk premium, before the opening of the market must reflect bearish sentiment at that time.

iv) Impact on market performance OLS regression results reported in Table 10.9 suggest that direct foreign investment (gross and net) has been positively related to the stock market rate of return. They further indicate that $1 billion of foreign investment inflows raise the monthly return by 18 percent (for gross flows) and 24 percent (for net flows) where t-statistics of regression coefficients are significant at a 0.05 level.[9] The contemporaneous relationship between foreign investment and market volatility is found to be positive (that is, increases risks), but statistically insignificant (see Tables 10.10-11).

In order to observe the direction of causality between foreign investment and market return and volatility, Granger causality tests were performed. A variable `x' Granger causes variable `y', if variable `x' helps in predicting variable `y'. In other words,

$$y_t = a_1 y_{t-1} + a_2 y_{t-2} + \ldots + b_1 x_{t-1} + b_2 x_{t-2} + \ldots + e_t$$
`x' causes `y' if $b_i \neq 0$ for some i.

The data includes observations from January 1992 to April 1993. The following regressions were estimated:

$$R_{mt} = a_1 R_{mt-1} + b_1 FII_{t-1} + u_{1t}$$
$$S_{mt} = a_1 S_{mt-1} + b_1 FII_{t-1} + u_{2t}$$

where R_{mt} is the return on the KSPI, FII is the foreign incoming investment and s_{mt} is the volatility in the market. Regression outcome presented in Tables 10.10 and 10.11 reveals that there is no statistically significant lagged effects of foreign investment inflows/outflows on stock market return which is broadly consistent with the efficient market hypothesis. This, combined with the results reported in Table 10.9, suggests that the significant relationship between direct foreign investment and market returns has been largely contemporaneous. As for the volatility, foreign investments − especially outflows − appear to have some significant lagged effects. Although there is no apriori reason to support the existence of a one-month lag, it might have been the result of increased transactions induced by foreign investment.[10] Foreign investment outflows also appear to have not been induced by the volatility of market returns.

In addition, regression estimates for disaggregated market performance data suggest that foreign investment was positive and significant (at a 0.05 level, in terms of t-statistics) in explaining monthly returns on many sectoral indexes, particularly in: chemicals, basic metals, fishing, transport and storage, construction, wholesale, machinery and equipment, wood and wood products, all of which have reportedly been the primary targets of foreign investment. The 0.05 level significance was found in more than two-thirds of the sixteen sectors examined (tables not attached).

v) Integration with global markets One of the goals of the Korean government was to make the equity market more efficient and integrated. It was hoped that market liberalization would not only provide the much-needed foreign capital to the market but make the investors think more rationally. The importance of fundamentals in the market should rise, while the speculation should decrease. The correlation of the Korean market index with world indices was also expected to go up after the liberalization.

Table 10.12 presents the results of the correlation between KSPI and various other global and developed-country indices. Contrary to our expectations, the correlation between KSPI and other indices went down dramatically after liberalization. The exception was the U.K. composite. The correlation between KSPI and the FT 100 increased from 0.59 to 0.70 after liberalization, which may reflect the fact that British investors are the largest shareholders among foreign investors in Korea's equity markets. After January 1992, it appears that the two markets started moving closer together. Figure 2 shows the co-movement of KSPI and MSCI. These moved very close in late 1988 and early 1989, when the Korean market was booming, but grew apart again later.[11]

Table 10.12 also shows the results of the *international capital asset pricing model* (ICAPM) estimate which is represented as:

$$E(R_{kt}) = R_{ft} + b[E(R_{wt}) - R_{ft}]$$
$$\text{where } b = Cov(R_{kt}, R_{wt}) / (Var(R_{wt}))$$

The results show that b went up from 0.23 to 1.09 after liberalization, when the return on IFCG was used as a proxy for R_{wt}. The R^2 also improved. Nevertheless, when MSCI was used as a proxy for R_{wt}, b turned out to be insignificant and R^2 went down. Since IFCG index comprises only emerging markets and MSCI only developed-country markets, it is obvious that KSPI will be more integrated with IFCG than with MSCI after liberalization

vi) Analysis of individual stocks To gain further insight into the market performance under liberalization, it is useful to examine the behavior of individual stocks. The 20 largest Korean stocks listed in the IFC index are likely to be in heavy demand by foreign investors. Let us consider the following regression:

$$R_{wt} = d + gR_{kt} + h_t$$
$$R_{wt} = a + b_k R_{kt} + b_w UR_{wt} + e_t$$

where R_{wt} is the return on MSCI index, R_{kt} is the return on the KSPI, R_{it} is the return on stock i and UR_{wt} is the residuals from regressing the world market return on the Korean market return. UR_{wt} which is same as h_t represents that part of the world return which is not explained by the return in the Korean market. R_{kt} and UR_{wt} are orthogonal to one another. After liberalization, the Korean betas of the large firms would be expected to fall, while the world betas would rise. This is because (post-liberalization) the share of foreign investors in these stocks will increase, which will increase the covariance between individual stocks and the world index. At the same time, the share of domestic investors would fall, which will decrease the covariance between the individual stocks and the Korean price index.

Table 10.13 presents the results for the top 20 companies. Of those, 13 have b_k falling, significantly after the liberalization, while 15 have b_w increasing, but insignificantly. To check if the results are sensitive to the size of the stocks medium- and small-sized companies are also examined (see Table 10.14). Of 17 medium sized companies, 12 stocks have decreasing b_k and 12 have increasing b_w. Of the 20 smallest companies, only eight are going down in b_k and 13 are going up in b_w (Table 10.12). The significance does not change much with company size. The pattern shows that a higher percentage of the large stocks, which tend to be favored by foreign investors, behave as

157

expected by the hypothesis.

Macroeconomics effects

Net foreign investment in the Korean stock market was $3.1 billion at the end of March 1993. Since this was less than 2.5 percent of the monetary aggregate (measured by M2), which stays within the normal operational range, these inflows do not appear to have complicated the authorities' management of money supply and price levels. This is particularly the case when increases in money supply stemming from foreign sources can be effectively absorbed by policy means (for example, less restrictions on Korea's foreign outward investments).

The impact of external inflows on foreign exchanges has also been slight. There have been isolated cases where drastic increases in foreign investment noticeably influenced the foreign exchange market. For example, in October-November 1992, market sentiment was quickly turned around, and 'National Shares' were made available for direct foreign investment. Mostly, however, the relative infrequency and modest size of in- and out-flows have not created added pressures to the government's management of external reserves and exchange rates.

Cross country experience

Markets that have liberalized foreign investment rules have consistently experienced huge price increases. In 1991, Argentina, Brazil, Colombia, and Pakistan eliminated all restrictions, allowing free entry and exit. According to Buckberg (1992), each witnessed December to December price ratio increases of roughly 40 to 1000 percent – Argentina more than 1000 percent, Brazil 43 percent, Colombia more than 140 percent, and Pakistan more than 180 percent. In Chile, Mexico, and the Philippines, price/earnings ratios have risen continuously for several years after the opening of their markets, suggesting that those markets were historically undervalued.

Buckberg's tests (1992) also show that openness is conducive to market integration. Of six opened markets – Greece, Jordan, Malaysia, Portugal, Thailand, and Venezuela – only Portugal rejects the *International Capital Asset pricing model*. After the opening up of markets, increases in both turnover and capitalization should reduce liquidity risk inherent in emerging markets and thereby reduce required returns and the cost of capital. Market capitalization rose permanently within a few years of opening up in countries such as Chile, Mexico, the Philippines, Turkey and Venezuela. Most of these have expanded in their number of participants, firms listed, value and capital flows.

Summary and conclusions

Korean securities markets have grown significantly in the 1980s. The excellent macroeconomic performance and phenomenal growth in new equity issues, especially in the second half of the 1980s, made the Korean Stock Exchange one of the largest emerging bourses. Although the Korean market has been sluggish over the past two years, it is now the world's fourteenth largest by market capitalization.

Along with stock-market growth, Korean authorities have gradually opened up the market to foreign investors. Since investment trust funds for non-residents were first allowed in 1981, many international funds have been set up. Since 1984, inflows of portfolio investment have been progressively liberalized. Initially, foreigners were allowed only limited investment in Korean stocks through investment funds. Foreign securities companies were later allowed to open representative offices while Korean companies were permitted to raise foreign capital through equity-linked bonds. In 1992, foreigners were allowed to invest directly in Korean stocks, subject to certain limits.

The major concerns expressed by the Korean government before the market opening were that the domestic market would be disturbed by foreign speculators and there would be huge inflows and outflows of 'hot' money. Experience to date, albeit limited, indicates that such fears are largely unfounded. There has been relatively insignificant turnovers by foreigners, and sales proceeds have been mostly reinvested, as part of portfolio realignment. Furthermore, empirical studies suggest that foreign investment has contributed to improved returns on equity since 1992, with insignificant (contemporaneous) effects on the volatility of market returns. At the macro level, considering the large domestic liquidity (W98 trillion of monetary aggregates on an M2 basis), foreign investment flows of W2.4 trillion appear to have raised no substantive problems with monetary control and thus, negligible effects on domestic inflation.

Liberalization of capital markets (or accounts) is an integral part of Korea's broader financial-sector reform, which (as envisaged) encompasses improvement in monetary policy and credit allocation, interest rate deregulation, development of securities markets, and foreign-exchange liberalization.

Notes

The author wishes to acknowledge the excellent research assistance by Ms. Achla Marathe. The findings, interpretations, and conclusions are those of the author, and should not be attributed to the World Bank.

References

Buckberg, Elaine (1991), 'Emerging Stock Markets and International Asset Pricing,' mimeo, MIT.

Gooptu, Sudarshan (1993) 'Portfolio Investment in Emerging Markets,' Working Paper No. 1117, The World Bank, Washington, DC.

Jun, Kwang W. (1992) 'The Korean Securities Market,' mimeo, The World Bank, Washington, DC.

Monthly Review (various issues), Korea Securities Supervisory Board, Seoul.

Park, Keith K.H. and W. V. Agtmael (1993), 'The World's Emerging Stock Markets,' *Probus Publishing Company,* Chicago, Illinois.

Schwert, G. William (December 1989), 'Why the Stock Market Volatility Change Over Time,' *Journal of Finance,* Vol. 44.

Figure 10.1
The relationship between foreign investment
and the Korean stock index

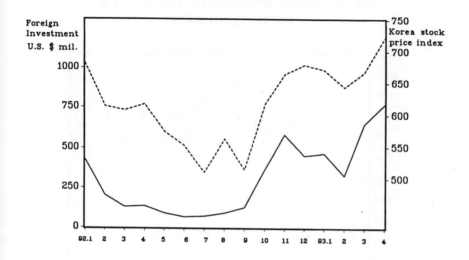

Note: Solid line represents foreign investment (gross), and dotted line refers to Korean stock market index. Data are from Korean Securities Supervisory Board.

Figure 10.2
The correlation between the Korean stock index
and the global index

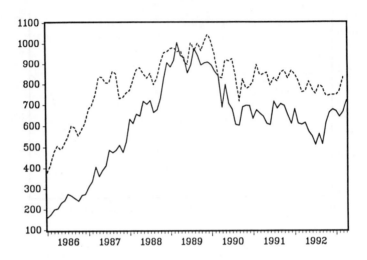

Note: Solid line represents Korean Stock Price Index, and dotted line refers to Morgan Stanley Capital International.
KSPI: Korean Stock Price Index
MSCI: Morgan Stanley Capital International

Figure 10.3
The relationship between foreign investment and market volatility

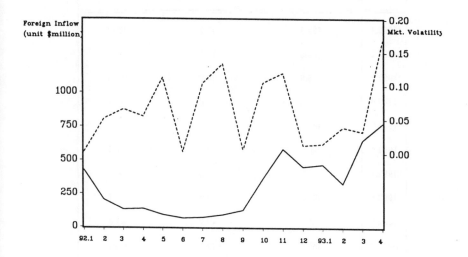

Note: Solid line represents foreign investment (gross), and dotted line refers to the standard derivation of return on Korean stock index.

Table 10.1
Foreign investment in Korean stock market

Month	Incoming Investment U.S. $ million	Outgoing Investment U.S. $ million	Net Investment U.S. $ million
1992.1	425.1	35.7	389.4
1992.2	202.9	16.0	186.9
1992.3	128.9	24.2	104.7
1992.4	135.5	47.6	87.9
1992.5	89.4	34.2	55.2
1992.6	65.6	48.3	17.3
1992.7	70.1	67.9	2.2
1992.8	89.4	52.3	37.1
1992.9	124.3	40.7	83.6
1992.10	361.0	49.7	311.3
1992.11	582.0	139.9	442.1
1992.12	449.5	96.4	353.1
1993.1	465.2	146.5	318.7
1993.2	324.5	129.8	194.7
1993.3	647.0	157.4	489.6
1993.4	770.0	167.4	602.6

Source: Korea Securities Supervisory Board.

Table 10.2
Descriptive statistic of variables for the period
1986.01-1993.04

RET – Return on IFC index measured in US dollars.
RETLC – Return on IFC index measured in local currency won.
RETM – Return on the Korean local market index.
SD – Standard deviation of RET.
SDLC – Standard deviation of RETLC.
SDM – Standard deviation of RETM.
P/E – Price earnings ratio of the stocks in the IFC index.
DIVYD – Average dividend yield of the stocks in the IFC index.

	Mean	Std.dev	Maximum	Minimum	Skewness	Kurtosis
RET	.017	.09	.265	-.19	.442	2.71
RETLC	.016	.088	.264	-.18	.495	2.85
RETM	.02	.083	.21	-.18	.33	2.50
SD	.07	.051	.256	.003	1.06	4.17
SDLC	.069	.051	.247	.003	.964	3.79
SDM	.055	.04	.168	.0003	.692	2.74
P/E	21.66	6.44	44.04	9.79	1.21	4.54
DIVYD	1.79	1.00	5.07	0	.486	3.18
P	410.84	148.49	703.63	124.95	.194	2.24
PLC	366.81	105.73	572.45	134.23	.005	2.29
KSPI	614.28	212.45	1003.31	160.42	-.394	2.48
R_f	.010	.002	.016	.007	.318	2.32

Source: IFC, IECDI, the World Bank, and international financial statistics, IMF.

Table 10.3
Descriptive statistic of variables before
market opening 1986.01-1991.12

RET − Return on IFC index measured in US dollars.
RETLC − Return on IFC index measured in local currency won.
RETM − Return on the Korean local market index.
SD − Standard deviation of RET.
SDLC − Standard deviation of RETLC.
SDM − Standard deviation of RETM.
P/E − Price earnings ratio of the stocks in the IFC index.
DIVYD − Average dividend yield of the stocks in the IFC index.
P − IFC price index measured in US dollars.
PLC − IFC price index measured in won.
KSPI − Korean stock price index.
R_f − Short-term money market rate used as a proxy for risk-free rate.

	Mean	Std.dev	Maximum	Minimum	Skewness	Kurtosis
RET	.019	.088	.213	-.19	.318	2.46
RETLC	.017	.087	.225	-.18	.388	2.61
RETM	.021	.084	.21	-.18	.289	2.52
SD	.067	.049	.215	.003	.856	3.09
SDLC	.066	.049	.204	.003	.788	2.79
SDM	.053	.036	.143	.0003	.89	3.35
P/E	22.13	6.97	44.04	9.79	.995	3.74
DIVYD	1.77	1.05	5.07	0	.621	3.03
P	419.14	161.82	703.63	124.95	.046	1.91
PLC	369.63	115.11	572.45	134.23	-.056	1.99
KSPI	613.46	233.42	1003.31	160.42	-.353	2.07
R_f	.010	.002	.016	.007	.318	2.32

Table 10.4
Descriptive statistic of variables before
market opening 1992.01-1993.04

RET – Return on IFC index measured in US dollars.
RETLC – Return on IFC index measured in local currency won.
RETM – Return on the Korean local market index.
SD – Standard deviation of RET.
SDLC – Standard deviation of RETLC.
SDM – Standard deviation of RETM.
P/E – Price earnings ratio of the stocks in the IFC index.
DIVYD – Average dividend yield of the stocks in the IFC index.
P – IFC price index measured in US dollars.
PLC – IFC price index measured in won.
KSPI – Korean stock price index.
R_f – Short-term money market rate used as a proxy for risk-free rate.

	Mean	Std.dev	Maximum	Minimum	Skewness	Kurtosis
RET	.008	.100	.265	-.126	.881	3.40
RETLC	.011	.099	.264	-.124	.844	3.36
RETM	.013	.084	.198	-.099	.504	2.33
SD	.085	.058	.256	.01	1.36	5.29
SDLC	.083	.056	.247	.009	1.25	5.22
SDM	.063	.053	.168	.002	.413	1.82
P/E	19.55	2.26	23.62	15.25	-.20	2.22
DIVYD	1.92	.68	2.63	.07	-1.42	4.32
P	373.51	46.14	438.32	300.56	-.18	1.65
PLC	354.15	43.73	419.18	286.43	-.15	1.60
KSPI	617.96	62.26	721.6	509.95	-.27	1.98
R_f	.011	.001	.012	.009	-.65	1.84

Table 10.5
Autocorrelation of variables for the period 1986.01-1993.04

RET – Return on IFC index measured in US dollars.
RETLC – Return on IFC index measured in local currency won.
RETM – Return on the Korean local market index.
SD – Standard deviation of RET.
SDLC – Standard deviation of RETLC.
SDM – Standard deviation of RETM.
P/E – Price earnings ratio of the stocks in the IFC index.
DIVYD – Average dividend yield of the stocks in the IFC index.

	ρ_1	ρ_2	ρ_3	ρ_4	ρ_5	ρ_6	ρ_7	ρ_8	ρ_9	ρ_{10}	ρ_{11}	ρ_{12}
RET	-.10	.14	-.08	.13	.04	.03	-.03	-.01	.16	.13	-.07	.05
RETLC	-.16	.11	-.11	.11	.03	.01	-.06	-.05	.14	.11	-.10	.04
RETM	-.10	.14	-.11	.14	.05	.07	.02	.01	.18	.20	-.001	.06
SD	.06	.05	-.01	-.07	.04	-.06	-.19	-.01	.03	.04	-.07	-.08
SDLC	.06	.05	.01	-.04	.02	-.08	-.21	-.01	.04	.03	-.05	-.09
SDM	-.07	-.17	.11	.04	-.01	.06	-.14	.09	.14	-.07	.03	-.03
P/E	.88	.79	.70	.61	.54	.48	.41	.34	.26	.15	.06	.01
DIVYD	.81	.73	.65	.56	.50	.45	.41	.37	.35	.30	.27	.25

Source: IFC and IECDI, the World Bank.

Table 10.6
Autocorrelation of variables
before opening the market 1986.01-1991.12

RET – Return on IFC index measured in US dollars.
RETLC – Return on IFC index measured in local currency won.
RETM – Return on the Korean local market index.
SD – Standard deviation of RET.
SDLC – Standard deviation of RETLC.
SDM – Standard deviation of RETM.
P/E – Price earnings ratio of the stocks in the IFC index.
DIVYD – Average dividend yield of the stocks in the IFC index.
P – IFC price index measured in US dollars.
PLC – IFC price index measured in won.
KSPI – Korean stock price index.
R_f – Short-term money market rate used as a proxy for risk-free rate.

	ρ_1	ρ_2	ρ_3	ρ_4	ρ_5	ρ_6	ρ_7	ρ_8	ρ_9	ρ_{10}	ρ_{11}	ρ_{12}
RET	-.11	.13	-.09	.15	.04	.01	-.03	.06	.16	.21	-.09	.13
RETLC	-.18	.10	-.12	.13	.04	-.02	-.06	.03	.13	.20	-.13	.13
RETM	-.07	.13	-.12	.17	.07	.05	.01	.07	.17	.27	.01	.15
SD	.09	.01	-.05	.04	.05	-.09	-.28	-.13	.02	-.01	-.11	-.07
SDLC	.06	.02	-.04	.06	.05	-.12	-.28	-.13	.04	-.03	-.08	-.08
SDM	-.02	-.15	.01	.22	-.08	.02	-.02	-.07	.14	.05	-.07	-.12
P/E	.88	.79	.70	.61	.55	.49	.42	.35	.27	.16	.06	.01
DIVYD	.86	.77	.69	.60	.55	.49	.46	.42	.38	.34	.30	.29

Source: IFC and IECDI, the World Bank.

Table 10.7
Autocorrelation of variables
after opening the market 1992.01-1993.04

RET – Return on IFC index measured in US dollars.
RETLC – Return on IFC index measured in local currency won.
RETM – Return on the Korean local market index.
SD – Standard deviation of RET.
SDLC – Standard deviation of RETLC.
SDM – Standard deviation of RETM.
P/E – Price earnings ratio of the stocks in the IFC index.
DIVYD – Average dividend yield of the stocks in the IFC index.
P – IFC price index measured in US dollars.
PLC – IFC price index measured in won.
KSPI – Korean stock price index.
R_f – Short-term money market rate used as a proxy for risk-free rate.

	ρ_1	ρ_2	ρ_3	ρ_4	$.\rho_5$	ρ_6	ρ_7	ρ_8	ρ_9	ρ_{10}	ρ_{11}	ρ_{12}
RET	-.04	.12	-.18	-.07	-.04	-.06	.04	-.24	.05	.03	.01	.01
RETLC	-.08	.12	-.19	-.06	-.02	-.05	.05	-.24	.04	.04	.01	.01
RETM	-.20	.15	-.12	-.11	-.04	-.13	.16	-.22	.07	.004	-.004	.03
SD	-.12	.02	.01	-.51	.01	-.17	.02	.22	.13	.02	.01	-.05
SDLC	-.06	-.02	.09	-.49	-.10	-.16	-.48	.23	.10	.03	.05	-.04
SDM	-.19	-.21	.19	-.34	.07	.10	-.30	.21	.05	-.25	.21	.05
P/E	.49	.24	.05	-.10	-.25	-.41	-.40	-.35	-.12	.02	.03	.05
DIVYD	.07	.10	-.04	-.07	-.13	-.21	-.21	-.13	00	-.02	.06	-.22

Source: IFC and IECDI, the World Bank.

Table 10.8
Market price of risk

$$\lambda = \frac{E(R_m) - R_f}{\sigma_m}$$

R_m − Return on the Korean local market index.
σ_m − Standard deviation of R_m
R_f − Short-term money market rate used as a proxy for risk-free rate.

Period	Mean	Maximum	Minimum
1987.01 - 1993.04	-0.45	51.05	-24.51
1987.01 - 1989.12	.19	5.33	-18.38
Before Opening	-0.62	5.33	-18.38
After Opening	.173	51.05	-24.51

Source: IFC and IECDI, the World Bank.

Table 10.9
Conteporaneous relationship between
foreign investment and market performance

Panel A: $Y_t = a_1 FII_t + u_t$					
Y	C	a_1	R^2	DW	F-stat
RETM	-0.04	0.18	.24	2.5	4.44
	(1.29)	(2.11)			
STDM	0.05	0.03	.02	2.0	.28
	(2.28)	(0.53)			

Panel B: $Y_t = a_1 FIO_t + u_t$					
Y	C	a_1	R^2	DW	F-stat
RETM	-0.01	0.33	.04	2.3	.64
	(0.32)	(0.80)			
STDM	0.05	0.16	.02	2.0	.38
	(2.01)	(0.62)			

Panel C: $Y_t = a_1 NI_t + u_t$					
Y	C	a_1	R^2	DW	F-stat
RETM	-0.04	0.24	.28	2.6	5.68
	(1.40)	(2.38)			
STDM	0.05	0.03	.15	2.0	.21
	(2.52)	(0.46)			

Source: Korea Securities Supervisory Board, IFC, and IECDI, the World Bank.
Note: In the parentheses are t-ratios in absolute value.

Table 10.10
Granger causality results: Foreign investment inflows

Panel A: $Y_t = a_1 Y_{t-1} + b_1 FII_{t-1} + u_t$				
Y	a_1	b_1	R^2	F-stat
RETM	-0.28	.051	.08	.59
	(1.02)	(0.76)		
STDM	0.28	.13	.47	4.64
	(0.99)	(2.10)		

Panel C: $Y_t = a_1 Y_{t-1} + b_1 NI_{t-1} + u_t$				
Y	a_1	b_1	R^2	F-stat
RETM	-0.29	0.06	.08	.59
	(1.03)	(0.74)		
STDM	0.33	.15	.52	4.03
	(1.17)	(1.96)		

Source: Korea Securities Supervisory Board, IFC, and IECDI, the World Bank.
Note: In the parentheses are t-ratios in absolute value.

Table 10.11
Granger causality results: Foreign investment outflows

Panel A: $Y_t = a_1 Y_{t-1} + b_1 FIO_{t-1} + u_t$				
Y	a_1	b_1	R^2	F-stat
RETM	-0.24	.18	.08	.44
	(0.92)	(0.74)		
STDM	0.23	.54	.45	4.65
	(0.76)	(2.14)		

Panel B: $FIO_t = a_1 FIO_{t-1} + b_1 X_{t-1} + u_t$				
X	a_1	b_1	R^2	F-stat
RETM	1.03	.082	.61	.58
	(10.05)	(0.76)		
STDM	1.02	0.06	.60	.13
	(7.70)	(0.37)		

Source: Korea Securities Supervisory Board, IFC, and IECDI, the World Bank.
Note: In the parentheses are t-ratios in absolute value.

Table 10.12
Correlation of Korean stock price index with global markets

KSPI − Korean stock price index.
IFCG − International financial corporation global composite index.
MSCI − Morgan Stanley capital international index.
S&P − S & P 500 composite US index.
UK − *FT* 100 UK composite index.
JAPAN − Japan's Nikkei index.

	Total Period 1984.12 - 1993.03	Before Opening 1984.12 - 1991.12	After Opening 1992.01 - 1993.03
KSPI, IFCG	.837	.880	.306
KSPI, MSCI	.896	.904	.072
KSPI, *S&P*	.456	.604	.474
KSPI, UK	.494	.599	.703
KSPI, JAPAN	.841	.935	.346

$$E(R_{kt}) = R_{ft} + \beta(E(R_{wt}) - R_{ft})$$

	Total Period 1986.11 - 1993.03	Before Opening 1986.11 - 1991.12	After Opening 1992.01 - 1993.03
KSPI, IFCG	0.29	0.23	1.09
t-stat	(2.26)	(1.73)	(2.56)
R^2	.05	.04	.29
KSPI, MSCI	0.44	0.49	0.08
t-stat	(2.84)	(2.98)	(0.18)
R^2	.09	.12	.001

Source: IFC, and IECDI, the World Bank.

Table 10.13

$$R_{it} = \alpha + \beta_k R_{kt} + \beta_w R_{wt} + e_t$$

20 Largest Korean companies listed in IFC index

Name	N	Before Opening β_k	β_w	After Opening β_k	β_w
POSCO	41	0.98	-0.10	1.33	-1.26
t-stat		(11.43)	(0.85)	(6.04)	(2.66)
Samsung Elec	72	0.95	0.19	0.64	-0.13
t-stat		(8.23)	(1.15)	(2.69)	(0.26)
Hanil Bank	44	1.04	0.15	1.04	-0.25
t-stat		(12.42)	(1.29)	(8.85)	(0.98)
Korea First	44	1.13	0.10	1.10	-0.14
t-stat		(10.00)	(0.64)	(8.37)	(0.51)
Choheung Bank	44	1.05	0.21	0.98	-0.17
t-stat		(12.31)	(1.83)	(6.15)	(0.48)
Commercial B	44	1.09	0.22	0.96	-0.23
t-stat		(12.91)	(1.92)	(5.82)	(0.66)
Bank of Seou	44	1.05	0.25	0.93	-0.18
t-stat		(11.76)	(2.04)	(5.60)	(0.49)
Kia Ind.	72	0.90	0.17	1.04	-0.55
t-stat		(7.17)	(0.95)	(3.95)	(0.96)
Ssangyong Oi	41	0.71	-0.17	0.77	0.64
t-stat		(4.63)	(0.82)	(3.51)	(1.35)
Lucky Ltd.	72	0.93	0.35	1.10	-0.45
t-stat		(9.59)	(2.49)	(4.73)	(0.90)
Hyundai Moto	72	0.90	-0.03	1.01	-0.91
t-stat		(8.91)	(0.19)	(3.07)	(1.28)
Daewoo Secur	41	1.44	0.09	1.23	-0.16
t-stat		(7.86)	(0.35)	(6.05)	(0.36)
KLTCB	44	1.02	0.04	0.75	0.06
t-stat		(8.61)	(0.27)	(3.49)	(0.13)
KAL	72	1.08	0.30	1.08	-0.20
t-stat		(8.68)	(1.66)	(3.47)	(0.30)
Gold Star	72	0.97	-0.28	0.94	-0.36
t-stat		(7.62)	(1.52)	(2.53)	(0.45)
Daewoo Elect	72	1.16	0.23	0.82	-0.24
t-stat		(6.93)	(0.97)	(2.38)	(0.32)
Lucky Secur	41	1.48	0.08	1.17	-.001
t-stat		(7.20)	(0.27)	(5.93)	(0.002)
Daewoo Heavy	72	1.07	0.38	0.81	-0.87
t-stat		(5.72)	(1.40)	(2.03)	(1.01)
Dongsuh Secur	41	1.45	-0.08	1.19	0.16
t-stat		(12.53)	(0.53)	(5.44)	(0.35)
Ssangyong Cem	72	1.02	0.09	1.07	0.72
t-stat		(9.71)	(0.59)	(3.58)	(1.12)

Table 10.14
$$R_{it} = \alpha + \beta_k R_{kt} + \beta_w R_{wt} + e_t$$
17 Medium sized Korean companies listed in IFC index

Name	N	Before Opening β_k	β_w	After Opening β_k	β_w
Kolon Ind	44	0.97	-0.02	0.49	1.65
t-stat		(6.03)	(0.10)	(1.62)	(2.51)
Chungbuk Ban	41	1.11	0.19	1.01	0.17
t-stat		(10.79)	(1.39)	(6.61)	(0.51)
KDLC	24	1.28	0.27	0.82	0.86
t-stat		(8.55)	(1.34)	(4.03)	(1.94)
Daewoo Telec	13	0.87	-0.33	0.51	-0.39
t-stat		(3.32)	(0.85)	(1.13)	(0.40)
Orion Electr	13	0.72	0.05	0.60	0.79
t-stat		(2.70)	(0.13)	(2.15)	(1.30)
Taihan Elect	72	0.68	-0.16	0.91	-0.69
t-stat		(4.20)	(0.70)	(3.07)	(1.07)
Samsung Cons	41	0.89	-0.08	0.99	-0.48
t-stat		(8.24)	(0.56)	(3.19)	(0.72)
Gyeong Nam	13	1.05	0.33	0.93	-0.12
t-stat		(6.70)	(1.44)	(6.08)	(0.37)
Daelim Ind	44	1.01	0.20	1.17	-0.24
t-stat		(6.64)	(0.97)	(4.39)	(0.42)
Sun Kyung	72	1.13	-0.28	0.32	-0.09
t-stat		(10.02)	(1.74)	(0.78)	(0.10)
Dongkuk Stee	41	0.69	-0.13	1.33	0.07
t-stat		(5.70)	(0.77)	(2.91)	(0.07)
Dong A Const	41	1.07	0.08	1.39	-0.36
t-stat		(8.55)	(0.48)	(6.41)	(0.77)
Kwang Ju Ban	13	0.92	0.27	0.90	0.37
t-stat		(5.87)	(1.17)	(4.78)	(0.89)
Hana Bank	44	1.07	0.17	0.95	0.28
t-stat		(5.89)	(0.69)	(3.29)	(0.46)
Inchon Iron	41	0.60	0.05	0.56	-0.85
t-stat		(5.28)	(0.32)	(1.30)	(0.91)
Korea Pacifi	72	-1.71	-2.83	1.20	-0.05
t-stat		(0.99)	(1.13)	(3.47)	(0.06)
Hanshin Secur	13	1.60	0.03	1.25	-0.14
t-stat		(9.38)	(0.13)	(7.08)	(0.38)

Note: In the parentheses are t-ratios in absolute value.

Table 10.15

$$R_{it} = \alpha + \beta_k R_{kt} + \beta_w R_{wt} + e_t$$

20 Smallest Korean companies listed in IFC index

Name	N	Before Opening β_k	β_w	After Opening β_k	β_w
Byuck San	72	0.92	-0.25	0.71	0.06
t-stat		(3.00)	(0.57)	(2.23)	(0.08)
Hanil Synthe	13	1.04	0.30	1.43	0.29
t-stat		(3.33)	(0.65)	(2.79)	(0.27)
Han Yang	72	1.49	-0.24	1.17	0.82
t-stat		(6.00)	(0.67)	(1.60)	(0.51)
Kwang Ju Hig	13	0.57	-0.03	1.39	0.73
t-stat		(1.38)	(0.05)	(2.72)	(0.66)
Hyosung Corp	41	0.75	-0.25	1.25	0.78
t-stat		(4.85)	(1.21)	(3.36)	(0.96)
Korea Steel	41	0.93	0.18	0.87	-0.35
t-stat		(6.91)	(0.97)	(1.97)	(0.36)
Sam Mi Corp	41	1.01	0.03	1.06	-0.09
t-stat		(5.66)	(0.12)	(2.39)	(0.09)
Hyundai Corp	72	0.95	-0.40	0.68	-0.24
t-stat		(9.81)	(2.89)	(2.68)	(0.44)
Lucky Metal	44	0.81	0.02	0.83	0.09
t-stat		(5.53)	(0.09)	(1.80)	(0.09)
Hanil Synthe	13	1.04	0.20	1.38	0.19
t-stat		(3.22)	(0.41)	(2.76)	(0.17)
Korea Machin	72	0.57	0.03	0.86	-0.86
t-stat		(4.42)	(0.15)	(2.21)	(1.01)
Han Shin Con	72	1.28	-0.06	1.06	1.06
t-stat		(6.98)	(0.22)	(1.44)	(0.67)
Dong Bu Stee	44	0.78	0.02	0.97	-0.39
t-stat		(5.82)	(0.11)	(3.59)	(0.67)
Ssang Young	13	1.42	-0.27	1.29	0.20
t-stat		(6.06)	(0.78)	(5.57)	(0.39)
Hanil Develo	41	0.83	-0.05	1.12	0.01
t-stat		(5.81)	(0.25)	(1.83)	(0.01)
Hanshin Secu	13	1.61	0.15	1.19	0.10
t-stat		(7.28)	(0.46)	(6.28)	(0.24)
Saeil Heavy	44	0.92	0.25	1.25	0.60
t-stat		(5.66)	(1.12)	(2.67)	(0.59)
Cheil Synthe	44	0.80	-0.12	0.50	2.03
t-stat		(3.89)	(0.43)	(1.56)	(2.87)
Kwang Ju Hig	13	0.85	-0.06	1.51	0.93
t-stat		(2.02)	(0.11)	(2.98)	(0.85)
Poongsan Met	41	1.23	0.19	0.92	0.37
t-stat		(7.38)	(0.83)	(3.05)	(0.57)

178

11 The US–Korea financial dialogue

James H. Fall III

In the years I have worked in Washington and the Treasury Department, I think it is somewhat remarkable to observe the shift in perspective with which we have viewed, analyzed and interacted with Korea. This is especially true with regard to financial issues.

Ten years ago, for example, there was considerable worry that Korea, with its external debt among the highest and fastest growing in the world, would be caught up in the worst of the global debt crisis. Now, any debt-ratio comparisons put Korea in an almost enviable position.

Several factors are quite clear when we look at Korea at this time:

1 Korea's credit standing is not in doubt by any measure.
2 Foreign financial institutions can generate profits in Korea – if not without some frustration.
3 Korea is capable of serious introspection and self-analysis on the need for positioning its financial sector to meet both realistic domestic demands, and foreign competition – particularly the increasingly fierce competition from Korea's neighbors in the Pacific Basin.

In short, Korean authorities know the country's priorities and areas of critical self-interest, but in the spirit of this book's title, I believe we must identify and seek solutions to remaining problems together.

The United States and Korea now confront the challenge of domestic renewal in order to keep pace with a rapidly evolving world. The US is facing up to its responsibilities to contribute to a growing world economy, and Korea also has responsibilities in this area. Clearly, we must work together to bring about the changes needed if all our futures are to be secure and prosperous.

What are we in the United States doing?

First, the US is focusing on reinvigorating macroeconomic coordination with our G-7 partners to spur economic growth. The Clinton Administration and Congress have implemented measures to reduce the US budget deficit and improve domestic savings and investment.

Second, there is a focus on 'export activism' as a component of the Administration's growth strategy. Broadening this to a 'market access activism' approach leads us in the financial sector to objectives which focus on opening financial markets abroad to US firms just as foreign firms have access to our market. Secretary Lloyd Bentsen expressed this view in during his confirmation hearings in 1993 when he voiced concern that some countries still do not give US banks and securities firms a fair opportunity to compete in their financial markets.

Our skill at developing a fully integrated global economy has been tested during the first two years of the Clinton Administration. The US successfully hosted the first APEC Leaders' Summit in Seattle last fall and valued the opportunity to solidify and convey our regional aspirations to our Asian friends. Korea will continue to play a growing role in this rapport.

Korea's rising global influence is demonstrated by several unique and some shared characteristics. Korea's importance to the US was borne our by the fact that it was the first bilateral visit of our President outside the G-7. Korea's role in the Uruguay Round, its high profile participation in APEC, the goal of OECD membership by 1996, and its border with one of the few remaining hard-line communist regimes will generate challenges and opportunities in the years ahead.

From our perspective, what are the cautionary signs? Let me pose several responses in the form of questions:

1 Can the Republic of Korea build on the achievements of its first 45 years?
2 Can Korea address its growing global reputation as a somewhat discriminatory or possibly hostile environment for foreign investment?
3 Can Korea, through a rigorous commitment on financial reform, fulfill the goals it has set for itself?

I would likely to briefly review herein several Treasury observations on the financial reform process – with some background on how the US Treasury's dialogue has evolved with our colleagues and friends at the Korean Ministry of Finance.

I believe we in Washington are on the edge of a shift in attitude in our discussions with Korea. This may manifest itself in a continued dialogue of greater intensity, for it is now Korea's chance to show what it can do for itself in a highly competitive global financial environment.

I ask the question: Can Korea meet and accommodate both its self-interest and global responsibility for the benefit of its own economy and the economic strength of the region, while simultaneously providing competitive opportunities for both foreign and domestic players in Korea? The answer to this question lies with the Korean authorities. One thing is certain, however. The positive fulfillment of these challenges points to greater prosperity for Korea.

I am reminded of an old Asian adage that I read recently in a museum in Washington which goes like this: *A person will sit on a hillside a long time with his mouth open before a roast duck will fly in.*

Of course, we hope there is no analogy here − that Korea will not be sitting and waiting for others to render a service. It is for Korea itself to act, especially in the financial area, if its aspirations are to be met.

With these opening remarks, let me give a brief overview of the background and status of our financial policy discussions with the Korean authorities.

The Treasury Department has been working closely with the Ministry of Finance (MOF) since February 1990 to resolve problems faced by US financial institutions in Korea. The Financial Policy Talks (FPT), as our discussions with the Ministry of Finance have been called, have focused on securing national treatment and market access for US banks and securities firms operating in Korea, and on encouraging broader liberalization of Korea's financial sector. Over the last three years, we have maintained our dialogue on financial policy issues with the Koreans through formal and informal rounds of the FPT and regular written correspondence.

In the early years of the FPT, discussions between Treasury and MOF officials focused on various issues on a case-by-case basis. Some of the priority issues for US banks and securities firms included (and still include):

1 Inadequate access to local currency funding sources.
2 Controls on foreign exchange and capital flows that impede foreign banks from competing in their natural lines of business.
3 Lack of transparency in financial regulations and enforcement.
4 Tight restrictions on introducing new products into the market.
5 Restricted access to Korea's securities market, such as:
   − A 10 percent ceiling on foreign investment in listed Korean firms (although indications are that the Korean government will raise this limit by a small amount in the near future).

181

— Stringent criteria for establishment of foreign securities branches (high capital requirements) and restrictions on foreign securities branch activities in Korea.

As the FPT dialogue progressed, it became apparent that many of the difficulties faced by foreign financial institutions in Korea were connected to structural distortions in the financial sector resulting from the highly regulated nature of the system and government's heavy-handed intervention. We therefore shifted our focus in the FPT from individual issues to the need for basic structural reform of the Korean financial sector.

In March 1992, our counterparts at the Ministry of Finance took a significant step forward in the FPT with the announcement that Korea would formulate a three-stage Blueprint for comprehensive financial sector liberalization. Treasury welcomed the move as an important shift away from the piecemeal approach to these issues taken in the past, and as a turning point in our dialogue. The Korean government also agreed to consult with the International Monetary Fund and World Bank during the Blueprint formulation process. The formulation of the short- and medium-term measures contained in Stages I and II of the Blueprint was completed in April and June 1992, and implementation of those measures is well underway. Although Stages I and II address a few of the individual issues faced by our financial institutions operating in Korea, the key areas needing attention are covered in the recently announced third and final stage of the Blueprint. The Government of Korea has recently accelerated the implementation of Stage III, and some important measures have already been undertaken.

After the Kim Administration took office in February 1993, the scope of the financial sector reform plan was expanded. A parallel package of reform measures to deregulate and enhance the competitiveness of the domestic financial industry was subsequently developed and incorporated into the new Five-Year Plan.

We are impressed with the comprehensive nature of the combined Blueprint and Five Year Financial Reform Plan measures. Of course, timely and consistent implementation will be key to international capital markets' assessment of Korea's commitment to liberalization. Prior to the completion of the Blueprint, Treasury outlined five areas that would be the focus of our attention, and I would like to review those very briefly and comment on each.

Treasury's assessment of Korea's financial sector reform package will focus on the extent to which the combined measures of the Blueprint and the domestic financial deregulation plan undertake the following:

182

1 Expedited interest rate liberalization and ceased reliance on 'window guidance.' The interest rate liberalization plan follows World Bank recommendations closely. Given the ROKG's history of backtracking on interest rate decontrol, however, implementation of Stage III of the liberalization plan in coming months will be crucial to the credibility of Korea's commitments in the Blueprint.

2 Eased controls on capital account and foreign exchange transactions, including restrictions on deferred payments for imports, further stock market opening, and underlying documentation requirements for foreign exchange transactions.

   − If commitments are carried out, the Blueprint could lead to fairly significant easing of underlying documentation requirements for forward exchange transactions by 1994-1995.

   − The exchange rate fluctuation band is scheduled to be widened sometime during the second half of 1994.

   − The Blueprint includes vague commitments to ease ceilings on foreign investment in the stock market in 1994-1995 and 1996-1997. Indications are that the Korean government will raise the ceiling from 10 to 15 percent during the second half of 1994, but further expansion of the ceiling has not been clearly delineated. Significantly, foreigners were permitted to invest in non-guaranteed convertible bonds issued by small- and medium-size Korean companies as of 1 July 1994.

   − The Korean government also expanded the repayment period for deferred credit operations in mid-1994, although Korea still lags far behind international norms in this regard.

3 Abandonment of directed credit schemes.

   − The main issues of concern to US financial institutions in this area are mandatory lending requirements to small- and medium-size industries (SMI) and limits on lending to the 30 largest conglomerates (*chaebol*).

   − US banks proposed to MOF a significant relaxation of ratio requirements for SMI lending and the exclusion of joint venture companies from the chaebol loan restrictions. According to the bankers, the Blueprint does provide some relief on the latter issue, but not until 1996, when the requirements will be imposed on only the 10 largest chaebol. SMI ratio requirements will not be reduced until 1996-1997; a date for the abolishment of the requirement is not specified in the Blueprint.

4 Adoption of more indirect means of monetary control.

   − The Blueprint did accelerate the liberalization of interest rates on

Monetary Stabilization Bonds to 1993 and envisions moving to an auction-based system for MSB allocation. Full use of open market operations as the major monetary policy instrument is not scheduled until 1996-1997.

- Of key concern to US banks, the mandatory underwriting of MSBs from trust deposits will not be abolished until 1996-1997, although the level of required purchases will be reduced somewhat in 1994-1995.

5 Improvement in foreign banks' access to local currency funding sources.

- The Blueprint does not address the *won* currency funding problem. For example, it does not include new measures to sanction discrimination against foreign banks in the interbank call market; MSB purchase requirements from trust accounts will remain for some time; CD issuance will still be subject to ceilings; and funding and lending limits will still be tied to the local rather than the global capital of foreign banks.

6 Enhanced regulatory transparency, openness, and consistency.

- According to US banks, Korea is moving to address issues of transparency but foreign banks continue to be hampered by ambiguous, unevenly applied regulations. Korea's financial sector reform plans (the Blueprint and the Five Year Financial Reform Plan) touch on these issues, but not in a meaningful way.
- We are somewhat concerned by language in the Blueprint that alludes to vague conditions having to be met before some key steps are taken.

In Korea's interest

As we have emphasized in our financial policy discussions with our counterparts, financial sector liberalization is not only in the interest of the US and other foreign financial institutions in Korea, but in Korea's interest as well.

Implementation of financial liberalization measures will strengthen and deepen Korea's own financial markets and enhance overall economic efficiency. Foreign competition contributes to the depth of the market, helps strengthen domestic industry and provides greater consumer choice. Foreign banks offer needed products and support Korea's domestic and international activities. Importantly, a forward-moving financial sector reform strategy will make Korea's foreign investment environment a more welcoming one and will be key to attracting the foreign investment and technology Korea seeks.

The best form of technology transfer is osmosis through a significant foreign direct investment presence in the economy. But if foreign firms can't finance themselves in Korea, they will look elsewhere. At a time when the low-wage countries of Southeast Asia and China are successfully making their markets more appealing to international investors, Korea is encumbered with a reputation as an extremely difficult place to do business.

Financial sector liberalization will help solve these problems by allowing the market to allocate resources more effectively, freeing the commercial banking sector to support Korea's economic development, and making Korea's investment environment more attractive to foreign investors.

Discussion

Hae-Wang Chung

The Korean government plans to liberalize its financial market gradually and tries to improve investment environment for the foreigners. Such endeavors are not just the result of US pressure. Rather, they result from the recognition of the fact that improving investment environment and liberalizing the financial market will increase the competitiveness of Korean products by upgrading the efficiency of the financial industry.

The government's plan for improving the investment environment is presented in the New Five Year Economic Plan. To improve the business environment for foreign firms, the plan calls for reducing the number of businesses closed to foreign investment and relaxing restrictions on foreign investment as well as imported technologies. Furthermore, it calls for facilitating foreign firms' business activities, even permitting acquisitions of land for business purposes and establishing an exclusive industrial complex for foreign investors.

As for the liberalization of financial markets, details of which Dr. Cho and Dr. Fall already addressed, I would like to present a brief historical overview of the process before further discussing the plan in order to clarify its contents and Korea's unique circumstances.

For the past 30 years, Korean financial institutions have contributed a lot to continued high economic growth by allocating limited resources efficiently. However, the efficiency diminished because of the expansion of the size of the economy, growing structural complexity, changes in the international economic environment, and strict control of the government on operations of financial institutions. The Korean government initiated liberalization of its financial industry in the early 1980s, starting with interest rates, foreign exchange and capital markets. During the process of liberalization, Korea experienced high trade surpluses, especially against the US, causing trade disputes between the two countries in the late 1980s. To reduce trade deficits, the US urged Korea to open its service sector, including the financial services industry, at the Uruguay Round of multinational talks.

US demands for opening Korean markets set off political turmoil in Korea. While most Koreans were fearful that more efficient foreign firms would dominate domestic markets, anti-American sentiments grew in Korea. In an effort to reduce conflicts, Korea and the US agreed to start Financial Policy Talks (FPT) in 1989.

In the beginning, the US asked Korea to loosen some of the trivial restrictions imposed on foreign banks and security firms operating in Korea. However, after several FPT meetings, the US requested a blueprint with a year-by-year time schedule. Upon accommodating the request, Korea decided to prepare a blueprint with three phases: short-term, mid-term, and long-term. The first phase plan was announced at the end of March 1992 and the second one was followed three months later. The final stage plan was supposed to be announced by 1993; however, presidential elections in both Korea and the US that year inevitably delayed the plan's presentation. In Korea, the newly elected President Kim Young Sam and his administration initiated efforts to reform the nation with an extensive anti-corruption drive. The new administration also presented a 100-Day economic revitalization plan which ended in June 1993, and announced the New Five Year Economic Plan (94-97) in late April.

Two major goals of Korea's new international economic policy under the Five-Year Economic Plan are to internationalize its economy and to become an advanced economy. The government wants to foster international trade and policy cooperation, which may encourage overseas activities of domestic firms.

Since the third phase plan was drafted under the new administration, its content was somewhat changed. Under the new plan the liberalization process will be accelerated. According to the new blue print, the Phase I plan would end by mid-1993, six months ahead of its original schedule; the Phase II and III plans will be respectably executed in 1994-1995 and 1996-1997, one year ahead of the original blueprint. The Phase III plan designates interest rate deregulation, indirect monetary control, efficient supervision of financial institutions, readjustment of business domain among firms, and foreign exchange and capital market liberalization.

To be more specific, the following is a brief summary of implementation plans:

Interest deregulation

The Korean government decided not to regulate the interest rate in order to increase the efficiency of the financial industry by encouraging interest rates to reflect market conditions. In Phase I (by the end of 1993), interest rates are to be deregulated for all banks and non-banks loans except for policy loans, deposits for two years or longer, corporate and financial bonds with less than two years maturity, and monetary stabilization bonds (MSBs), and treasury and public bonds.

Between 1994 and 1995, in Phase II, interest rates are to be deregulated for short-term deposits and loans eligible for BOK (the Bank of Korea) rediscount. By 1996, deposits whose interest rates are tied to the market rate, e.g., MMFs (Money Market Funds), are to be introduced. Thus, all interest rates will be deregulated by the end of 1996.

Indirect monetary control system

According to the Blueprint, the central bank will use indirect instruments such as open market operations for controlling the money stock. In 1993, the rates for treasury bonds, RP's, and MSB's are to be revised to become more flexible. Between 1996 and 1997, reserve requirement ratios will be lowered on a gradual basis; open market operations dealing in treasury and public bonds will be actively used as major monetary policy instruments.

Promotion of money markets

Presently, the money market is highly segmented, despite continued growth of trade volume; that is, short-term interest rates do not reflect the market conditions. As a result, implementing indirect control of money supply would be difficult. By 1993, the call market is to be completely deregulated; short-term financing companies are to be promoted to function as money market brokers. Between 1994 and 1995, the market will be expanded by introducing commercial papers with diverse maturities and allowing short-term financing companies to participate in the foreign exchange market.

Liberalization of foreign exchange and capital transactions

On the foreign exchange side:

After the exchange rate system based on the market average rates were introduced in March 1990, the daily fluctuation band has been expanded in steps. In September 1992, the foreign exchange regime changed to adopt a negative list system — foreign exchange transactions are restricted only in exceptional cases.

According to the Blueprint, further restrictions on foreign exchange transactions would be relaxed. In 1993, the daily fluctuation band for foreign exchange rates is expanded from plus or minus 0.8 percent to plus or minus 1.0 percent. Between 1996 and 1997, a freely fluctuating exchange rate system will be implemented.

Government applies position limits to nation-wide commercial banks differently from regional banks. Previously, such position limits were set to control banks' over-bought position only. In 1993, government will start to weight both over-bought positions and banks' own equity standing.

In 1994, underlying documentation (UD) will be waived for forward transactions involving foreign currencies and limits for UD-waived foreign exchange deposits payable in won will be abolished. Between 1996 and 1996, underlying documentation will be waived for even ordinary transactions so that firms are solely responsible for the foreign exchange risks.

On the capital transaction side:

Currently, the regulations on foreign direct investments both in and out of the country have been continuously relaxed by adopting a negative list system. Furthermore, foreigners have been allowed to invest directly in the Korea Stock Exchange since 1992. To give more freedom to Korean businesses and financial institutions, government has relaxed the restrictions on offshore financing and allowed limited offshore borrowing.

In 1993, all FDI's (Foreign Direct Investment) in Korea is under a notification system. Also, the government expanded the scope of institutional investors in overseas stock markets and raised their investment limits. Furthermore, the government extended the settlement date from 90 to 120 days for deferred payments of imported raw materials used exclusively for export. Between 1994 and 1995, the government will expand the sectors eligible for FDI and simplify the procedure for FDI. Institutional investors will invest in foreign stocks freely; the limit for foreigners' investment in Korea Stock Exchange will be raised. In addition, international organizations will be authorized to issue floating rates for bonds denominated in Korean won in 1995; foreigners will be authorized to invest directly in bonds tied to stocks - convertible bonds; and bond type funds will be authorized. Finally, the period for import on deferred payment will be further extended.

The Blueprint also deals with other areas such as relaxing credit controls for large and small businesses and reducing requirements for opening branches of foreign securities firms, investment trusts, and investment consulting services.

So far, I have discussed the main issues of the Blueprint. If I may say my personal opinion about the plan, I believe that the Korean government will strictly adhere to its schedule and complete the liberalization of the financial market until the end of 1997.

Jin-Ouk Kim

Regardless of the Korean government's efforts to induce more foreign investment and technical transfer, it is my regret to see that not a few foreign investors have already left Korea and some investors are now considering to withdraw their investments from Korea. It is also observed that the total amount of new investment is down from previous years.

During 1993, this unfavorable trend leveled off, or even improved to a limited extent. In the opinion of the author, such a limited improvement is the result of, among others, the reduction of the kinds of businesses restricted to foreign investment, and government's efforts to ease administrative constraints toward the foreign invested companies. However, said improvement of 1993 does not reach the level of the foreign investment in 1991 as indicated in Table 13.1.

To find a way of turning around such an undesirable trend, we need to explore its origins. Below I address some of the factors which led to this decline.

Disputes between Korean and foreign partners

When a joint venture company is established based upon more or less equal equity participation of Korean and foreign investors, the company is to be managed jointly by Korean and foreign investors. Many of such disputes arise from different ways of thinking, different cultures and lack of trust, which could be resolved or prevented by establishing better communication and through mutual effort of understanding the other party, and by naming the management of good communication. However, quite often, a deadlock in management decisions arises from fundamental issues, such as a conflict of interests between the joint venture company and the foreign investor. This could involve, for example, export restrictions by the foreign investor of the products manufactured by the joint venture company.

A foreign investor usually imposes restrictions of export of the products of a joint venture company to avoid competition between the joint venture

190

company's and its affiliates' products in the same market. Such a restriction was not a problem when the local market was big enough to accommodate the production capacity of the joint venture company. But such becomes a problem when the joint venture company cannot sell all of their products locally due to the competition of local markets caused by newcomers into the market and therefore it needs foreign markets to survive.

Inflows of foreign direct investment

		(in million US$)		
		1991	1992	1993
Country:	US	296.3	379.2	340.7
	Japan	226.2	155.2	285.9
	Europe	824.3	282.9	307.4
	Others	49.2	77.9	110.3
	Total	1,396.0	894.5	1,044.3
Industry:	Chemicals	161.2	220.0	241.2
	Machinery	85.1	38.2	49.8
	Electronics & electrical machinery	124.1	66.6	45.2
	Transportation equipment	49.9	40.0	44.1
	Hotels	31.1	31.8	75.7
	Banking	77.6	39.3	57.0
	Others	867.0	452.6	531.3
	Total	1,396.0	894.5	1,044.3

Note: On an approval basis.
Source: Economic Cooperation Bureau, ROK Ministry of Finance

To solve this problem, certain alternatives need to be worked out, such as allowing a joint venture company's export of the products under different trademarks or even under the same trademark, but clearly identifying the origin of the products to maintain discriminative prices in the same market. It may hurt the interest of foreign partner, but it would definitely improve the relationship between the partners.

Another example of conflict of interest or mistrust between partners comes from when the foreign investor establishes a new company in a market where the joint venture company has exported its products. It is expected for Korean partners to be given opportunities to make an investment to the said new venture together with the foreign partner, or at least the joint venture company should be given an alternative way to be compensated for their lost market. However, unfortunately, the Korean partner is generally neglected by the foreign partner.

There are also many other reasons creating mistrust to an extent which cannot necessarily be overcome.

Labor problems

Korean labor is no longer cheap, compared with other developing countries. In fact, it may be said the cost of labor in Korea is too expensive in view of its productivity and level of per capital income. It is, therefore, mandatory in Korea to create a consensus that curbing the increase of the labor cost should be accepted not to aggravate further non-competitiveness of Korean products. The role of Korean government and mass media is important for people reaching such consensus.

It is also advised that the multinational foreign investors offer Korean employees the job opportunities in their affiliates in other countries which will serve as an incentive to work at the joint venture companies and to reduce labor disputes. Korean white-collar employees and skilled laborers may be valuable in other affiliated companies of foreign investors.

Land ownership deregulation

The size of a factory site that foreign invested companies may own is very tightly regulated. For example, the factory site cannot be larger than double the size of the factory building. If the factory site is larger than regulated, the excessive land is subject to five times higher tax than normal property tax rate. Furthermore, a factory construction completion certificate can not be obtain, and the foreign invested company may be compelled to sell the excessive land. Such a restriction should be lifted or eased for a foreign invested company, to purchase and own enough site for future expansion.

Another example is that the current law prohibits any incorporated company to own the residential house under the Housing site Regulation Act. Therefore any company, including a foreign invested company, cannot purchase and own any house for their expatriate officers. Such restriction shall be lifted, considering the rent for an adequate house in Korea is unreasonably expensive. To give an idea of housing expenses, executive-level residential housing costs about US$10,000 per month.

In 1994, the government eased the restriction to a limited extent. The brief of said deregulation is as follows:

> In principle, foreigners must obtain prior approval from the government in order to purchase land in Korea. In limited instances, however, qualifying foreigners may purchase land by merely reporting the purchase to the government before entering into a contract. Namely those foreigners with F-2 visa (long-term residence visa) can purchase residential land of less than 660 m2 (one house per one household). In addition, manufacturing companies can now purchase land required to carry on its manufacturing activities by reporting the purchase. However, there are limits on the size of land which can be purchased depending on the type of business for the companies (these limits apply to Korean companies as well).

> Other than the above two instances, foreigners must still obtain approval from the government. As described below, however, foreigners can now purchase land with government approval. This is in contrast to the previous law where purchases by foreigners were severely restricted.

Other issues

Foreign exchange restriction shall be properly lifted. Foreign exchange and capital transaction has been liberalized to some extents in the first half of 1994. The main content is as follows:

1 The negative list of current foreign exchange transactions is lessened, and most of the items which need the approval by the Bank of Korea ('BOK') are only to be validated by foreign exchange banks.
2 Validation of foreign invisible transactions is made immediately at the time of payment, while until now, the validation has been made at either the time of contract or payment.
3 At the time of payment validation by banks, the previously required recommendation of the Minister concerned is abolished.
4 Capital transactions less than US$100,000 is validated by a foreign exchange bank without requiring the approval of the BOK.

Foreign loan restrictions shall be properly lifted. Presently, domestic interest rates are higher than prevailing international interest rates, and the domestic money supply is being restricted for economic stability. Also, since 1986, procurement of foreign capital has been restricted for fear that an influx of foreign exchange, coupled with the accumulation of trade surplus, may lead to the revaluation of the Korean currency. For these reasons, domestic companies as well as foreign invested companies are desiring more access to low-cost foreign capital.

Due to the large disparity between domestic and foreign interest rates, a massive sudden liberalization could result in an influx of foreign capital which in turn could lead to a revaluation of the Korean currency. Rapid appreciation of the won would hinder the international competitiveness of Korean enterprises. In order to increase opportunities for use of foreign capital, with the least amount of side effects, certain measures shall be implemented.

In 1994, the government allowed foreign firms bringing advanced technology into Korea to borrow from abroad funds amounting up to 75 percent of their invested capital starting January 15, 1994, compared with the current 50 percent. The borrowings are to be used for the import of productive facilities and raw materials and the reimbursement of debts. Furthermore, foreign manufacturing companies operating in Korea were newly allowed to borrow up to 50 percent of invested capital for the import of facilities.

Korean government shall take more initiatives to induce foreign investment. The government should undertake to (1) reduce the corporate tax rate applicable to foreign invested companies, (2) expand the scope of permissible real estate acquisition by foreign invested companies (this will be accompanied by simplification of the relevant procedures) and (3) create industrial complexes for the exclusive use of foreign invested companies. In addition, for the promotion of stability in labor relations, a new bureau will be established to handle foreign invested companies matters exclusively. Business restrictions to foreign investment shall be reduced significantly, and the procedures for reporting of investment or technology transfer shall be simplified substantially. Furthermore, there shall be continuous and vigorous efforts to ease administrative constraints and to correct any unfavorable treatment toward foreign invested companies. Opportunities for utilization of domestic and foreign currency capital shall be increased for foreign invested companies, starting with those in the high-tech industries.

Joonmo Cho

The paper by Thomas Chiang, Bang Nam Jeon and Kap-Soo Oh addresses three important issues in the process of Korea's financial restructuring: (1) ownership linkages between the banking and commerce sector, (2) the scope of services provided by banks and nonbank financial institutions, and (3) the abolishment of various price regulations maintained in the financial sector.

For the purpose of suggesting some answers to these issues, the authors investigates thoroughly the cases of the US, UK, Japan and Germany. There is no doubt that such experiences of the other developed countries provides some valuable lessons in directing future financial policies for Korea. However, we have to be very cautious in arguing pros and cons according to the majority rules as in this paper.

In the US, the key factor which has been taken into account in making any policy is the prohibition of capital concentration.1 As we all know, there are many Anti-Trust Laws which prevent one conglomerate firm from growing to take the monopoly power in any market. There is no exception even in the banking sector. There are a lot of regulations which prevent the major banks from opening more than two branches within a state. It is frequently criticized that the average size of the US bank is so small in comparison with the size of their economy. If an economies of scale exists in the banking sector, this legal restrictions requires economic inefficiency.

On the other hand, many people believe that the banking sector was the key sector in inseminating and in fostering the Ferman industrialization during the 19th century. This tradition seems to last even now. According to the authors' investigations, the Ferman government has been so generous to the banking sector. For instance, only limit to the banking sector is that a bank's investment including shares in banks and commercial firms (if the shares exceed 10 percent of a commercial firm's capital) may not exceed the bank's capital. Also many Ferman banks have significant influences on commercial firms though the proxy votes by banks of their clients' share and the presence of bankers on most of the largest corporations' management. It is not quite surprising if we look at the Ferman history of industrialization.

What about Korea? Do we have to follow the German paradigm, the US's or another? The answer is that we have to look at our own history instead of borrowing a good case from elsewhere. During the past two decades between 1960 and 1980, Korea experienced the rapid economic growth. In their rapid growth, the role of government and the banking sector was indispensable. The banking sector plays a major role of the channel between the government and the commerce sector. That is, the government was able to convey their intention about the industrial policy to the commerce and to enforce necessary reward-penalty schemes through credit rationing of the banking sector. Inevitably, some large conglomerates (chaebols) emerged and the competitiveness of the banking sector vanished (they served the Korean government faithfully!).

Bearing these facts in mind, we have to ask the following questions. The first one is whether the commerce including chaebols should be allowed to participate in the bank ownership under the rationale of promoting the world competitiveness in the banking sector. Does the capital growth of chaebols and of banks necessarily lead to the growth of Korea? By the way, is the economies of scale really working in the banking sector?

Many people argued that the high interest rate is the killer to the Korean firms. Let's say that the interest would go down if the chaebols were allowed to have the bank ownership. This might promote the competitiveness of our products in the world market. Even if we all accept this argument, what about the housing market? Even if we all accept this argument, what about the housing market? The low interest rate would definitely cause a higher demand for houses, the rental rate going up. As we all know, the high rental rate has been another killer to Korean people and many firms (especially small and mid-sized firms). As we know, the housing market has not cause any big trouble in Germany or in the US. The perspective of the partial equilibrium analysis on the financial market is silent in answering those welfare-type issues.

Finally, the authors provided an interesting evidence of cointegration in the US, Germany, Japan and the UK. This results seem to indirectly suggest that the cointegration would be rejected and the macroeconomic variables would fail to be harmoniously related in a stable fashion because those variables are determined in an ad hoc fashion by the government instead of market itself. Even if it was of interest, the empirical study for the Korea case should be executed in order to provide some concrete suggestions to the Korean government.

Stanley Judd

Investment companies have enabled investors to achieve several goals, including: (1) diversity of company or industry risk, (2) professional management, (3) lower costs through economies of scale, and (4) integrity of the means of investment. There are now over 3,000 investment companies registered under the Investment Company Act of 1940. They have assets of over $1.7 trillion, which can be roughly divided in thirds. In other words, approximately a third in equity funds, a third in bond funds, and a third in short-term money-market instruments. We also have 18,000 investment advisers registered under the Investment Advisers Act of 1940.

In Korea, too, statistics reflect the continuously growing popularity of Korean investment trusts. In 1980 there were six investment management companies, which are the firms that manage investment funds. In June 1990, that number increased to 14. Meanwhile, the total number of investment funds grew from 72 to 271 in the same period. In 1980 there were about 350,000 unit-holders. Ten years later, the group numbered almost 4.5 million. The level of net assets of the funds in June 1990 was nearly 30 times their level at the end of 1980.

The interest in international investment has greatly accelerated in order to diversify country risk, among other things. For example, from 1985 to 1992, the number of US closed-end investment companies — companies whose shares are not redeemable — significantly investing in foreign securities grew from eight funds with total net assets of over $1.1 billion, to 73 funds with total net assets of $13.1 billion.

The interest in foreign investment is likely to continue to grow. A recent item in the Wall Street Letter of June 28, 1993, states that Prudential Securities and Shearson Lehman Brothers have set their course on having brokers increase their clients' foreign investments. The article goes on to state that they are following in the footsteps of Merrill Lynch, which last summer encouraged brokers to get their clients to put 20 percent of their assets in international markets by the end of the decade.

Responding to the interest in foreign investment, investment managers have accommodated by creating several types of funds. 'Country' funds are investment companies which invest in the securities of issuers from one country. 'International' funds denotes investment companies that invest in the securities of issuers from many countries, but not the United States. Meanwhile, 'global' funds are investment firms that invest in the securities of issuers from many countries, including the US. In addition, the interest in foreign investment has caused many foreign investment advisers, or their subsidiaries, to register under the Investment Advisers Act of 1940.

As of March 31, 1993, approximately 312 entities with foreign business addresses from 32 countries were registered under the Advisers Act. A number of foreign advisers, possibly 30 or more, operate U.S. registered funds.

In Korea, three US registered funds are in place. They include the Korea Fund, a closed-end fund with about $240 million in assets; the Korea

Investment Fund, a closed-end fund with about $50 million in assets; and the Korea Capital Trust, an open-end investment company. This last firm issues redeemable securities and usually maintains a continuous offering of its shares, with about $6 million in assets. There are also 13 Korean investment managers registered under the Investment Advisers Act.

Why are closed-end funds so popular as a means of foreign investment? Some believe that the manager of a closed-end fund can pursue a longer term investment strategy more easily than can the manager of an open-end company because he is not required to provide liquidity to meet redemption requests or to invest funds from further subscriptions for shares. Thus, the size of the pool of assets to be managed in a closed-end is likely to be more stable than that of an open-end company. For this reason, closed-end funds may be particularly well-suited for emerging markets and venture capital investments where a longer term view may be necessary.

From the view of the nation in whose market a fund invests, the closed-end structure may be preferable in an emerging securities market because there is no risk that the fund will be forced to sell portfolio securities to meet redemption requests. Thereby, they avoid the potentially adverse effects of forced sales on securities prices. Moreover, an open-end company must be able to determine its current net asset value whenever an investor wishes to redeem, and that may be particularly difficult if the market is thin and/or unstable.

Finally, and perhaps most importantly, a policy of the Commission requires that not more than 15 percent of the assets of an open-end fund be illiquid – or incapable of being sold for their stated value within seven days – and that standard may be difficult to achieve with satisfactory diversity in an emerging market. One should note that the sole Korean fund which is registered as an open-end company has a subclassification under the Investment Company Act of as a non-diversified company. While the policy of the company is to come within the definition of a 'regulated investment company' under the Internal Revenue Code, and while that definition requires some degree of diversification, it is not required to be as diversified as is a diversified company under the Investment Company Act.

The US has historically been a strong advocate of national treatment and the free international movement of goods, services and capital. The International Banking Act of 1978 adopted the policy of national treatment, defined as parity of treatment between foreign and domestic banks in like circumstances. According to the National Treatment Study prepared by the US Department of the Treasury in 1990, the concept of national treatment has evolved in practice from de jure national treatment to de facto equality of competitive opportunity. In that study the Treasury Department stated, 'When implemented worldwide, national treatment, defined as equality of competitive opportunity, offers the best hope of achieving global economic efficiency and prosperity.'

The experience of foreign investment companies under the Investment Company Act illustrates how national treatment in the de jure sense can result in non-national treatment in the de facto sense. The Investment Company Act requires that a foreign investment company must obtain an order of the Commission permitting the foreign investment company to register under the Investment Company Act and to make a public offer of its securities, before it uses the mails or any means of interstate commerce to sell its securities. In order to grant such permission, the Commission must find that by reason of special circumstances or arrangements it is practically feasible for the Commission to enforce the Act against the foreign investment company and that the issuance of such order is otherwise consistent with the public interest and the protection of investors.

Those provisions of the Investment Company Act would seem to be a model of national treatment in the de jure sense. They permit a foreign investment company to register under the Act and use the mails or any means of interstate commerce to offer its securities if the Commission can enforce the same law against the foreign investment company that it enforces against domestic investment companies.

Nevertheless, those provisions have prevented foreign investment companies from registering under the Act and from using the mails or any means of interstate commerce to sell their securities, except in a handful of exceptional cases. Thus, they have resulted in non-national treatment in a de facto sense. That may occur because a foreign company is most likely to have been formed under a basic law that differs from the basic law, such as a state's corporation or business trust law, under which US companies are usually formed. They may therefore be unable to comply with the provisions of the Investment Company Act, which assume certain structures.

For example, the Act requires a managed investment company to be under the supervision of a board of directors of which at least 40 percent of the members are independent of the fund's management. Foreign investment companies formed on a contractual basis, such as those formed in Korea, may have difficulty complying with that requirement.

The practical result is that anyone who wishes to use the US mails or any other means of US interstate commerce to offer the securities of an investment company generally must form the company as a US domestic company. There is no restriction, however, on the formation of such a company by foreigners.

On January 2, 1992, Korea generally permitted foreign investment in Korean equity securities subject to the following limits: a foreign investor could own up to 3 percent of a company's equity, and all foreigners as a group could own up to 10 percent of a company's equity. In the year that followed, a total of 1,572 investors registered to invest in the Korean stock market. That total included 678 individual investors and 894 institutional investors. Of the 894 institutional investors, 572 were investment companies. Total inflow amounted to $2.7 billion, of which $655 million was remitted. Net inflow from the US was $573.1 million, about 27.7 percent of total net inflow.

According to some investment advisers interested in investing in the equities of Korean companies, the 10 percent cap on investment by foreigners in a company's equity has been reached in about 80 good quality companies. As a result, there is as much as a 10-point spread between the bid and the asked prices of the securities of those companies which may be purchased by foreigners. For example, there may be a 25 percent premium on the sale of such a security and a 35 percent premium on the purchase of the same security. As a result, an investment manager may be restrained in his management of a portfolio in that he would be disinclined to sell a security that he can imagine repurchasing in the future.

One investment adviser told me that premiums in transactions between foreign owners of Korean securities have gone as high as 80 percent. I was also advised that individual foreign investors are inhibited from investing in Korea by the huge amount of red tape connected with the acquisition of a security by a foreign investor.

What would professional investors interested in the Korean stock market like to see happen? From my conversations with a few advisers and investment managers interested in investing in the Korean stock market, it seems to me that they would like to see Korea do the following:

1 increase the amount of securities that may be purchased by foreigners;
2 simplify the process by which an individual may acquire a Korean security;
3 enable foreign investment advisers and analysts to obtain the same kind of information from Korean companies that they may obtain from US companies.

In the US, company spokespersons often meet privately with financial analysts to discuss a company. Should a spokesperson inadvertently disclose material inside information in the course of such a meeting, the company proceeds immediately to issue a press release containing the same information. The development of a sophisticated understanding as to what information is material inside information and what is not, may increase the total information that is available to inquiring financial analysts. In this connection, Korean financial experts have suggested that it would be important to improve the skills and acumen of market participants.

US investment managers also would like to be able to sell US investment funds in Korea, or to be allowed to establish funds in Korea, just as Koreans are allowed to establish funds in the US. Investment managers in the US also would like to be able to provide Koreans with investment advice either directly or through Korean subsidiaries.

Several years ago the Commission recommended to the US Congress that it amend the Investment Company Act. The amendment proposed to make it possible for the Commission to permit the sale in the US of foreign funds which can not comply with all the provisions of the Act, provided they are subject in their home country to a scheme of regulation that has the same purposes as the Act. The first problem with that approach is how it can be accomplished while preserving the protection intended to be provided investors by the Investment Company Act. The second problem is how a level playing field can exist between US funds and foreign funds if foreign funds are exempted from provisions of the Investment Company Act to which US investment companies are subject.

Possible means of solving those problems are: (1) harmonization of regulation; and (2) reciprocal recognition of regulatory systems through bilateral memoranda of understanding that also provide for cooperation and coordination between regulating agencies.

In its report issued in May of 1992 on the regulation of investment companies, entitled 'Protecting Investors: A Half Century of Investment Company Regulation,' available through the Government Printing Office, the Division of Investment Management recommended to the Commission that it propose legislation to the Congress that would incorporate the aforementioned policies. With regard to international investment advisers, the Division of Investment Management recommended in the Protecting Investors Report that the Investment Advisers Act should be interpreted as applying only to acts or effects occurring in the US. The interpretation furthermore held that the foreign business of a foreign adviser registered under the Act should not normally be deemed to be subject to the Act, and that foreign advisers should be permitted to share personnel with registered subsidiaries offering advice in the US without requiring the registration of the foreign parent company. The staff has proceeded to implement those interpretative positions.

The Commission's Division of Investment Management has made legislative recommendations concerning foreign investment companies. These recommended changes would give to US investors a broader choice among investment companies and investment advisers. I believe that the Division perceives that as being in the interests of US investors. Similarly, it would be in the interest of foreign investors if they, too, were given a broader choice among investment companies and investment advisers.

Part III
INDUSTRIAL COOPERATION AND
BUSINESS RELATIONS

12 Foreign direct investment by firms from developing and developed countries

Jongmoo Jay Choi, Kyoung Kim and Rajan Chandran

Concomitant with a phenomenal increase in foreign direct investments (FDI) in recent years by firms from less developed countries (LDCs), as opposed to the conventional FDIs by multinational corporations (MNCs) from developed countries, there is a burgeoning academic literature on the foreign direct investments by these new unconventional multinational firms. Many of these studies have examined the FDI behavior of these firms in a particular country, but the stylized facts about the FDIs by these MNCs from LDCs (LDC-MNCs) are not yet generally understood. The stylized facts are needed both as a basis for comparison to those of MNCs from developed countries (DC-MNCs) and as a prelude to new theoretical interpretations.

This chapter surveys the literature on FDIs by LDC-MNCs, particularly those from newly industrialized countries in Asia, in order to establish the stylized facts on these investments as opposed to FDIs by DC-MNCs. Concentration on the Asian firms helps control extraneous variables, as these firms operate in relatively homogeneous home-country environments (e.g., the stage of economic development, national policy orientations, the resource endowment, cultural factors, etc.). The extent to which the conventional theories of FDI are consistent with these stylized facts will also be discussed. Suggestions are then made for a theoretical framework which synthesizes the conventional theories and the real risk diversification motive of the firm. To aid theoretical interpretations of unconventional versus conventional FDIs, preliminary empirical evidence is presented on the pattern of FDI inflows and outflows in Korea.

Major characteristics of multinationals from Asian developing countries in contrast to conventional multinationals

The characteristics of LDC firms and their FDI behavior are compared with those of DC firms in the following categories: the size of the parent company, the ownership pattern of their subsidiaries, the geographic location of FDIs, the motivation for international investments, and the competitive advantages of the parent firm.

The size of the parent company

The conventional theory of FDI is based on the proposition that MNCs possess oligopolistic advantages in comparison with indigenous local firms. Large firms in concentrated industries tend to have these advantages. Thus company size is an important factor in foreign investments. This hypothesis is generally supported by early empirical studies (e.g., Caves [1974], Horst [1972]), although there is some evidence (Franco [1976], Giddy and Young [1982]) that smaller firms are also becoming active in FDIs.

In evaluating MNCs from LDCs as opposed to DCs, comparing their absolute sizes alone is not appropriate because LDC firms are generally much smaller than their counterparts from developed countries (Lecraw [1981]). Therefore, a relative comparison of the firms making international investments in each sample rather than the comparison of their absolute sizes is more appropriate.

Table 12.1
Distribution of foreign manufacturing subsidiaries of LDC-MNCs

Sales of Parent	Number of Subsidiaries
Less than $5 million	26 (17.7%)
At least $5 million but less than $50 million	27 (18.3%)
At least $50 million but less than $100 million	21 (14.3%)
At least $100 million but less than $500 million	42 (28.6%)
$500 million or more	31 (21.1%)
Total	147 (100%)

Source: Wells, Louis T., Jr., *Third World Multinationals: The Rise of Foreign Investment from Developing Countries* (1983), The MIT Press, Cambridge, p. 31.

Evidence from the works of Chen (1983) and Jo (1981) suggests that the size is not a critical factor for LDC firms to go abroad because small and medium-sized firms are as active as large ones in international investments. Wells (1983), in particular, reports in Table 12.1 that out of 147 foreign

206

subsidiaries of *LDC-MNC*s in his sample, 26 subsidiaries or 18.3 percent were established by companies whose sales were <u>less</u> than $5 million, while 31 subsidiaries or 21.1 percent were owned by companies whose sales were more than $500 million. Among the foreign subsidiaries established by *US*-based manufacturing firms, Rhodes (1974) reports that 34 percent of the new subsidiaries was established by companies whose sales were less than $50 million whereas 17 percent was by those whose sales were more than $1 billion. It is thus likely that, within both DC and LDC firm groups, relatively small companies as well as big ones go abroad if they possess firm-specific assets exploitable in international markets.[1] However the absolute size of the LDC firms is generally much smaller as seen above.

The pattern of subsidiary ownership

There exists a significant difference for MNCs from developing and developed countries in terms of equity participation in foreign subsidiaries. Firms from developed countries generally prefer a wholly-owned subsidiary (Franco [1976], Rhodes [1974]) whereas LDC-MNCs in general opt for a joint-venture (Fong and Komaran [1985], Heenan and Keegan [1979], Wells [1977]). In the case of a joint-venture, DC firms prefer a majority ownership while firms from LDCs tend to choose a *minority* ownership.

In Table 12.2, Lecraw (1977) indicates the ownership pattern of local subsidiaries of firms that invested in one less developed country, Thailand. It is interesting that more than 50 percent of DC-MNCs in that sample have a majority ownership while 86 percent of LDC-MNCs have a minority ownership. Industrial organization theory suggests that conventional multinationals from developed countries which possess high technology and other intangible assets avoid a joint venture with a local partner because of the fear of losing their information and technological advantages. Furthermore, these firms often integrate operations of various subsidiaries and internalize transactions to retain the oligopolistic benefits from the standpoint of the parent corporation.[2]

Table 12.2
Ownership patterns of foreign firms in Thailand

Home Country	*% Foreign Ownership*				
	100%	*99.5-50.1%*	*50%*	*49.9-0%*	*Total*
US	10	47	15	28	100%
Europe	23	45	12	20	100%
Japan	25	51	10	14	100%
LDCs	2	7	5	86	100%

Source: Lecraw, Donald, 'Direct Investment by Firms from Less Developed Countries,' *Oxford Economic Papers*, March 1977, p. 448.

LDC-MNCs, in contrast, tend to possess a standardized technology without a distinctive oligopolistic advantage so that they would have less to lose from a joint operation. Instead, they may need additional capital or the marketing capability of local partners. This makes them more amenable to the joint venture with the local firm. Moreover, unlike multinationals from developed countries, LDC firms lack a well-structured international network of operations, and their foreign subsidiaries are likely to operate independently of the parent company. In addition, given their standard technologies, the bargaining leverage of the LDC firms relative to the host government is weaker than multinationals from developed countries. This is another reason why LDC firms often opt for joint ventures with local partners, because local partners can provide local contact or serve as their advocate vis-a-vis the host government.

The geographical location of investments

A striking difference also exists in the geographical location of FDIs. DC-MNCs tend to invest a majority of their capital in developed economies while LDC-MNCs concentrate their investments in less developed areas, often in their neighboring countries.

Table 12.3 reports the geographical distribution of outward direct investment stocks of various countries. With the exception of Japan, a majority of investments from the developed countries are in developed economies. Moreover, except for the US, this pattern of concentration has accelerated over the past decade. On the other hand, a majority of outward investments from LDCs are concentrated in underdeveloped regions.

Table 12.3
Stock of outward direct investments

(Millions of US$)

A. FDIs by developed countries

Home country		DCs	LDCs	Total
US	1975	45,427(81.3%)	10,459(18.7%)	55,886(100%)
	1985	75,907(79.8%)	19,197(20.2%)	95,104(100%)
UK	1974	11,620(81.1%)	2,707(18.9%)	14,327(100%)
	1984	24,536(85.7%)	4,084(14.6%)	28,620(100%)
W. Germany				
	1976	7,261(73.0%)	2,681(27.0%)	9,942(100%)
	1985	20,327(80.5%)	4,913(19.5%)	25,240(100%)
Canada				
	1975	4,778(91.6%)	439(8.4%)	5,217(100%)
	1983	13,062(93.2%)	950(6.8%)	14,012(100%)
Japan	1975	1,404(27.2%)	3,760(72.8%)	5,164(100%)
	1985	10,850(44.5%)	13,551(55.5%)	24,401(100%)

B. FDIs by less developed countries, as of 1980

Home country	DCs	LDCs	Total
Korea	36.5(25.7%)	105.4(74.3%)	141.9(100%)
Taiwan	44.0(43.4%)	57.4(56.6%)	101.4(100%)
India	8.1(7.0%)	107.7(93.0%)	115.8(100%)

The FDI data for developed countries (Panel A) covers manufacturing only. The data for LDCs (Panel B) includes primary and service industries as well. *Source:* For the Taiwanese data, Alice H. Amsden, 'Exports of Technology by Newly-Industrializing Countries: Taiwan', *World Development*, May/June 1984, p. 498; For the Indian data, Sanjaya Lall, 'Multinationals from India' in Sanjaya Lall ed., *The New Multinationals: The Spread of Third World Enterprises*, John Wiley & Sons,1983, p. 28; For other countries, UNCTC, *Trans-national Corporations in World Development: Trends and Prospects*, United Nations, NY, 1988.

This difference in the geographical distribution of FDIs can be explained by the motivation of firms making these investments. Firms from developed countries, possessing advanced and large-scale technologies go to developed countries for offensive motives, i.e., to exploit their technological and oligopolistic advantages. They seek investment opportunities for incremental monopolistic profits in wealthy countries where there is high potential demand for high-technology products. On the other hand, firms from developing countries have technologies that are more labor-intensive and appropriate for small-scale operation in LDC environments. Moreover, they often make investments for defensive purposes to protect their existing markets, although the defensive investments are also seen in the case of the follower-firm in developed countries. In the same vein, the geographical or cultural proximity plays an important role in selecting a host country by multinationals from LDCs.[3]

The defensive objective also applies to investments by LDC firms in countries which were previously served by exports. These take place when it becomes difficult for the LDC firms to preserve their existing markets through exports due to rising labor costs at home and trade barriers in the importing country. An empirical study by Wells [1983] finds that there exists a strong relationship between the past export performance of manufactured goods and the subsequent direct investments from one LDC to another.

The motivation for FDIs

As expected, there are variations with respect to the motivation of the firms making direct investments depending upon home country and other factors. Several common traits nevertheless exist with regard to the motivation of LDC firms in contrast to firms from developed countries. Various authors (Chen [1981], Euh and Min [1986], Ting and Schive [1981]) cite the following factors as reasons for going abroad by Hong Kong, Korean and Taiwanese firms: to secure raw materials, to seek lower labor costs, to facilitate exports and overcome trade barriers, to take advantage of host government incentives, and to avoid competition in small home markets and seek growth overseas.

Lecraw (1977) reports, in Table 12.4, the survey results of DC and LDC firms that had subsidiaries in Thailand. Except for 'threats to existing markets' which was cited as an important motivation by both groups, a rather clear distinction is seen between the DC and LDC firms. For firms from developed countries, 'exploiting high production technology' and 'exploiting marketing expertise' were rated highly, while for firms from LDCs 'diversification of risk' and 'small home market' were cited as important motivations for FDIs.

Table 12.4
Motivations for foreign direct investment in Thailand

	DC-MNCs	LDC-MNCs
1 Threats to existing markets:	8	6
2 Diversification of risk:	1	7
3 High local return:	3	6
4 Investing accumulated local funds:	1	3
5 Exploit experience with high technology production:	8	1
6 Exploit experience with labor-intensive technology:	1	5
7 Relatives or countrymen-business associate in LDC:	1	5
8 To export capital equipment:	2	4
9 A source of cheap labor:	3	1
10 To export to the developed world:	2	1
11 Exploit marketing expertise:	7	1
12 Small market at home:	2	6
13 Circumvent tariff and quotas in developed countries:	1	2

Note: Numbers are average rating by firms in the group on a scale of 1 = no importance, 10 - very important.
Source: Lecraw, Donald, 'Direct Investment by Firms from Less Developed Countries', *Oxford Economic Papers,* March 1977, p. 444.

Thus, LDC firms appear to go abroad mainly for defensive purposes, and much of their motivation is related to the fear of losing existing export markets and to the desire to diversify. Threats to export come from such locational factors as rising labor costs and competition in the home country and trade barriers on their exports in the host country. Therefore, a large portion of FDIs by LDC firms appears to be motivated by locational factors.

Multinationals from developed countries, in contrast, seem to be more concerned with exploiting market imperfections and firm-specific factors (e.g., to exploit their high technology, marketing expertise, and other oligopolistic advantages) and are generally more 'offensive' in nature.

The competitive advantage

Existence of a certain competitive advantage is essential in the theory of multinational firms and a necessary condition for FDIs. The oligopolistic theory of FDI (Caves [1971], Hymer [1976]) assumes that the competitive advantages of MNCs over local competitors come from market imperfections, and include technology, marketing and management expertise, economies of scale, superior access to finance and so forth.

The major competitive advantage of LDC-MNCs is more mundane: the possession of small-scale and labor-intensive technology appropriate to local conditions (Kumar and Kim [1984], Lecraw [1981], Ting and Schive [1981], Wells [1978]). Possessing such an asset may enable LDC-MNCs to compete successfully with DC-MNCs in developing countries where local markets are relatively small. However, when LDC firms make direct investments in developing countries, they must compete not only with DC-MNCs but also with local competitors. In this case, LDC-MNCs must find relative advantage not only against DC-MNCs but also against local competitors which lack technology but are more familiar with local conditions.

212

Table 12.5
Competitive advantages of Hong Kong firms

Advantages over local firms	Score
1 Longer experience in production and operation:	5.6
2 Better management skill:	5.4
3 More advanced technologies:	5.2
4 Better connections with the export markets:	4.6
5 More appropriate technologies for local conditions in the host countries:	4.1
6 Government policies in the host countries in favor of foreign firms:	3.6
7 Greater flexibility and adaptability:	3.4

Advantages over DC-MNCs	Score
1 Better understanding of the conditions in LDCs:	6.8
2 Lower costs for managerial and technical staff:	5.3
3 Greater flexibility and adaptability:	5.2
4 Closer language and cultural affinity:	4.9
5 More appropriate technology for the local conditions in the host countries:	4.8
6 Better connections with export markets:	2.5
7 Longer experience in production and operation:	2.2

Note: Scales range from 0 (no importance) to 10 (extreme importance).
Source: Chen, Edward K. (1981), 'Hong Kong Multinationals in Asia: Characteristics and Objectives', in Krishna Kumar and Maxwell McLeod eds., *Multinationals from Developing Countries*, Lexington Books, pp. 116-7.

In Table 12.5, Chen (1981) reports the survey results on the competitive advantages of Hong Kong firms over local firms in host LDCs and over DC-MNCs operating in the same countries. As expected, the competitive advantages of LDC-MNCs from developed countries do not necessarily coincide with those over local firms in the host country. This is because LDC-MNCs are typically positioned at an intermediate level between DC-MNCs and local firms in terms of technology and operational capabilities. Their advantages over the local firms lie basically in firm-specific assets (e.g., more advanced technology, longer experience in production and operation, etc.) whereas those over the DC-MNCs stem mainly from location or country-specific factors (e.g., better cultural understanding, ethnic ties, lower payrolls for expatriate managers, etc.) This relative position of LDC-MNCs vis-a-vis DC-MNCs or local indigenous firms is also consistent with Lecraw's [1993] finding that Indonesian multinationals have gone abroad not only to exploit their ownership advantages but also to access and develop advantages they did not previously possess.

Theoretical interpretations

Stylized facts about the characteristics of LDC multinationals as opposed to multinationals from developed countries discussed in the previous section are summarized in Table 12.6. Since the accepted theories of FDI were developed in the context of conventional MNCs from developed countries, a question arises as to how new FDIs by LDC firms are to be interpreted theoretically.

Table 12.6
Comparison of major characteristics between
conventional MNCs and LDC-MNCs

	DC-MNCs	LDC-MNCs
1. Size of parent company	Company size is not an important factor for FDI	Company size is not an important factor for FDI
2. Patterns of subsidiary ownership	Wholly-owned or majority ownership is dominant	Joint-venture or minority ownership is dominant
3. Direct investment by area	A majority of direct investments concentrates in developed countries	A majority of direct investments concentrated in LDCs
4. Motivations for FDI	To exploit superior technology and marketing expertise (i.e., offensive)	To overcome threats to export markets (i.e., defensive motivations)
5. Competitive advantages	Advanced technology, marketing and management skills, and economies of scale	Appropriate technology for local conditions, greater flexibility and adaptability

214

Wells (1977) argues that the product life cycle theory of Vernon (1966) is applicable to FDIs by LDC firms as well as by firms from developed countries. The product life cycle theory was originally developed to explain how the pattern of FDIs from a technologically advanced country such as the US evolves in relation to trade flows through various stages of the product's life cycle. Wells accepts the product life cycle theory as an explanation of the FDIs from LDCs as well as from developed countries, because the LDC firms are the recipient of technologies from DC-MNCs and also the agent of transfer of standardized technologies to poorer developing countries. However, it should be pointed out, that the technologies transferred by LDC-MNCs are standardized only from the standpoint of DC-MNCs but not from the standpoint of LDC-MNCs. For instance, direct investments are often made in LDCs by Hong Kong firms in growth industries, not in technologically standardized or mature industries as the theory suggests (Chen [1983]). In addition, the theory fails to explain the reverse direct investment that occurs when LDC firms go to developed countries to secure advanced technologies and/or superior marketing skills.

Rugman (1981) contends that the internalization theory is sufficiently general to accommodate FDIs by LDC firms as well as those by conventional MNCs. The internalization theory elaborated by Buckley and Casson (1976, 1985) posits that various imperfections in product and factor markets prevent firms from earning adequate economic rents from their firm-specific assets. This causes the firms to create internal markets within their corporate network rather than engaging in external transactions. Rugman defends the generality of the internalization theory by pointing out that the MNC is itself a creature of internalization under market imperfections.

The internalization theory, however, is at odds with one important aspect of FDIs by LDC firms. Compared to multinationals from developed countries, LDC firms in general lack valuable firm-specific assets that can be profitably internalized. Instead, as Giddy and Young (1982) point out, the primary advantage of LDC firms is their adaptive abilities to host-country locational factors. The locational factors are also important in understanding those FDIs by LDC firms when direct investments are viewed as an alternative to exports to the host countries. In the internalization theory, the locational factors, however, are treated as an exogenous variable rather than a key factor which affects the firm's investment decisions systematically.

The eclectic theory of Dunning (1980) synthesizes the existing FDI theories by incorporating the location-specific factors along with the ownership-specific endowments of enterprises, and the firm's ability to internalize markets to their own advantage. Owing to the inclusion of the locational factors, the eclectic theory can explain why MNCs make FDIs in a certain country as opposed to others, and is applicable to LDC-MNCs as well as DC-MNCs (Agarwal, 1977). In the case of FDIs by LDC firms, Chen (1984) argues that 'pull factors' (i.e., the location-specific factors) are more important than 'push factors' (i.e., the ownership-specific factors). Given its synthetic nature, the eclectic theory, however, lacks a coherent and focused explanation of its predecessor theories.

It is also noteworthy that a significant portion of FDIs by Asian LDC firms is the 'trade-oriented' type suggested by Kojima (1973, 1978) to explain Japanese FDIs. Kojima argues that the bulk of the Japanese manufacturing investments abroad has been 'trade oriented' whereas the US investments have been 'anti-trade oriented.' A part of Japanese direct investments abroad has been made in LDCs by small and medium-sized firms and in standardized industries that have been losing a comparative advantage in Japan but still have a comparative advantage in the host LDCs. Kojima contends that the Japanese direct investments strengthen the competitive advantages of the host country and increase their exports to developed countries because the technologies transferred by Japanese MNCs are more suitable to the host country than the advanced technologies transferred by large US MNCs whose main motive for FDI is local sale.

It is debatable whether Kojima's hypothesis is valid in a larger context, especially his contention regarding the anti-trade orientation of US firms. Many manufacturing subsidiaries of large US firms produce goods abroad for export back to the US or in the world market (Choi and Hawkins, 1984). However, it is very interesting that the FDIs by LDC firms, especially by firms from Asian newly industrialized countries, share certain traits with those by traditional Japanese MNCs in many respects. Ozawa (1979) documents that small- and medium-sized Japanese firms are active in the direct investment scene in unsophisticated products and in developing countries with low production costs, and that the Japanese firms tend to accept a minority ownership in their subsidiaries abroad. Although the recent Japanese direct investments by large corporations with advanced technologies and established brand names are explicable by the oligopolistic theory, Kojima shows that the earlier investments by smaller Japanese firms in mature industries were motivated by locational factors such as rising labor costs in the home country and the adaptation to the host country. Despite its controversy, the Kojima's hypothesis is thus potentially applicable to a portion of FDIs by firms from newly industrialized Asian countries and provides a testable proposition in terms of whether these firms follow the pattern of small Japanese MNCs (Pyun, 1985).

Finally, the direct investment behavior of LDC-MNCs can also be examined from the perspective of real risk diversification. Diversification is prominent in the theory of portfolio investment, but has not been fully incorporated in the mainstream FDI literature. Rugman (1975) and Agarwal (1977), however, document that the benefits of real asset diversification can be substantial at the firm level. International investment provides an opportunity for the firm to diversify across geography and industry, and thereby improve on their expected return-risk tradeoff. Exchange rate is another variable that affects the firm's international investment decisions because of its impact on the firm's cash flow and the cost of capital as well as through its impact on the firm's operational risk.[4] Choi (1989) developed a theoretical model of corporate international investment encompassing the gains of international diversification and exchange risk. Diversification is also relevant in modelling the political stability-seeking motive of Hong Kong firms that invest abroad because of the political uncertainty at home. The real risk diversification hypothesis thus provides another plausible framework to explain FDI behaviors of LDC-MNCs.

It should be noted that the real asset diversification theory actually is quite consistent with the traditional industrial organization theory based on market imperfections. In perfect capital markets, any gains from diversification can be obtained directly by individual shareholders so that the diversification at the firm level would be superfluous. Justification of the diversification motive at the level of the firm therefore requires the presence of market imperfections which limit individual shareholder activities or the agency cost which separates the managerial decisions from the shareholder interest. As a rule, market imperfections are greater in the international context than in the domestic market because of the government restrictions on international portfolio investments and heterogeneous rational economies. Moveover, multinational firms generally possess some assets that make them a superior agent over individuals in exploiting market imperfections. The real asset diversification theory is also related to the internalization theory. Given market imperfections and the possibility of uncertain valuation gains, the firm's desire to internalize its transactions within the firm, rather than dealing with unaffiliated customers in the external market, is a manifestation of its diversification motive.

Direct investments in and out of Korea: A case study

To facilitate theoretical interpretations outlined above regarding different factors influencing FDIs originating in DCs versus LDCs, preliminary empirical evidence is presented in this section on the determinants of inflows and outflows of foreign direct investments in the case of one Asian developing country − South Korea. Korea is an interesting case because it has significant levels of both inflows and outflows of FDIs. This permits simultaneous examination of FDI behaviors by both DC and LDC firms in a given country: inflows are the result of FDI decisions by DC-MNCs (conventional) while outflows reflect decisions by LDC-MNCs (Korean).

A general conceptual framework that can be used is the eclectic paradigm proposed by Dunning (1980). Dunning proposes a framework where FDIs result from the interaction of three factors: firm ownership-specific factors, industry-specific factors, and location-specific factors. No guidance, however, is provided in that theory as to what variables constitute these factors. Selection of specific variables is relegated to underlying specific theories (e.g., oligopoly theory) or empirical work. Theories of DC versus LDC firm FDI behaviors surveyed above, as well as existing empirical work, help us to select these variables. For now, foreign direct investment inflows and outflows, K_i, is expressed as a function of country-specific (C), industry-specific (I) and firm-specific variables generally:

$$K_i = f(C, I, F), \quad i = \text{inflows, outflows.} \tag{1}$$

Most inward FDIs in Korea come from developed countries where the primary motive for international investment is local sale or local production. DC-MNCs invest in Korea to combine their R&D and other oligopolistic advantages with the advantages of local production or local sales. In these circumstances, country-specific variables such as relative wage rate or market size are likely to be important. At the industry level, inward FDIs for local sales are likely to be in technology or marketing-intensive industries while those for local production tend to be concentrated in labor-intensive industries. For outward FDIs, Korean firms go abroad in labor-intensive industries where labor costs are lower abroad, and where they possess intermediate technological or managerial advantages vis-a-vis local firms. In the current empirical work reported here, we utilize industry data. Therefore, firm and industry variables are combined with an eye towards capturing the salient features of industry characteristics. However, country variables are also included as control variables. By analyzing the determinants of both inward and outward FDIs of Korea, we can compare determinants of FDIs by firms from foreign developed countries with those of FDIs abroad by Korean firms.

Existing empirical work by Owen (1982), Lall (1983), Kim and Lyn (1987), Dunning (1980) and others have identified six types of firm or industry-specific determinants of FDIs: technology, product differentiation, capital intensity, economies of scale and competition, skill levels, and labor intensity. We use these variables. In addition, two country variables -- general relative wage level, and economic growth -- are used as locational control variables. The following equation is hypothesized to estimate Korean FDI inflows or outflows, K_i:

$$K_i = a_0 + a_1 R\&D + a_2 AD + a_3 FA + a_4 CON + a_5 SK + a_6 LC + a_7 W \text{ and} + a_8 Y \quad (2)$$

where R&D is total research and development expenditures as a percentage of total industry sales; AD is total advertising expenditures as a percentage of total industry sales; FA is capital intensity as measured by the ratio of net fixed assets to total industry sales; CON is the industry concentration ratio as measured by the total sales of four largest firms (in sales) divided by total industry sales; SK is industry labor skill level as measured by the ratio of average industry wage rate to that in total manufacturing industries; LC is labor intensity as measured by the ratio of labor costs to total costs in the industry; W is an average wage rate in Korean manufacturing industry relative to the same in the US; and Y is annual real growth rate of Korean gross national products. Equation (2) is estimated for FDI inflows and outflows separately. Expected signs of these variables for FDI inflows and outflows respectively are summarized in Table 12.7 and draw from the existing literature on FDIs by DC versus LDC firms surveyed in previous sections. Exact definitions of industries as well as data sources are indicated in the footnote of Table 12.8.

Strictly speaking, the first three variables, R&D, AD and FA, are ownership-specific variables while the next three, CON, SK and LC, are industry-specific variables proper. However, given our use of industry FDI data here, all these variables are measured at the industry level. The last two variables, W and Y, are location-specific country variables. Given the potential multicollinarity caused by factor correlations, these variables are used selectively in each group. The data used are the annual data for nine manufacturing industries at the two-digit SIC level for the period of 1983-90.

Table 12.8 presents the estimation results from the pooled time-series and cross-section regression using the generalized least square method. The results on inflows indicate the significance of R&D, in both full and reduced equations, at the five percent level. In addition, capital intensity and labor skill variables are significant in the reduced equation at least at the 10 percent level. The location variable, the relative wage rate, is also significant at the five percent level in the full model. These results are consistent with conventional industrial organization theory based on market imperfections. However, the overall support for conventional theory is weak, because other variables found significant in the test of conventional FDI theories, such as advertising expenditure or industry concentration ratios, are insignificant here.

Consistent with inflows, the outflows equation shows significance for R&D, capital intensity and labor skill. The signs of these variables are the same for outflows and inflows. This shows that, to some extent, FDI decisions by Korean firms are influenced by some of the same factors affecting conventional FDIs by DC-MNCs. However, unlike inflows, the outflows equation shows some significance for advertising expenditure and the labor intensity variable. The resulting effect on advertising expenditure confirms the earlier description of the distinguishing characteristics of Asian LDC-MNCs in terms of their desire to diversify markets out of fear of protection by the host government. The significance of the capital intensity variable is consistent with the notion that Korean firms attempt to reduce operating leverage by international diversification. This is consistent with the risk reduction motive for foreign direct investment.

Policy implications for the US

It is important to analyze the foreign direct investments from the newly developing countries of Asia for various reasons:

First, FDIs by DC-MNCs is shifting to the European Common Market and the newly emerging markets of Eastern Europe and Latin America. This means a decrease in the inflows of new FDIs to the United States from leading DC-MNC's. To replace this, some states, such as Tennessee and California, aggressively court FDIs from the DC-MNC's of Europe and Asia, and now approach some of the LDC-MNCs on a targeted basis.

Second, since many of these LDC-MNCs are willing to take minority ownership, the state government could arrange for local partners in their states who need capital infusion. Money in exchange for their local contacts and marketing expertise could be a powerful selling tool.

Third, given that the technological and operational capabilities of these

LDC-MNCs lie at an intermediate level (between those of DC-MNCs and local LDC firms), it would be beneficial to exploit their trading strengths and plan for exports from the US back to developing countries. In addition, many of these companies could impart their aggressive trade-oriented culture to the small and medium-sized US firms with which they form partnerships or otherwise get in contact.

Summary and conclusions

A recent phenomenon in international corporate investment is a surge of direct investments by LDC firms. These investments differ from those by conventional MNCs from developed countries. Existing literature has paid scant and fragmented attention to these new direct investments by LDC firms.

This paper examines the main characteristics of FDIs by multinationals from LDCs, especially those from Asian developing countries, in contrast to investments by conventional multinationals from developed countries. From the survey and synthesis of the existing literature, five stylized facts have been identified in terms of the following respects: the size of the parent company, the ownership pattern of subsidiaries, the geographical location of FDIs, the competitive advantage of the parent firm, and the motivation for international investment. The stylized facts are then examined in light of the existing theories of FDI, and suggestions are offered as to a plausible framework for explaining this relatively new phenomenon. To aid theoretical interpretations of new LDC-based FDIs versus conventional FDIs from DCs, preliminary empirical evidence is presented on the determinants of FDI inflows and outflows in the case of Korea. Policy implications for states seeking to woo direct investments from abroad are suggested.

Table 12.7
Expected signs of explanatory variables

	Inward FDI	Outward FDI
R&D	+	-
AD	+	-
FA	+	-
CON	+	-
SK	+	-
LC	+	-
W	-	+
Y	+	+

These signs assume that the inward FDIs are those of conventional developed country firms while the outward FDIs are those of developing country firms. To the extent that Korean firms do not exactly belong to either classification, the signs can deviate from the above. R&D measures technology, AD measures product differentiation, FA measures capital intensity, CON measures economies of scale and competition, SK measures general skill levels, LC measures labor intensity, W measures relative wage level, and Y measures economic growth. For exact data definitions, see text or Table 12.8.

Table 12.8
Pooled cross-section and time-series estimation of Korean foreign direct investment flows

	Inflows		Outflows	
Constant	2.686	1.894	6.986**	6.295**
	(1.07)	(1.17)	(3.16)	(4.19)
R&D	3082.8*	3981.4**	1166.1	1271.8*
	(3.12)	(4.81)	(1.34)	(1.65)
AD	36.03		-119.6**	-1173**
	(0.81)		(-3.04)	(-2.85)
FA	0.510	-5.030*	-2.743	-6.772*
	(0.20)	(-1.67)	(-1.21)	(-1.81)
CON	3.734		-1.547	
	(1.24)		(-0.58)	
SK		5.606**		3.836*
		(2.72)		(1.67)
LC	-10.27		-13.21*	
	(-1.21)		(-1.77)	
W	15.74**		9.775	
	(1.98)		(1.39)	
Y	-0.368		13.28	
	(-0.03)		(1.07)	
R^2	0.52	0.47	0.35	0.24
DW	1.25	1.40	1.93	1.62

**Significant at 5 percent. *Significant at 10 percent on a two-tail test.
Data definitions: R&D = total R&D expenditure as a percentage of total industry sales; AD = total advertising expenditure as a percentage of total industry sales; FA = capital intensity as measured by the ratio of net fixed assets to total industry sales; CON = four-firm concentration ratio as measured by total sales of four largest firms in sales divided by total industry sales; SK - industry skill level as measured by the ratio of average wage per employee in each industry to average wage per employee in total manufacturing industry; W = the ratio of average wage rate in Korean manufacturing industry to average wage rate in US manufacturing industry; and Y = annual growth rate of real gross national product. Data period is 1984-90.
Data sources: Bank of Korea; *Financial Statements Analysis*; Korea Investors Service Inc., *Financial Report of Korean Companies*; and IMF, *International Financial Statistics*.

Notes

1 The size classification in each group is arbitrary and not directly comparable. This weakens the proposition mentioned in the text considerably. However, the basic point on the role or size in FDI decisions remains valid.

2 Even among MNCs from developed countries, the ownership pattern of the subsidiary varies, however, depending upon industry characteristics and other factors. For example, firms in high technology industries tend to exhibit higher equity ownership by the parent.

3 White (1981) reports that a similar phenomenon is observed in the case of MNCs from Latin America.

4 For a theoretical analysis on the impact of real exchange risk on asset demand, see Choi (1984). An empirical work on the determinants of aggregate capital flows in Korea during the floating exchange rate period is found in Choi (1991).

References

Agarwal, J.P. (January/February 1977), 'Theories of Foreign Direct Investment: A Summary of Recent Research and A Proposed Unifying Paradigm', *Economic Affairs,* pp. 31-45.

_____ (September 1985), 'Intra-LDCs' Foreign Direct Investment: A Comparative Analysis of Third World Multinationals', *The Developing Economies,* pp. 236-53.

Amsden, Alice H. (May/June 1984), 'Exports of Technology by Newly-Industrializing Countries: Taiwan', *World Development,* pp. 491-502.

Buckley, P.J. (1976), and Casson, M., *The Future of the Multinational Enterprise,* The Macmillan Press, London.

_____ (1985), *The Economic Theory of the Multinational Enterprise,* The Macmillan Press, London.

Caves, Richard (February 1971), 'International Corporations: The Industrial Economics of Foreign Investment', *Economica,* pp. 1-27.

_____ (August 1974), 'Causes of Direct Investment: Foreign Firms' Shares in Canadian and United Kingdom Manufacturing Industries', *Review of Economics and Statistics,* pp. 279-293.

Chen, Edward K. (1981), 'Hong Kong Multinationals in Asia: Characteristics and Objectives', in Krishna Kumar and Maxwell McLeod eds., *Multinationals From Developing Countries,* Lexington Books.

_____ (1983), 'Multinationals from Hong Kong', in Sanjaya Lall ed., *The New Multinationals: The Spread of Third World Enterprises,* John Wiley & Sons.

_____ (May/June 1984), 'Exports of Technology by Newly-Industrializing Countries: Hong Kong', *World Development,* pp. 481-490.

Choi, Jongmoo Jay (September 1984), 'Consumption Basket, Exchange Risk and Asset Demand,' *Journal of Financial and Quantitative Analysis,* pp. 287-298.

_____ (Spring 1989), 'Diversification, Exchange Risk, and Corporate International Investment', *Journal of International Business Studies,* pp. 145-155.

_____ (1991), 'International Investments During the Flexible Exchange Rate Period: Firm Behavior and Policy Choices in Korea,' *Pacific-Basin Capital Market Research,* Vol. 2, North Holland.

Choi, Jongmoo Jay and Hawkins, Robert G. (January 1984), 'The Impact of US Foreign Direct Investment on US Balance of Payments: A Simulation Analysis', *American Business Review.*

Dunning, John H. (Spring/Summer 1980), 'Toward an Eclectic Theory of International Production: Some Empirical Tests', *Journal of International Business Studies,* pp. 9-31.

Euh, Yoon D. and Min, Sang K. (June 1986), 'Foreign Direct Investment from Developing Countries: The Case of Korean Firms', *The Developing Economies,* pp. 149-168.

Fong, Pang E. and Komaran, Rajah V. (Summer 1985), 'Singapore Multinationals', *Columbia Journal of World Business,* pp. 35-43.

Franco, Lawrence G. (1976), *The European Multinationals,* Graylock Publishers.

Giddy, Ian H. and Young, Stephen (1982), 'Conventional Theory and Unconventional Multinationals: Do New Forms of Multinational Enterprise Require New Theories?', in Alan Rugman ed., *New Theories of The Multinational Enterprise,* St. Martin's Press, NY.

Heenan, David A. and Keegan, Warren J. (January-February 1979), 'The Rise of Third World Multinationals', *Harvard Business Review,* pp. 101-108.

Horst, Thomas (August 1972), 'Firm and Industry Determinants of The Decision to Invest Abroad: An Empirical Study', *Review of Economics and Statistics,* pp. 258-266.

Hymer, Stephen H. (1976), *The International Operations of National Firms: A Study of Direct Foreign Investment*, The MIT Press, Cambridge, MA.

Jo, Sung-Whan (1981), 'Overseas Direct Investment by South Korean Firms: Direction and Pattern, in Krishna Kumar and Maxwell McLeod eds., *Multinationals from Developing Countries*, Lexington Books.

Kim, W. S. and E. O. Lyn (Summer 1987), 'Foreign Direct Investment Theories Entry Barriers, and Reverse Investments in the US Manufacturing Industries,' *Journal of International Business Studies*, pp. 53-66.

Kojima, Kiyoshi (June 1973), 'A Macroeconomic Approach to Foreign Direct Investment', *Hitotsubashi Journal of Economics*, pp.1-20.

_____ (1978), *Direct Foreign Investment: A Japanese Model of Multinational Business Operations*, Praeger Publishers, NY.

Kumar, Krishna and Kim, Kee Y. (Spring/Summer 1984), 'The Korean Manufacturing Multinational,' *Journal of International Business Studies*, pp. 45-61.

Lall, Sanjaya (1983), 'Multinationals from India' in Sanjaya Lall, ed., *The New Multinationals: The Spread of Third World Enterprises*, John Wiley & Sons.

Lecraw, Donald (March 1977), 'Direct Investment by Firms from Less Developed Countries', *Oxford Economic Papers*, pp. 443-57.

_____ (1981), 'Internationalization of Firms from LDCs: Evidence from the ASEAN Region', in Krishna Kumar and Maxwell McLeod eds., *Multinationals from Developing Countries*, Lexington Books.

_____ (1993), 'Outward Direct Investment by Indonesian Firms: Motivation and Effects,' *Journal of International Business Studies*, Vol. 24, No. 3, pp. 589-600.

Owen, R. F. (1982), 'Inter-Industry Determinants of Foreign Direct Investments: A Canadian Perspective,' in A.M. Rugman, ed., *New Theories of the Multinational Enterprise*, St. Martin's Press, NY.

Ozawa, Terutomo (March 1979), 'International Investment and Industrial Structure: New Theoretical Implications from The Japanese Experience', *Oxford Economic Papers*, pp. 72-92.

Pyun, Chong S. (December 1985), 'Japanese Direct Foreign Investment in Developing Countries: An Analysis and Extension of Kojima Hypothesis,' *The Korean Economic Review*, pp. 189-206.

Rhodes, John B. (Summer 1974), 'US New Business Activities Abroad', *Columbia Journal of World Business*, pp. 99-105.

Rugman, Alan M. (September/October 1975), 'Motives for Foreign

Investment: The Market Imperfections and Risk Diversification Hypothesis', *Journal Of World Trade Law*, pp. 567-73.

_____ (1981), *Inside The Multinationals: The Economics of Internal Markets,* Croom Helm, London.

Ting, Wen-Lee and Schive, Chi (1981), 'Direct Investment and Technology Transfer from Taiwan', in Krishna Kumar and Maxwell McLeod eds., *Multinationals from Developing Countries*, Lexington Books.

United Nations Center for Transnational Corporations (1988), *Transnational Corporations in World Development: Trends and Prospects*, United Nations, NY.

Vernon, Raymond (May 1966), 'International Investment and International Trade in the Product Cycle', *Quarterly Journal of Economics*, pp. 190-207.

Wells, Jr., Louis T. (1977), 'The Internationalization of Firms from Developing Countries', in Tamir Agmon and Charles Kindleberger eds., *Multinationals from Small Countries*, The MIT Press, Cambridge.

_____ (Spring 1978), 'Foreign Investment from The Third World: The Experience of Chinese Firms from Hong Kong', *Columbia Journal of World Business*, pp. 39-49.

_____ (1983), *Third World Multinationals: The Rise of Foreign Investment from Developing Countries*, The MIT Press, Cambridge.

White, Eduardo (1981), 'The International Projection of Firms from Latin American Countries', in Krishna Kumar and Maxwell McLeod eds., *Multinationals from Developing Countries*, Lexington Books.

13 Technology policies in Japan and the US: Implications for Korea

Youn-Suk Kim

Korea's industrial technology has been developed from imported technology, mostly from Japan and the United States. Having realized successful industrialization, Korea now faces the problems of competing in a dynamic international economy as patterns of foreign investment and product cycle series change dramatically with serious implications for Korean industries. Korea's emphasis on internationalization is driven by the standardization of markets and products, re-engineering, consolidation and efficiencies in production, and technological innovation with imported technology from Japan and the US.

This chapter discusses the technological implications of three countries, and examines the technology policies of Japan, the United States and Korea in the post Cold-War era. Analyzing trade imbalances and production structures among the three countries, how does technology contribute to the changing trade-production pattern? How has the education system or human capital formation supported technology application in production? And finally, what bearing does US-Japan technology competition have on Korea's strategy?

Trade imbalance and technology paradigm

The United States and Japan, two of the world leaders in technology, present striking differences in scientific and technical institutions that generate new knowledge, and in their impact on the global market. It is well-known that Japan leads in manufacturing products, while the United States has provided continuous leadership in basic sciences and breakthroughs in technology which require creative thought and imagination. The complexity and dynamic nature of technology relations between the two countries have been complicated as the industrial weakness of the United States has been exposed by its massive, continuing trade deficits. Japan's R&D has been an industry-driven operation: more than 80 percent of the funding came from industry. In contrast, much of the US R&D has come from government-driven expenditures for the common defense of the Western Hemisphere.

Until the end of the Cold War, United States policy focused on the threat to security posed by Soviet power, thus concentrating on defense R&D. Japan, however, had the advantage of being able to concentrate almost exclusively on commercial R&D, allowing their government to make cost-effective use of its national resources. The American trade account has been in deficit for over two decades, raising concern about its competitiveness in global markets. Any improvement in the US trade deficit is at risk unless the United States alters its production to cope with Japan's challenge. Japan assumed a large portion of the world market in steel and automobiles which played to Japan's strengths in mass production and standardized process technology. And Japan has been advancing into the market of semiconductors, computers, and other hi-tech industries. In the current conditions of international disequilibrium Japan has become a conspicuous target of American hostility because of its enormous competitiveness in merchandise trade.

The US trade deficit has, however, declined since the end of 1987. The yen's recent rise has been successful in reducing Japan's trade surplus. A decline in relative prices indicates that US-produced goods are becoming less expensive relative to Japanese produced goods. At the same time, the Clinton Administration has adopted a policy aimed not only at raising the value of the yen, but also at reducing trade barriers and pushing Japan to stimulate its economy and consumption.[1] Though US-Japan competitiveness has been commonly appraised by such measures as movements in merchandise trade, a more sophisticated evaluation should include some measure of productivity in association with technology.

Technology has emerged as a key logistical factor of international competition. Technology serves a catalyst for multiplying and synergizing factors of production like the availability of capital and the quality of the labor. Technological innovation implies economic gains through the commercialization and use of inventions providing gains from the trade of new products and services.

The product-cycle theory maintains that the flow of technology is restricted, and that products undergo predictable sequences in production and marketing over time. The product cycle implies that a series of shifts over time in major trading commodities influences the product composition of trading countries.

For example, the US has an export monopoly in a new product; after Japanese production of that product begins, some Japanese manufacturers becomes competitive in export markets. The US imports the now-established product of Japan, and Korea follows a path similar to what Japan did. In a similar vein, the 'Flying Geese' paradigm is a Japanese version of the product cycle, which implies that Japan, with its larger economy and higher technology level in Asia, is in the lead position, and production of new products passes back (down) to less developed Asian countries. Conspicuous in contemporary technological development, particularly in regard to the product cycle and new products, are theories of product growth and product maturity (see Yamazawa, et al., 1993).

Japan's R&D system has been geared to 'latecomer catch-up' to close the gap with the US. The strength of its R&D system has been in its integration with the production process. The decision to import technology from abroad has been based on a clear understanding of the country's potential and the constraints to which it is subject. 'MITI engages in painstaking discussions with scientists and engineers, research scholars, industry leaders, and financial analysts – the people in the know – to find out where technology is headed and where the most promising commercial opportunities lie. The information it collects and processes is about as thorough as could be obtained. National research projects thus emerge from an ongoing process of national consensus-building based on extensive give-and-take between government and the private sector' (Okimoto, 1989, p. 73). Along with the product cycle series, a substantial proportion of Japan's targeted industries seem to be characterized by economies of scale. New technology leads to producing more goods with the same input or producing the same quantity of output with less input. Technology is accompanied by expanded production through economies of scale and the learning-curve effect, which result in lower cost curves.

The United States has been stressing American interests while maintaining the open system of science and technology research that the United States values and wishes to preserve as it has brought about pioneering technology and basic science. Balancing the two has been at the heart of US policy.

Economists argue that a country finds new technology is cheaper to purchase than it is to develop, since R&D costs have already been incurred. For example, imitators can on average make a new product for much less cost and time that it took the inventors. Edwin Mansfield's study on technological progress in the American economy over 30 years showed that imitators can on average make a new product for two-thirds of the cost and time that it took the innovators (see Mansfield, 1990, pp. 17-30).

The imported technologies made Korea attain efficiency and effectiveness through the operation of the learning curve and economies of scale. Especially Korea's imported technology is characterized by modification and adaptation, the country develops its way of using technology and capital goods including reverse-engineering. Machinery and technological application are handled in simpler ways than originally designed to better suit the workers were in industrialization. The major feature of Korean technological policy was the fostering of indigenous technology through research centers established in both public and private sectors. Conspicuous in its policy is the stress on a factor mix in which labor and conventional technology are the dominant elements with incremental improvements on its tradeable products.

Korea's imported technology has resulted in structural change, cost reduction, and indigenous innovation in industrial production.[2] Korea is now finding it increasingly difficult to rely on imported technology for product innovation and process technologies which it must have for meeting challenges in global competition. Korea must muster the human capital, financial and other resources for domestic R&D needed to maintain a continued industrial growth path, complemented by imported technology from Japan and the United States.

Japanese technology policy

Japan concentrated on wide-scale application of improvement engineering to borrowed technology, with an emphasis on consumer goods for expanding exports. The government adopted policies which encouraged and actively guided technology imports. 'Before the capital liberalization of the late 1960s and 1970s, no technology entered the country without MITI's approval; no joint venture was ever agreed to without MITI's scrutiny and frequent alteration of terms; no patent rights were ever bought without MITI's pressuring the seller to lower the royalties or make other changes advantageous to Japanese industry as a whole; and no program for the importation of foreign technology was ever approved until MITI and its various advisory committees had agreed that the time was right and that the industry involved was scheduled for nurturing' (see Johnson, 1982, pp. 16-17).

The Japanese work ethic is considered to be derived from its rigid educational system, which has helped bolster Japan's industrial growth.

Education also has a direct linkage to industrial growth. The work ethic, difficult to analyze, is likewise important in education and training designed to meet the increasing demand for a modern workforce. In the business environment, as well, several factors influence productivity: a high literacy rate; commitment to a lifetime career in a specific firm (thus it pays for industry to invest in advanced engineering training); interest in engineering rather than science; positive response to work quality circles, which increase productivity while fostering continuous improvement in the quality of products. Furthermore, work quality circles develop workers' capabilities, and build their morale.

Japanese culture and education are the foundation on which workers' human capital is built. A strong work ethic is stressed in early education, as well as a concern for others and accommodation to the group. Japan is a country with flexible social ingredients which accommodate its smooth adjustment to change, and the success of technological policy has been a product of socio-cultural factors (see Kim, 1994, pp. 129-137). The Japanese culture and business environment are team- and group-oriented, and this characteristic is taught early: how to work in a group, to place the group ahead of individual concerns, and to help those in the group who need assistance. Thus, workers are prepared to cooperate in the industrial workplace as Japan moves ahead with a technology-oriented society.

Japan has created its powerful industrial economy in the presence of a vested socio-cultural value system, a system which has endured while the country emulated the US economy. Indeed, the Japanese value system has nurtured economic growth as well as social evolution while itself largely remaining intact. The attitudes associated with the Japanese value system transfer easily into behavior in the workplace. The Japanese educational system emphasizes competence in the majority of its students rather than concentrating on the top five to ten percent. This is an important phenomenon because the bottom fifty percent of high school students eventually comprises the majority of the manufacturing labor supply. This gives Japan the economic advantage of having knowledgeable workers, and thus pre-eminence in manufacturing.

In the 1950s and early 1960s the Japanese government − i.e., the Ministry of International Trade and Industry − approved all transactions regarding importation of technology. In its purchase of technology Japan has focused on more complex, high value-added industries at the expense of less complex technology. As a result, a greater amount of Japan's exports have come from these more complex manufacturing industries. Relaxed government controls lead to greater access to imported technology, a part of Japan's technology policy vis-a-vis the United States. Another characteristic of Japan's technology policy is its emphasis on commercial application and its increased R&D spending relative to GNP.

Japan's R&D funding is derived from world-class corporations; for example, Matsushita Electric alone invested in R&D more than $2 billion in 1988. Industrial laboratories are well-equipped and staffed with some of Japan's best engineers and scientists. Much research is stimulated by incentive systems which promote commercial innovations through rewards to engineers. Most research outcomes are patented as properties of individual corporations. Japanese companies initially bought separate patent rights from the United States and eventually made them complete 'packages,' including both the manufacture and the promotion of the product. This was facilitated by the fact that in the United States corporations would sell technology to foreign industries rather than to domestic companies to reduce potential home-country competition.

Japan undertook improvement engineering, improving the product quality of the imported technology beyond that of the original imported technology. At its best, Japanese production represents high quality products with improved functioning, simplicity, and attractiveness. While the United States has placed more emphasis on research for new products and breakthrough technology, Japan has stressed innovating manufacturing processes for commercial gains from improvement engineering. For example, Bell Laboratories invented the transistor, the laser, optical fibers, and stored-program control. The case of the transistor is a rather telling example of how Japan took advantage of American technology. American Telephone & Telegraph, the parent company of Bell Laboratories, did not exploit fully the transistor, so it sold nonexclusive rights to the use of its patents. In 1953 the US virtually gave away the technology, selling to a struggling Japanese company for $25,000 the license to make a radio called the Sony.

The Japanese government has played a catalyst role in nurturing industry-based cooperative research. Government-initiated R&D projects are established at central laboratories open to industry, while the individual firms pursue proprietary research needed to bring a product to market. Even government-financed imported technologies are associated with the central laboratories so that individual companies take advantage of government initiatives.

Liberalization of laws has made this process easier than it used to be. MITI's objectives were to expand the technology market by encouraging competition among sellers and by restricting imports wherever unused capacity or excessive domestic competition resulted from importing technology.

Furthermore, because of Japanese import restrictions and foreign direct investment controls prior to the recent opening and liberalization of trade, US firms had to be content with the licensing of their technologies and patents. This practice was attractive to US firms in the short run since most fees and royalties received were considered profits. This fast and easy money increased cash flow and allowed growing companies to finance additional investment and R&D without the need to increase bank borrowing. Japan has been quick to make use of US government-induced research. Some US technical research comes from government laboratories whose work is funded directly by the American taxpayer. Under federal law, all non-classified research resulting from these laboratories are in the public domain, available to anyone at nominal cost, a situation of which Japanese industries took full advantage. This has boomeranged on the US economy, resulting in recurring weakness in particular sectors.

Japan's industries have pressed their advantage in production processes through the initial licensing of US firms' technologies. For example, RCA sold its television technology to Japanese whose products eventually dominated the world market. The same occurred with Ampex, which sold its video-recording secrets and then went out of business when Japanese firms captured the VCR market. Japan's R&D is very much focused on innovation, a process which takes a long time. Sony worked on VCR technology for twenty years before making mature products in the late 1970s. NEC corporation acquired complex technology and additional computer manufacturing techniques from Honeywell, and then proceeded to market NEC supercomputers.

In recent years, major Japanese manufacturing companies have set up research labs in the US, hiring the cream of the US research crop. If this practice becomes significant, this combination of the best Japanese and American elements could become a formidable presence. Prestowitz describes how in industry after industry Japan took advantage of US technology, whether for consumer goods or industrial products, and how the successes of Japanese industry were helped by US technologies (see Prestowitz, 1988; April 1991, pp. 22-29).

In some areas Japan has bested the United States in terms of technology trade because the pace of technological change has become so rapid that no single nation seems to be able to monopolize the technology frontier. While

234

much US technology was transferred to Japan in the period from 1950 until 1992, continuous imports of industrial goods by the United States have resulted in its massive trade deficits with Japan. Thus Japan has been enjoying high returns from imported technology because it has made strategic use of management, allocation of investment, and domestic R&D to capitalize on the use of that technology. The Japanese government has played a major role in the importation of technology along with forming human capital. Japan's Ministry of International Trade and Industry served to organize and guide many industries from automobiles and electronics to semiconductors. The situation is changing; for example, both US firms and the US government are restricting the use of their patents. Because Japan now faces a serious challenge in the transfer of technology from the United States, it has engaged in different tactics, such as cross-licensing and patent-registering campaigns.

US technology policy

The US advantage in technology lies in the production of high-technology capital products and consumer goods, and the evidence is strong that this advantage has been growing. US technology exports are today about five times those of Japan. For example, US technology exports in 1987 were more than $1 billion while technology imports were less than half of this amount, as reported in *The Wall Street Journal*. Since then US exports of technology have soared, totaling $10.7 billion in 1991, while US imports of technology were only $2 billion. In contrast to Japan's trade balance, Japan's import of technology in 1991 was $2.4 billion while its technology export was only $1.9 billion (see Shoken, 1992, pp. 42-43).

The industrial weakness of the United states is exposed by its continuous imports of industrial goods. US industries have been placed at a severe disadvantage because of higher labor costs and managerial weakness resulting in lower productivity growth rates vis-a-vis Japanese industry and, in some cases, inferior quality of products. These major difficulties have been generally recognized. In comparison with the Japanese condition, culture and educational policy in the United States have not promoted high levels of productivity among average workers, and many high school students graduate with inadequate preparation for jobs in modern industry. Many workers cannot understand complex charts, blueprints or mathematical problems. In today's computerized and technical environment, such persons are less and less employable. US businesses must allocate large amounts of time and funds to train their employees so that they may become productive. Furthermore employers must cope with problems of worker turnover, which discourage their investment in worker training other than in very narrow, specific job skills.

Even the cultural emphasis on independence may work against high productivity of United States labor. American workers may be generally reluctant to admit that they do not understand a procedure for fear of being belittled, as well as for concern over the future of their job. Any condition which hampers learning on the job reduces productivity.

The new development may in fact point to an upgrading and reshaping of the US workforce and a re-engineering, restructuring and renewing of American industry within the world economy. It is crucial to acknowledge a basic difference between the two countries when comparing Japanese and United States work and management techniques. In the United States, investment decisions are made by management.

The success of the Japanese management style has forced US industries to adopt some quality control concepts and integrate them in the overall management processes. Cross-fertilization of technology and management has become increasingly evident as US productive facilities owned by Japanese have influenced production in America. Thus, as the US becomes more competitive, so does Japan and vice versa. In Japan, the group initiation of quality circles reaches upward so that investment decisions are made collectively, including marketing, finance, operations, R&D and quality control.

The US government and American businesses have awakened to the Japanese challenge and have learned from earlier mistakes. There are signs in the current economic recovery that US strength in innovation, creativity and free enterprise are expanding as shown in gains in overall labor productivity and in the success of the manufacturing export sector.

Nevertheless, American industries must be reassessed in the light of international competition in industrial technology. Product standardization, process innovation, high quality production, and incremental improvements are all Japanese strengths. The US comparative advantage industries in the 1960s, 1970s and 1980s have become relatively disadvantaged industries in the 1990s. Thus, the present situation requires that the US incorporate its high-tech or computer directing operations into manufacturing to renew industries and expand exports. It appears to be the US contention that hi-tech investment in one industry leads technical progress in other industries, through a 'spillover' effect.

It is well-known that US workers are both highly paid and productive in the economy of mass production and mass consumption. In terms of real gross domestic product generated per employed person, the US still stands at the top of all industrial countries including Japan. But in terms of rate productivity change, Japan is ahead of all major industrial countries. In some sectoral levels, US industries no longer lead in all fields as demonstrated in its trade statistics. Japan's productivity levels are above those of the US in steel, general machinery, electrical machinery, transportation equipment, and precision machinery and equipment, and its manufacturing is currently ahead in consumer electronics, advanced materials and robotics.

US-Japan industrial competition is centered on such lucrative products as computers, telecommunication equipment, home and office automatics, optoelectronics, semiconductors, biotechnology and medical instruments, and aerospace industry products (Kim, May 1990, pp. 501-503). Though the United States leads the world in most cutting-edge and defense-related technological areas, Japan is rapidly closing the gap.

The United States has realized how serious the situation has become. It is trying to establish some mechanism similar to what Japan has been doing all along, including government support for the development and maintenance of hi-tech industry. In 1987 the US responded to the Japanese challenge in the semiconductor industry with Sematech, formed as a government-backed consortium whose sole purpose is to bolster the US semiconductor technology. The consortium, based in Austin, Texas, was formed by fourteen American chip makers. The American semiconductor industry continues to lead the market in the area of new and innovative technology.

The US government announced its hi-tech push through macroeconomic policy, R&D policy and reallocation of resources (See Tyson, 1992, pp. 274-296). The US has the largest share of high-tech production and exports in global markets, and American industries are overwhelmingly successful in big system software, computers, aerospace, basic science, inventions, and new product design. These areas are where the US can meet Japan's industrial challenge head on and thus can improve the bilateral trade balance. Technology policy of the Clinton administration is crafted for the creation of high-paying jobs, export promotion, and an upgraded workforce. Hi-tech industries have shown distinctive features in that their costs fall rapidly as production builds up. And these leading-edge industries get replaced fairly frequently, mainly because of short product cycles.

Hi-tech advances in science and semiconductor technology have become

America's dynamic comparative advantage industry, requiring more research in this field in order to maintain the level of competitiveness. Since America has a broad technological base of business, university and government, US technological policy should accordingly cultivate government-business cooperation and stronger government support in hi-tech innovation. American business, which already funds 68 percent of industrial R&D, will have its share of total funding increased to the Japanese levels of 84 percent. The US industrial strategy is to shift key defense industries (aerospace, electronics and communication) to civilian use, thus ensuring a minimal loss of manufacturing jobs. As defense-related industry and university labs have been integrating and downsizing in response to defense budget cuts, the Clinton administration is facilitating the process with an industrial policy influenced by Japanese style.

The United States has established the Defense Advanced Research Projects Agency (DARPA) which has a $2 billion budget with $500 million in defense conversion programs in areas of regional technology alliances, agile manufacturing and dual-use critical technology partnerships. This agency influenced many commercially successful innovations ranging from packet-switched telecommunications to artificial intelligence. The agency was a catalyst in strengthening American companies such as Sun Microsystems, Inc., the leading computer workstation maker since the 1970s.

DARPA involves commercial ventures just like those of MITI's Agency of Industrial Science and Technology (AIST). DARPA supported microchip fabrication such as the Very High Speed Integrated Circuits program (VHSIC), and the spin-off of the program has resulted in development of the high-resolution X-ray lithography systems needed to produce the next generation of computer memory chips. DARPA subsidized dual-use civilian and military technology ranging from packet-switched data networks to carbon fiber materials. In 1992, DARPA also initiated a high-definition display manufacturing consortium to cope with Japan's lead on the manufacture of thin electronic screens critical to weapons systems, commercial display systems and high-definition television. For hi-tech industry the Clinton administration has initiated the industrial policy of direct subsidies, tax subsidies, protection from foreign competition, procurement regulations and preferential access to credit, as seen in Japan's industrial policy.

Industry-led and public-private funded consortia like Sematech which was created five years ago to revitalize the American semi-conductor chip industry emerges as a strategic option for American technology policy. US hi-tech leads in world markets such as semiconductors and threatens to surpass the Japanese in high-definition TV, electronic books, wireless phones and other devices. Apple Computer Inc. and Compaq Corporation are flooding the Japanese market, slicing personal computer market share from NEC. This turnaround illustrates the role the US government can play in hi-tech industry.

Granted that the US had underestimated the importance of education and training, private sector investment, and market responsiveness, America has recently begun to respond with a specific policy program for forming suitable human capital and industrial policy. Indeed, human capital formation is posited as the foundation on which a technology — more or less sophisticated, more or less innovative — can be based. And although the structural restraints will not be overcome easily, there are already positive signs. A significant change in the US government outlook has taken place as the new administration focuses on enhancing US industrial competitiveness. We see evidence of a widespread consensus that government and business must work together to ensure an effective policy for managing the hi-tech sectors of the economy. This policy will promote the dissemination of new knowledge and technology, and it will increase the portion of the benefits that accrue to the US innovators.[3]

The best US hope lies in the hi-tech industry where America enjoys an overwhelming lead in software and microprocessors, the two most profitable segments of the computer industry, the benefits of communication deregulation which spurred growth in wireless telephone, the US skill in meshing software and hardware, and the high quality of research at US universities and the interplay between industry and academe.

At present global competition depends increasingly on the skills of a country's labor force. The United States has mapped out a civilian technology agency and plans to increase funding for existing R&D civilian programs. This seems to imply the introduction of more integrated American-style industrial policy. The relationship between worker productivity' and investment in education has become a major policy issue in the US and Japan.

US-Korea technological cooperation

Japan and the United States continue to express a desire for a stable world economy, more open global markets to allow for trade growth, bilateral stability, and recognition as major economic powers. In order to enhance and bolster trade and welfare, trading countries should strive toward dynamic, multilateral equilibrium. Technology is spread among nations about as unevenly as physical capital and human capital. Korea relies heavily upon imported technology from the United States and Japan, both contractual and informal. Contractual methods include direct foreign investment, which also brings technology into Korea; foreign licensing which allows the local licensee to use a technology within constraints stipulated by its foreign owner; and technology consultants, which provides the local firm with technologies included in turnkey plant contracts. Foreign training and imported capital goods are also important informal means of technology transfer.

The time has come for Korea to engage in selected leading-edge goods production to sustain its export and growth. Korean workers' skill levels are tied to capital requirements, and technological changes are sought as a by-product of the faster growing income that is to result from the efficient and selective use of scarce factors. Thus, Korea emerges as a growing market for its trading partners, offering goods other countries need and buying from them goods it needs itself.

Korea faces a difficulty in the changing world economy. Japan's competitive strength is strong in world market and Korea will have a continuing problem in reducing the bilateral trade imbalance. In trilateral trade Korea's option would most likely be a technical complement with the United States to overcome the trade imbalances of both Korea and America. Tensions in Korea-Japan economic relations have developed as Korea's trade deficit with Japan surged to new highs in 1990-91. Since normalization of relations between the two countries in 1965, the trade imbalance has persistently been in Japan's favor, reaching a cumulative total of $66.2 billion in 1991. Korea's allegations of Japanese trade barriers focus on the higher import tariffs, non-tariff barriers such as the complex inspection systems and exclusive distribution channels. Japan (Korea's chief source of technology transfer in the 1960s and the 1970s) is unwilling to cooperate because technology transfer to Korea would enable the latter to compete with Japan in third-country markets.

It is not generally realized how precariously Korea is placed. To export, Korea must import intermediate goods from Japan, thereby incurring further trade deficits. This structural weakness creates the imbalance of bilateral trade: favorable trade with the US but unfavorable trade with Japan (Kim, February 1990, pp. 79-87). Thus, actual US-Japan imbalance is even greater than is apparent since Korea's exports include Japanese parts and components.

Korea's relative similarities to Japan extends to geography, culture,

240

tradition, history and ethnic background. And although there are certain characteristics of the Korean economy resembling those of contemporary Japan, Korea remains fundamentally different from Japan. Its population is one third the size of the latter, and Korea's GNP is about one-twelfth of Japan's. Japan is the second largest economy and the largest capital exporter in the world, with net foreign assets amounting to $513.6 billion. Japan's export growth was realized after development of the domestic market and economies of scale realized there while Korea remained mostly export-oriented. Also, Korea's large industries are dependent on imported technology and materials. Yet the US seems to treat the two countries together, threatening protective policies against both. Failure to differentiate between them may invite irreversible damage to both the US and Korea.

Regarding Korea-US relations, the US role in building Korea's technological competence dates back to the early 1950s. Because of the geopolitics of the Cold War, Korea was one of the biggest recipients of US technical assistance during the 1950s and 1960s. Korea has also sent a large number of students overseas for education, mostly to the US, and these educated Koreans become elite engineers, scientists and managers who can increasingly move into responsible positions, promoting Korea-US business linkages. Korea has relied on the import of capital goods and related technical assistance as the principal means of getting new technology. Much technology has also been transferred through the repatriation of Korean students with work experience in the US and through the temporary employment of Americans having technical expertise. The vital aspect of these processes lies in the assimilation of the technology into the local industrial fabric.

Korean industrialization began with technologies at the mature and declining stages in the product life cycle. Korea has assimilated imported technologies and strengthened technological efforts. Having realized a successful industrialization, Korea now faces formidable constraints in the export-led economy. Because of Korea's rising labor costs, Southeast Asian countries and China offer challenges in labor-intensive industrial exports, and other newly industrialized countries, such as Taiwan, Hong Kong and Singapore, present stiffer competition in the world market. Technology is crucial to Korea for maintaining its position vis-a-vis the other Asian NICs, as well as increasing its competitive strength vis-a-vis Japan. The shift to leading-edge goods or middle-level technology production will enable Korea to compete more effectively in the markets of the advanced countries.

Korea can provide Southeast Asian countries and China with technologies suitable to its factor endowments and to its workers in particular (Kim, 1989, pp. 217-223). Criticism of imported technology from the US and Japan has centered on the problem of absorption. Technological cooperation between Korea and the United States can overcome such constraints for mutual gains from technology, trade and investment. If the two countries are to make the most of their opportunities and challenge Japan in Asia, it would be desirable that they develop economic policies that stress suitable technologies.

Utilizing its cheap labor and land, China is being transformed into the world's emerging manufacturing center. On the basis of purchasing parity, the World Bank has already announced that China is one of the world's economic giants, with a per capita GDP amounting to $2,460 and GDP of $2,890 billion. China has achieved much in the last 15 years since it adopted the policy of reform and openness by bringing a portion of the population − the 260 million people in coastal areas along the Yellow River and the Southeast China Sea − into the market-oriented economy.

Korea's trade with Southeast Asian countries and China could be significant to US interests. Since Korea's economy complements the US economy in many ways, the US could capitalize on its close ties with Korea and move into Asian markets in association with this partner. The US's enormous financial capacity and its inherent technological advantages could combine well with a disciplined, highly skilled Korean workforce and Korea's proven record as a shrewd trader in the world market. Pursuing this partnership could yield remarkable economic potential to produce quality products at low cost.

In conclusion, Korea as a medium-level country might actively seek US investment as a partner to facilitate joint ventures of R&D and production, and engage in fields like HDTVs, next generation automobiles and semiconductors, and new materials for the purposes of formulating a technological and industrial alliance, thus alleviating the growing trade deficits of the two countries, and preventing their competitiveness from further eroding. Korea, associated with the US economy, could play a major role as a regional balancer, providing stability for a new order in Northeast Asia and the Asia-Pacific region as a whole.

Table 15.1
Foreign technology transfer to Korea

(Unit: US$ million)

Source	1962-1971	1972-1981	1982-1991	Total
Foreign licensing (FL)				
US	8.4	180.5	2,724.6	2,913.5
Japan	5.0	198.5	1,807.6	1,911.1
All Others	3.7	169.0	1,112.1	1,284.8
Total	17.1	548.0	5,644.3	6,109.4
Technology consultancy				
US	3.1	22.7	778.9	804.7
Japan	12.1	28.5	306.8	347.4
All Others	1.6	22.0	497.5	521.1
Total	16.8	73.2	1,583.2	1,673.2
Capital goods imports				
US	547.0	8,192.0	45,493.0	54,232.0
Japan	1,440.0	18,692.0	75,629.0	95,761.0
All Others	870.0	9,935.0	50,402.0	61,207.0
Total	2,857.0	36,819.0	171,524.0	211,200.0
Direct foreign investment (DFI)				
US	120.3	370.7	2,063.7	2,554.7
Japan	98.0	928.0	2,988.8	4,014.8
All Others	45.7	301.3	2,345.8	2,694.8
Total	264.0	1,600.0	7,398.0	9,264.3

Source: Korea Industrial Technology Association for DFI and FL; Korea Engineering Services Association for Technical Consultancy data; and Korean Society for Advancement of Machinery Industry for Capital Goods data, calculated and quoted from Linsu Kim's "Absorptive Capacity and Industrial Growth: A Conceptual Framework and Korean's Experience" East Asian Institute Reports, Columbia University, March 1993.

Table 15.2
Korea's import dependency ratio (KIDR)
of parts and components (PsCs), 1992

(Unit: % based on Amount)

Industry	(A) KIDR of PsCs	(B) Source of import	Japan's portion of (A)
Semiconductor	65%	Japan, US, Malaysia Germany	50%
Computer	60	US, Japan, Taiwan	40
Large color TV	60	Japan, US, Germany	40
Laser disk player	30	Japan, US	95
Programmable logic controller	35	Japan, US	80
Automobile (export)	20	Japan, US, Germany	70
NC controller machine	45	Japan, Germany	90
Robot	75	Japan, US	85
Camera	50	Japan	100
Ship	10	Japan, Germany US, France	60
Total	45%	-	60%

Note: Large color TV means 25 inches and over.
Source: Korea Development Bank, *Trend of [Korea's] Industrial Technology* (in Korean), Technology Division, Korea Development Bank, September 1992.

Notes

1 On September 16, 1993, US Under Secretary of the Treasury Lawrence Summers went to Japan just when the Japanese government announced its emergency economic measures. On the next day he demanded the Minister of International Trade and Industry to reduce income tax by issuing deficit bonds. He argues that Japan's Ministry of Finance has not done enough in increasing fiscal expenditure. At the same time the White House emphasized Japan's need to stimulate home consumption. These pressures from the US administration are keenly felt by Japan's Kasumigaseki (Ministry of Foreign Affairs) bureaucrats. This is because Summers gave a statement on August 19 in the midst of the rising yen value to the effect that the recent rise in the yen value is likely to impede the economic growth of Japan and the world, apparently as a gesture of a helping hand to the Hosokawa administration in Japan. The reason why the US

government is extending a helping hand to Japan is, it is rumored, that President Clinton has given a secret promise to Premier Hosokawa so that while Japan makes an effort to cut its trade surplus, the US would stop pressing for a higher value of the yen. See *Yomiuri Shimbun* (daily newspaper), September 18, 1993.

2 By modifying imported technology and implementing reverse engineering, Korean industries husbanded their supplies of capital while utilizing abundant labor supplies. See Ira C. Magaziner and Mark Partinkin, 'Fast Heat: How Korea Won the Microwave War,' *Harvard Business Review,* January 1989, pp. 83-92; Youn-Suk Kim, 'Korea's Technology Policy for Industrialization,' *Korea Journal of Population and Development,* July 1992, pp. 85-98.

3 The Clinton administration also strives to reverse the trend toward greater foreign ownership of critical US industries.

References

Johnson, Chalmers (1982), *MITI and the Modern Japanese Miracle: The Growth of Industrial Policy,* 1925-1975, Stanford University Press, Stanford.

Kim, Youn-Suk (1994), 'Japan's Technology Policy and the United States,' *Human Systems Management,* vol. 13, no. 2.

_____ (May 1990), 'Prospects for Japanese-US Trade and Industrial Competition,' *Asian Survey.*

_____ (February 1990), 'Korea-US Trade Friction and the Japan Factor,' *Asian Profile.*

_____ (1989), 'Managing Technological Transfer with Korea as a Catalyst,' *Human Systems Management,* vol. 8, no. 3.

Mansfield, Edwin (1990), 'Intellectual Property, Technology, and Economic Growth,' in *Intellectual Property Rights in Science, Technology, and Economic Performance,* edited by Francis W. Rushing and Carole Ganz Brown, Westview, London.

Okimoto, Daniel I. (1989) *Between MITI and the Market*, Stanford University Press, Stanford.

Prestowitz, Clyde V., Jr. (1988), *Trading Places: How We Are Giving Our Future to Japan and How to Reclaim It,* Basic Books, New York; and (April 1991) 'More Trade Is Better Trade: Life After GATT,' *Technology Review.*

Shoken, Daiwha, ed. (1992), *Japan in the World: Economic Geography*. (in Japanese), Nippon Enterprising Publisher, Tokyo.

Tyson, Laura (1992), *Who's Bashing Whom,* Institute for International Economics, Washington, DC.

Yamazawa, I., et al. (March 1993), *Dynamic Interdependence among the Asian Pacific Economies, Keizai Bunseki* (EPA), no. 129.

14 Managed trade, direct investment and external balance

Catherine Mann

Slow growth at home in recent years has focused policymakers' attention on negotiating improved access to foreign markets. Market access for exports and investment are seen as key parts of a policy package to revive domestic economic activity and increase jobs. Policymakers' views are bolstered by some economic theories that suggest that appropriately designed and implemented government interventions into clearly imperfect markets could increase exports, jobs, and incomes. Yet, an important question is whether these market-access policies can affect external balance, and through what transmission mechanisms. From purely an accounting standpoint, unless market access yields a net improvement in external balance, domestic economic activity will not improve.

In the United States, there is a certain schizophrenia in the policy community about how US external balance might respond to successful market-access negotiations. Even among those advocating this approach, few expect 'voluntary import expansions' or foreign government's 'leveling the playing field' for US investors to close the overall US external imbalance. In other words, it is well known and agreed that domestic savings and investment are the fundamental determinants of external balance. But with respect to the bilateral deficit with Japan, opening the Japanese market to more US exports and investment can be seen as central to closing the bilateral gap. Since Japan's bilateral deficit represents some 50 percent of the global US deficit, a significant improvement in that bilateral deficit would seem to lead to a narrowing of the overall external deficit. Can we reconcile the macro view that external balance is determined by savings and investment with the micro view that market access for goods and investment can reduce a large bilateral deficit?

This chapter will not dwell on the merits or demerits of managed trade or policies to facilitate direct investment. It should be noted, however, that these policies are difficult to design from an economic standpoint and impossible to implement from a political standpoint. Moreover, the increasingly complex interrelationship between trade and foreign investment may make proper policy design all the more difficult, and mistakes more costly.

Instead, suppose these policies are appropriately designed and implemented. What are the channels of transmission of these primarily microeconomic policies to external balance which is driven by macroeconomic forces? Moreover, given that external imbalance is merely a reflection of internal imbalance, there must be a consistent story of how these micro policies are transmitted on both sides of the macroeconomic identity.

A key linkage between micro policies and macro outcomes is business behavior. The transmission mechanisms of how the micro policies affect external and internal balance is through the firm's pricing strategy and investment choices, and therefore exports, investment and business savings (profits).

The second section of this chapter presents the familiar macroeconomic frameworks for external balance. From an accounting standpoint, external imbalances are mirrored in internal imbalances, between absorption and expenditure or between savings and investment. It then respecifies several elements of the macroeconomic equation in terms of the microeconomic foundations of a firm's pricing strategy and investment choices. An illustrative example of an exchange rate change shows the linkages between international competitiveness, investment choice, and internal and external balance.

The third section focuses on how market-access policies can affect the international competitiveness of a firm's products, its profitability and exports, and thereby affect both internal and external balance. Similarly, market-access policies can affect a firm's decision to invest at home or abroad, and thereby affect internal balance, as well as affect external balance through trade links. However, this section argues such policies can only have a temporary affect on internal and external balance unless they permanently change business profit rates. Since the business profit rate depends on the world interest rate, market access will change only the geographical composition of trade and investment, not the overall magnitude of internal and external balance.

Frameworks for internal and external balance

This section presents the standard macroeconomic framework for analyzing aspects of internal and external balance starting with the simple national income and product accounts (NIPA). Then, to highlight the roles for microeconomic policies, the accounting identities are made behavioral using simple behavioral specifications of the variables in the NIPA.

Simple accounting identities

The national income and product accounts give us the simplest relationship between macroeconomic elements of the economy. Start with the basic accounting framework for national output:

$$[1.] \quad Y = C + I + G + X - M$$

The first reformulation focuses on the broadest of macroeconomic aggregates, domestic expenditure ($E = C + I + G$) and domestic output (Y), and shows the identity between internal and external balances. An excess of domestic expenditure over domestic output, an internal deficit, is associated with an excess of imports over exports, an external deficit.

$$[2.] \quad Y - E = X - M$$

The second reformulation focuses on the balances for actors in the economy: households, business, and government. The value of domestic output (Y) can be defined as the return to labor (Wages, W) and capital (Profit, R), or $Y = W + R$. Accounting for taxes on the household sector (Th) and on the business sector (Tb), or $T = Th + Tb$, yields the following expansion of identity (1):

$$[3.] \quad X - M = (T - G) + (W - Th - C) + (R - Tb) - I$$

Recall that ($T - G$) is the government savings identity (Sg), ($W - Th - C$) is the household savings identity (Sh), and ($R - Tb$) is the business savings identity (Sb). Therefore, we can rewrite the accounting identity in the familiar form that relates external balance to the savings and investment balance:

$$[4.] \quad X - M = Sg + Sh + Sb - I$$

These accounting identities merely identify macroeconomic associations. They do not reveal how policies or behavior can change the aggregates and thereby change the balances.

Simple behavioral specifications

External balance (X - M) is common to each of the reformulations shown above. One simple behavioral specification of external balance is a partial equilibrium specification of the determinants of exports and imports. In this partial equilibrium model of external balance, exports are a function (x) of foreign income (Y*) and the relative price of exports (Px) to competing products (P*). Imports are a function (m) of domestic income (Y), and the relative price of imports (Pm) to domestic products (P). These observations yield a standard behavioral specification of the trade balance:

$$[5.] \quad X - M = x\,(Px/P^*, Y^*) - m\,(Pm/P, Y)$$

Thus, microeconomic market-access policies that focus on changing the relative price of exports have the potential to increase exports and, so long as the marginal propensity to consume imports is less than one, to improve external balance.

Are there similar factors on the side of internal balance? That is, even if market-access policies change exports, without a change in internal balance, external balance cannot change. We must look for channels through which market-access policies can affect internal balance.

One simple behavioral specification relates business savings (profits) (r) to price (P), costs (C) and quantity sold in domestic and export markets (Q=Qd+Qx).

$$[6.] \quad R = r\,(P, C, Q)$$

where price is a function of costs and the mark-up (V). Costs are a function (c) of wages (w), intermediates (m), capital (Pk), and production technology, such as economies of scale (l(Q)); C=c(w, m, Pk, l(Q)). V is function of the elasticity of demand (z) and market structure (s). Consequently, P = c(w, m, Pk, l(Q))*V (z, s).

Another simple behavioral specification relates a firm's decision to invest at home or abroad (i) to the relative marginal product of capital at home and abroad (k/k*), the relative price of capital in the home versus the foreign

250

market (Pk/Pk*), the world price of financial capital (q) and the depreciation rate (d).

$$[7.] \quad I = i\,(k/k^*,\ Pk/Pk^*,\ q,\ d)$$

These two behavioral specifications afford a variety of channels through which market-access negotiations could affect internal balance by affecting business savings (profits) and investment.

A behavioral specification of the accounting identity

Putting the behavioral pieces together with accounting identity (3) shows channels through which market-access policies could affect internal and external balance.

$$[8.] \quad x(Px,\ Y^*)-m(Pm,\ Y) =$$
$$r(c(w,\ m,\ Pk,\ l(Q))^*V(z,s),\ Qx+Qd)\ -\ i(k/k^*,\ Pk/Pk^*,\ q)$$

where the foreign and domestic aggregate prices and the depreciation rate are suppressed, taxes and government spending are assumed to be zero, and consumption is assumed to equal wage income. These assumptions allow a strict focus on the business profit and investment channels.

An illustrative example: An exchange rate change

Before turning to a discussion of market-access policies, tracing through the effects of an exchange rate change provides a good illustration of the linkages between international competitiveness, profits, investment choice and the two accounting balances.

Suppose the domestic currency depreciates. So long as the domestic firms pass through some of the depreciation, the foreign currency price of exports in the destination country will fall, and the quantity of exports will rise. If the effect of the depreciation on import prices and volume is within the normal range, external balance improves with a depreciation. On the savings side of the macro identity, business profits increase because more units are sold, and the unit mark-up is either the same or larger (depending on the degree of pass-through, the importance of imported intermediates, economies of scale in the cost function, and any changes in foreign market structure and elasticity of demand.) Thus, the macroeconomic identity is preserved − internal and

251

external balance both improve − and the link between the two sides of the identity is the pricing behavior and profit outcome of the firm.

Now consider the effect of the depreciation on investment choices. A depreciation will make the relative price of foreign capital more expensive to the extent that capital is purchased in the destination country − land or construction materials, for example. Thus, on the margin, investment will increase in the home country, and the savings-investment imbalance deteriorates. On the side of external balance, more investment at home raises domestic income and imports, so external balance worsens. The macroeconomic identity is again preserved through the transmission of the relative price of capital to investment, income and imports.

This very simple example illustrates not only basic channels of transmission but shows also that the same exogenous exchange rate change can have different effects on internal and external balance through the two channels of transmission: the goods channel and the investment channel.

Market-access policies and macroeconomic balances

The US and other countries participate in a variety of negotiating forums where the objective is to improve the environment for trade and investment for all the participants. Two examples are the Uruguay Round and the North American Free Trade Agreement. Neither of these negotiations explicitly promotes exports or foreign investment.

The US also undertakes a variety of negotiations on a bilateral basis, some of which are broad-based agreements and some of which are sector-specific. For example, Bilateral Investment Treaties with many countries focus on improving the overall climate for US investment in the specific country. The US-Japan Semiconductor Accord focuses on market access for particular foreign products in Japan.

Multilateral negotiations

The US has relatively lower rates of tariff protection, relatively transparent non-tariff barriers, and a relatively free investment climate compared to other participants in multilateral negotiations. Accordingly, if the Uruguay Round and NAFTA are completed and ratified, the US is likely to benefit relatively more from the zero-for-zero tariff principles, tariffication and increased transparency of non-tariff barriers, and liberalization of investment

252

regulations. That is, barriers that face US exporters that effectively raise the cost of exporting to foreign markets are likely to fall, exports and business profits are likely to rise, and internal and external balance both improve.

Moreover, improvements in the investment climate effectively will reduce the foreign cost of capital and/or raise the marginal product of capital in the foreign markets, thus contributing to greater outward investment. If exports follow foreign investment (and the empirical work suggests that there is a mild complementarity), then the United States can expect an improvement in both internal and external balance through this channel as well.

Will this superior trade and investment environment lead to permanent improvements in internal and external balance? Not necessarily. In this simple example, a permanent improvement in the macroeconomic balances requires a permanent change in the business savings rate. That is, unless the negotiations permanently change the business profit rate, improvements in business savings associated with reductions in costs of exporting will ultimately be spent on consumption, investment and imports, thus returning the macroeconomic balances to their initial levels.

Bilateral negotiations

How much do these arguments apply to more narrowly focused market-access negotiations such as the US-Japan Semiconductor Accord or the Bilateral Investment Treaties? That is, can sector- or country-specific market-access negotiations change business' international competitiveness and investment strategy, and can these affect internal and external balance overall? The simple answer is that these more narrowly focused negotiations are less likely to lead to the permanent change in the business savings rate necessary for permanent changes in the magnitude of internal and external balance. They might, however, alter the sectoral and geographical composition of external balance.

Market-access negotiations include policies that increase the volume of or the competitiveness of certain exports in a particular destination market. For example, 'voluntary import expansions' or market-share targets address principally the quantity of certain exports sold to a particular market. Reducing tariff barriers or dismantling distribution networks where imported goods are treated differently are examples of policy changes that address the relative price of particular exports.

Within the context of our model, tariff barriers or restrictive distribution networks represent costs of bringing a US export to the destination market.

Suppose we start with the presumption that a business has a hurdle rate that it must meet to enter any market. We can specify this simply that price minus average cost must be positive. An alternative specification requires that the rate of return in the new market be equal to the company average. A business will price the export into the market so long as it can achieve the minimum hurdle rate. Given that the protected market has higher costs, fewer products will meet the hurdle rate and, for those that do, the price will be higher. Consequently, the business loses export sales in this market.

How would successful market-access negotiations work? Eliminating barriers would reduce costs. Businesses could cut prices and still achieve the desired hurdle, and some products could now be exported profitably. Exports increase as does business savings. Initially, these improvements in savings and exports improve internal and external balance. However, these one-time improvements will damp out.

The schematic in Chart 1 shows the dynamic paths for exports to the target market, overall savings, overall imports and exports, and internal (S-I) and external (X-M) balance. The horizonal line from the origin for each panel indicates the equilibrium path for that variable given the hurdle rate for the business. This hurdle rate is h* for all panels except the panel for exports to the target market, where the zero line is defined for the hurdle rate prior to the market-access negotiations, h > h*.

Suppose market access negotiations are successful, shown here taking place at time T0. Costs facing businesses in the target market fall to C', which we will assume for simplicity reduces the hurdle rate to h*. Exports to this market increase (shown in panel 1), as do business profits. Overall savings initially rises, shown in the second panel. However, unless the overall profit rate on business sales changes, that is, unless h* changes, the extra-normal profits gained from sales to the formerly protected market will be spent on consumption, investment, or imports. Overall savings falls back toward the rate consistent with hurdle rate h* as business spends the extra-normal profits. The third panel shows the dynamic path of overall exports and imports if all the extra-normal profits are spent on imports. At the end of the adjustment period, shown here at Tn, both imports and exports will be greater, but the overall internal and external balance (and overall savings) will return to the original paths defined for the hurdle rate h*, as shown on the fourth panel.

Voluntary import expansions or market-share targets offer an alternative approach to improving a bilateral external deficit. Suppose the outcome of the negotiations is a one-time increase in sector-specific exports or suppose market share is a target. These quantitative arrangements allow extra-normal profits on sales into the protected market. Bilateral external balance improves, and, temporarily, overall internal and external balance may also reflect similar improvement. However, the extra-normal profits ultimately will be spent in other markets, and internal and external balance will return to being driven by macroeconomic determinants. Moreover, as both economies grow, the relative importance of magnitudes contained in the negotiated solutions will shrink, and the evolution of the bilateral external deficit will depend once again on macroeconomic factors.

Changing the regulatory climate for foreign investment has been a particular focus of market-access negotiations, including efforts to reduce the costs of entry by foreigners and equalize the treatment of foreign and domestic owned firms. These types of initiatives effectively reduce the relative cost of foreign capital or raise the relative rate of return on foreign capital.

Suppose such market-access negotiations for investment are successful in increasing US investment abroad. Will this lead to an improvement in internal and external balance? As before, there may be a temporary improvement in internal and external balance as businesses adjust investment strategies to exhaust extra-normal profit potential at the new location. However, in the longer-run, internal and external balance will not be affected by these sectoral negotiations.

The business savings rate or the hurdle rate is a key ingredient in this analysis. Where does it come from, and is it amenable to change with trade negotiations or market-access policies? Business decisions on whether to create a new product, enter a new market, or make a new investment depend fundamentally on whether the action will yield a return greater than that which could be obtained by investing the necessary capital in risk-free bonds. Thus, a riskless world interest rate must be a main driver of the hurdle rate. Broad-based trade negotiations and more-narrowly focused market-access negotiations are unlikely to change the world interest rate. Specific market-access negotiations can affect the return to or riskiness of a particular investment or market, and thus change the sectoral or geographical composition of internal and external balance.

Conclusion

This chapter considers the linkages between microeconomic policies that are often part of market-access negotiations and the macroeconomic balances between savings and investment as well as exports and imports. Market-access negotiations may affect the sectoral or geographical composition of internal and external balance, but cannot affect overall internal and external balance unless they permanently change the business savings (profit) rate. Since this profit rate ultimately depends on the world interest rate, market-access policies cannot systematically improve overall internal and external balance.

15 Technological policy and development in Korea

Woo-Hee Park

War-devastated only 40 years ago, Korea has metamorphosed into a modern society, with an economy that ranks approximately twelfth and thirteenth in the world in terms of trade volume and gross national product respectively.

Technology is one factor, among others, which has contributed to the rapid growth of the economy, but relatively little work has been done on the technology policies and their consequent effects on economic development in Korea. This paper attempts to explore the nature of the interaction between technological policies and industrial development. It is hoped that an interpretative framework emerges within which we can enlarge our understanding of the Korean experience of technological development during the last 30 years.

Growth of the Korean economy

Since the beginning of the 1960s the economic life of Korea has undergone astonishing change. In 1962 the Republic of Korea promulgated its first economic development plan, projecting rapid economic growth; five subsequent plans have been equally ambitious. Achievements have been impressive: since 1962 real GNP has already, as of 1985, risen seven times; by 1991, according to the figures in the first row of Table 15.1, it has risen tenfold. The rate of growth of GNP, in constant prices, has exceeded 8 percent on the average; GNP per capita has increased from US$477 in 1962 to $2,003 in 1985, and is expected to increase to $2,910 (all in constant US dollar at 1980 prices) at the end of the Sixth Five-Year Plan. Over the 20 years 1967-86 with which we are particularly concerned in this study of technological input, the rates of growth peaked during the interval of the Third Five-Year Plan, suffered a decline during the world's recession of

1980-1983, and recovered thereafter.

Table 15.1
Macroeconomic indicators of the growth
of the Korean economy: 1962-91

	Absolute figures						
	1962	1966	1971	1976	1981	1986	1991
Gross National Product (millions of US dollars in 1980 prices)	12,607	18,060	28,717	36,509	61,010	93,300	130,000
Population (1,000 persons)	26,513	29,436	32,883	35,860	38,723	41,839	44,690
GNP per capita (US dollar in 1980 prices)	477	613	873	1,297	1,575	2,331	2,910

	Rates of growth					
	1962-6	1967-71	1972-6	1976-81	1982-6	1978-91
Gross National Product	7.8	9.7	10.1	5.6	7.6	7.0
Population	2.7	2.2	1.7	1.55	1.55	1.30
GNP per capita	5.0	7.3	8.2	4.0	5.9	5.6

Sources: 1962-81; Governments of the Republic of Korea, The Fifth Five-Year Economic and Social Development Plan 1982-1986, Seoul; and ibid., 1986-91; The Sixth Five-Year Plan, Economic Planning Board, Seoul.

At least two important factors have contributed to the rapid growth of the economy, namely soaring exports and vigorous investment. Exports of commodities, in real terms, increased at an average rate of 23.2 percent annually during the decade of most rapid growth, 1970-80. Throughout the years of the Fifth Plan 1981-6 an annual growth rate of exports of approximately 8.9 percent was attained; throughout the Sixth Plan one of 9.0 percent was projected, and achieved. Only about 3.5 percent of GNP was exported in 1962; by 1986 the percentage has risen to 29, and by 1991 to 38

Table 15.2 Number of technology contracts approved by the Korean government, by industry: 1962-84

Year	1962-6	1967-71	1972-6	1977	1978	1979	1980	1981	1982	1983	1984	Total
Agriculture & horticulture	0	6	-	0	1	2	1	1	3	5	5	24
Food	2	6	7	0	1	9	5	15	21	20	24	110
Pulp & paper products	0	4	3	3	2	0	0	2	2	0	1	17
Fabrics, woven	5	2	10	2	2	1	4	4	4	3	2	39
Chemical fibers	2	5	14	1	6	12	3	6	23	27	29	128
Cement	1	11	9	3	10	7	9	5	9	6	10	80
Oil refining & chemicals	5	59	85	25	42	54	36	38	44	50	64	502
Pharmaceuticals	2	17	8	1	4	0	5	17	12	6	20	92
Metals	1	28	45	17	24	26	19	19	24	22	21	246
Electrical & electronics	5	65	84	32	51	42	47	33	60	80	77	576
Machinery	6	58	116	56	115	102	59	70	62	82	123	849
Ship-building	0	1	10	6	12	3	5	19	14	21	17	108
Communication	3	13	10	0	4	8	6	3	12	7	0	66
Electric power	0	2	7	8	11	6	4	8	8	4	4	62
Construction	1	3	4	3	4	2	8	4	6	9	7	51
Others	0	5	22	11	7	14	11	3	4	18	28	123
Total	33	285	434	168	296	288	222	247	308	360	432	3,073

Source:'Technology Imports Annual,' 1984, Ministry of Science and Technology, Republic of Korea.

percent.

In studying the import of modern technologies, most of which are applied to the production of intermediate rather than final goods, the growth of exports is a less significant factor than is the growth of investment. The modern technology is embodied in capital goods whose purchase and installation comprise investment; and many of the intermediate goods produced as a consequence of the investment are themselves allocated to further investment. It is therefore worth looking at the course of Korean investment in heavy and chemical industries in some detail.

The establishment of the heavy and chemicals industries

As has already been noted, during the periods of the First and Second Five-Year Plans, Korea built up substantial productive and export capacities in relatively labor-intensive light industries, such as textiles, wigs, rubber footwear and toys. Entering these activities relatively late in their product cycles, the Korean firms were nonetheless quick to apply the appropriate manufacturing techniques and to master the design and marketing skills needed for successful entry into international commerce.

But by the beginning of the 1970s, the Korean government had realized that the country's interests might best be served by integrating backwards into heavy industry. The time seemed propitious: in 1971 Japan announced a new policy which was to reorient the economy, away from 'pollution-prone' and 'natural-resource-consuming' heavy and chemical industries to 'clean' and 'brain-intensive' industries. On the international front, Japan was to stress a greater reliance than before on exports which would compete in quality, variety and sophisticated design, rather than in price.

Sensing that this was a trend which would be followed by many of the developed countries, Korea began to attract Japan's fading industries such as metal castings, bicycles, sewing machines, ceramics, leather products and the like. Furthermore, in 1972, at the start of the Third Five-Year Plan, the Korean government decided to make the chemical-process industries the focus of investment activity. It entered into chemicals, petrochemicals and iron and steel. New to the country, the manufacture of these commodities required resources that were scarce in Korea, particularly foreign capital and technology. To acquire these resources on the very large scale that capital-intensive industries require, the government had to systematize entry into these industries and to shape an environment within which they could flourish.

The first of these efforts resulted in guidelines to aspiring firms: first, suppliers of technology and of foreign loans would be selected in a competitive manner; second, projects funded by foreign loans should be internationally competitive in scale, and prices of their products must be in the neighborhood of international prices; third, in order to assure sound financial structures, entrepreneurs undertaking heavy and chemical projects would be expected to provide capital for at least 40 percent of the total investment. This was to be facilitated by improvement of the development financing systems, fostering the capital market and stronger savings promotion campaigns. Foreign capital was to be limited, in principle, to no more than 60 percent of the total investment. Foreign funds were to be utilized primarily for the acquisition of capital goods and advanced technology not locally available, rather than as equity. Fourth, although priority was to be given to loans on favorable terms, direct foreign investments were to be encouraged, especially when they would help to secure dependable sources of raw materials, expand markets for products or provide advanced technology. In this case, however, the foreign share was expected, in principle, not to exceed 50 percent; and fifth and finally, only the most modern techniques, those representing the current 'state of the art' in the developed countries, were to be chosen.

Various incentives were offered to Korean and foreign firms willing to invest in the new industries. A National Investment Fund was established whose purpose was to offer loans at less than market rates for the purchase of plant and equipment and even for the provision of working capital. These loans were extended for periods of longer than five years.

Tax privileges under the Foreign Capital Inducement Act and other tax laws were granted. Income and corporation taxes on enterprises with foreign capital were waived, or were reduced in proportion to the percentage of the total equity which foreign investors held. In the event of capital expansion, both income and corporation taxes were also waived or reduced in proportion to the foreign share. Such exemptions or reductions were to hold for five years from the initial reckoning date prescribed in the Income Tax Law and the Corporation Tax Law respectively, and were to be extended at half the rate for the ensuing three years. Enterprises with foreign capital were also exempted from acquisition taxes from the date of registration, and from property taxes rom the initial reckoning date prescribed in the respective tax laws. Even before the registration of an enterprise with foreign capital, it might be exempted from acquisition and property taxes on the property acquired for the original business purpose of the enterprise.

Creating an hospitable environment for the development of the heavy and chemical industries involved the Korean government in substantial investment in supporting facilities. Industrial sites were selected upon governmental initiative. In order to support construction of the selected industrial sites, the Industrial Site Development Promotion Law was enacted in 1973. The Gumi Electronics Industry Complex, the Changwon Machine Industry Base, the Yeocheon Chemical Industry Base and several others were constructed by the Industrial Sites Development Corporation and/or the Water Resource Development Corporation, both governmental organizations being established under the law. For these industrial complexes the government provided the infrastructure, such as harbor facilities, water supply systems and roads.

The acquisition of technology

Under the four successive Five-Year Development Plans 1962-81, foreign technology has been imported in company with foreign capital. Four laws govern the import of foreign technology into Korea: the Foreign Capital Inducement Law (1966), the Foreign Exchange Control Law, the Law Concerning Establishment of Free Export Districts and the Science and Technology Promotion Law. The Foreign Capital Inducement Law is the major policy instrument with respect to attracting both foreign capital and foreign technology. This law stipulates the criteria for screening technologies to be imported, and establishes priorities and procedure for their import. The various financial and administrative inducements given to suppliers of desirable foreign techniques are also based on this law. Preference ratings are assigned in the following order:

1 technology with high potential to expand export markets;
2 technology for manufacturing components and developing new processes for the capital goods industry;
3 technology which would be costly to develop domestically in time and expense; and
4 technology whose spill-over has the potential for cost reductions and productivity increases.

If a contract concerning the import of technology lacks any of the above provisions, it should be augmented by guarantees of the quality of the product by the supplier of the technology, and for the provision of any improvements

263

in the technology developed by the supplier during the contract period. The guidelines also limit payments for imported technology generally to three percent of the net sales of the resulting product and the contract period for such payments to three years, except in cases where the payment takes the form of a lump sum. Finally, the guidelines require the deletion of any clause that denies the importer of the technology rights to acquire other products or technologies sold in competition to those of the supplier or that prevents the importer of the technology from exporting to foreign countries in which the supplier does not exercise exclusive selling rights. The application of these guidelines will be observed in each of the four following sections of this chapter.

Since April 1979, the regulations governing the import of foreign technology into Korea have been relaxed. Before, the Korean government's role was active; it took part in any negotiations involving large expenditures and it vetted all agreements for lesser sums. By 1979 the government had recognized that most large Korean firms had accumulated experience in screening the proposals of prospective suppliers and conducting negotiations with them. Moreover, the government had found it difficult to keep up with the pace at which new contracts were being submitted to it for approval; in the 15 years from 1962 to 1976 the government had to approve a total of 752 agreements; in the next three years it had to approve as many again (see Table 15.2). By the dual devices of raising the ceiling on the value of contracts needing approval and exempting an increasing number of industries from the regulations, the government has kept the approval scheme to manageable proportions.

How has Korea acquired 'Western' technologies? At what cost? What have been the nature and scope of the technologies imported? From where? These are questions that will be answered in detail, but it might be useful to see what data are available for the Korean economy overall.

The first point is that technology is not a phenomenon that lends itself to measurement: we will not find aggregate statistics on technology imports. What we will find are statistics on items − e.g. numbers of contracts containing clauses related to the provision of technology, imports of capital goods in which technologies are embedded, and investment and income flows to and from abroad − which are indicators of technology imports. Let us commence by addressing the first of the questions posed: how does Korea acquire 'Western' technologies? A comparison of imports of technology into the five newly-industrialized countries of Argentina, Brazil, India, Mexico and Korea carried out by the World Bank and reported in Westphal, Kim,

Lin-Su and Dahlman (1984, Table 15.3) reveals that Korea's outstanding characteristic is the large fraction of its total gross domestic investment represented by imported capital goods. In the interval from 1977 through 1979, over a quarter (27.2 percent) of Korea's investments was comprised of imported capital goods, whereas the next highest figure (11.8 percent) was that of Mexico. To interpret these statistics we will draw upon our own observations that, unlike the three Latin American countries in the sample, Korea has not relied upon direct foreign investment as a source of foreign technologies. Korea has hired technology but has not hired production; Korea has welcomed foreign techniques but has not encouraged foreign ownership. Together with the modern capital goods that Korea has imported in such large quantities has come the know-how to operate them; but in the main Korea has purchased both the capital goods and the know-how, rather than letting foreign firms possess them.

To support this generalization we can draw upon some additional data provided by Westphal, Kim, Lin-Su and Dahlman (1984, Table 2). During the period 1962-81 the total amount of foreign investment in assets embodying technology new to Korea was, in current prices, US$ 1,249 million. Over the same period the Koreans paid royalties on licenses for new technology equal to US$ 565 million. If one assumes that all royalty payments were on a current basis, at the rate of 5 percent of sales revenues, and that foreign investment in modern technologies was undertaken at a capital: output (revenue) ratio of 4:1 and with 50 percent local participation, the average annual revenues attributable to technologies acquired through investment would have been $625 million and those attributable to technologies acquired through licenses would have been $11,300 million. This works out to $18 of revenue generated by Korean firms utilizing foreign (licensed) technology for each dollar generated by foreign firms operating in Korea under their own technology. A check against this crude comparison can be made by utilizing the figure for the total value-added 1962-81 in the production of goods utilizing imported technology, reported by Westphal, Kim, Lin-Su and Dahlman as $156,000 million, in constant 1975 prices. Dividing this figure by 20, the number of years in the period 1962-81, one obtains an annual average value-added of $7,900 million. Since value-added in production is less than sales revenues, excluding as it does the value of purchased components, the total annual figure for value-added of $7,800 million does not seem out of line with the total annual figure for revenues, $625 million plus $11,300 million or $11,925 million.

Since our thesis − that Korea imports foreign technology chiefly by means of licensing — is sustained by the evidence, we shall proceed to examine the sources, destinations and cost. Table 15.3 provides a summary of the sources and applications of technologies obtained over the 20 years 1962-81 through agreements with foreign suppliers. Nearly two-thirds of the agreements were approved in the last five years, during the Fourth Plan. Payments to foreigners for technology, mainly royalties on production but also including service, administrative, legal, travel and accommodation charges, are bunched even more towards the most recent years: data from the Economic Planning Board reveal that in the period of the First Five-Year Plan, 1962-6, payments were $0.8 million; in the Second, $16.3 million; in the Third, $96.5 million; and in the Fourth, $451.9 million. Yearly figures for 1982 ($115.7 million), 1983 ($149.5 million) and 1984 ($213.2 million), the first three years of the Fifth Plan, show that payments are accelerating, and no reduction is expected during the period of the Sixth Five-Year Plan 1986-91.

From Table 15.3 one observes that Japan has been the leading supplier of foreign technology, Japanese firms being the signatories on 55 percent of the total number of contracts approved by the Korean government. The United States is the second most important supplier, and Western European countries minor contributors. The machinery industry in Korea has initiated the largest number of contracts, 28 percent of the total; with the electrical and electronics, and the oil and chemical industries, accounting for 19 percent and 16 percent respectively.

As to the content of the contracts providing for the import of technology, the bulk of them are concerned with know-how. Scrutinizing 1,720 contracts authorized between 1962 and 1980, the Economic Planning Board discovered that 50.2 percent covered the provision of know-how only, and another 23.8 percent licenses and the know-how necessary to exploit them. Of the remaining contracts, 21.2 percent granted licenses only and 4.0 percent permitted the use of trademarks. In a subsequent scrutiny covering 603 contracts authorized in the three years 1981-3, the Korea Industrial Research Institute (KIRI), the umbrella association covering all capered research institutes, found roughly similar percentages of 48.4 percent, 37.2 percent, 5.8 percent and 8.6 percent respectively. As to the form that the know-how took, of the 516 contracts in KIRI's sample calling for the provision of know-how (either alone or together with licenses), 20 (3.8 percent of the 516) provided it solely in the form of blueprints and designs, 24 (4.7 percent in the form of visits from foreign consultants, and the remainder (472 or 91.5 percent) in the composite forms of blueprints, operating manuals, consultation, training and supervision. Just as advanced technology has been acquired by Korea chiefly through the device of contracts with foreign suppliers, so most of those contracts have been broadly written so as to assure the provision of all the necessary knowledge, in its many modes.

The demand for foreign technology, in whatever form, reflects in part a recognition on the part of the Korean government and Korean firms that capital can be more easily raised for technically advanced projects. Foreign capital, particularly, is more readily available to those Korean firms which adopt the technology that is generating profits to producers in developed countries. Lenders appear to attribute lower risks to absorbing the most advanced technology than to developing a less-advanced but more readily absorbed technology, or even an already existing, obsolete technology.

The demand for foreign technology in Korea also may reflect a lack of confidence in domestic capacity for research and development. It appears on occasion that even simple techniques, well within the capability of Korean firms, are acquired from abroad. Perhaps the reason is to enhance public acceptance of the final products; perhaps to establish links with foreign suppliers; perhaps to gain experience in negotiating with foreign firms and in securing approval from government ministries.

Table 15.3
Cumulative number of technology contracts approved
by the Korean government, by country of supply, 1962-84

	US	Japan	West Germany	UK	France	Others	Total	% of Total
Industry								
Agriculture & horticulture	9	14	0	0	0	1	24	0.78
Food	34	48	1	4	4	9	110	3.58
Pulp & paper products	8	7	1	0	0	1	17	0.55
Fabrics, woven	18	11	2	1	1	6	39	1.27
Chemical fibers	27	57	5	3	24	12	128	4.17
Cement	12	53	4	5	3	3	80	2.6
Oil refining & chemicals	122	297	17	23	14	34	502	16.3
Pharmaceuticals	27	33	12	6	2	12	92	2.99
Metals	41	155	7	14	6	23	246	8.01
Electrical & electronics	151	355	21	4	8	37	576	18.7
Machinery	140	528	62	39	17	63	849	27.6
Ship-building	16	19	12	7	9	45	108	3.51
Communication	19	31	4	0	0	12	66	2.15
Electric power	36	14	4	0	2	6	62	2.02
Construction	19	16	0	4	1	11	51	1.66
Others	29	57	10	1	5	21	123	4
Total	708	1700	162	111	96	296	3073	100

Source: 'Technology Imports Annual,' 1984, Ministry of Science and Technology, Republic of Korea

The inadequacy of research and development

Of the possible reasons for the import of technology, the only one that can be investigated on an aggregate basis with the data available is that of inadequate R&D. Even then most of the comparisons are with developed countries, from which Korea would be expected to emerge badly. The first bloc of figures in Table 15.4 makes this comparison, from which it is seen that Korea's total investment in R&D, as a fraction of GNP, runs between a third and a half that of the four major developed countries. The second bloc of figures in Table 15.4 reveals that this gap is expected to be almost completely eliminated by 1991, at the end of the Sixth Five-Year Plan. Then it will be the smaller size of the Korean economy, relative to those of the developed countries, that will restrict its expenditures in R&D.

When the basis of comparison is other developing countries, Korea may have become superior only after the recession of 1980-1, when both GNP and the fraction devoted to R&D resumed their rapid rise; even then we cannot be certain that those other developing countries listed in Table 15.4 have not raised their standards too.

Shifting our attention to more detailed figures, the ratios of expenditures on R&D to total revenues of Korean industries indicate that Korean firms currently spend from a third to a quarter as much as do firms in developed countries. The discrepancy is least for Japan, most for West Germany. As might be expected there is considerable variability industry-by-industry, Korean chemical firms incurring a much smaller ratio than their foreign counterparts and Korean general machinery firms a nearly equal ratio. Even more notable is the variation between different industries within Korea, electrical (and electronic) firms spending five-and-a-half times as much on R&D, per won of sales, as did chemical firms.

Table 15.4
Expenditures on research and development
in some developed and developing countries

Country	Year	Total R&D Expenditure		Public R&D Expenditure	
		Relative to Korea in 1982 (Korea - 1)	As a % of GNP	Relative to Korea in 1982 (Korea - 1)	As a % of the govt's total budget
US	1982	93	2.5	142	4.9
Japan	1982	39	2.2	23	2.9
France	1980	38	1.8	30	6.2
W Germany	1981	44	2.7	19	4.8
Korea	1982	1	0.9	1	2
	1984	2	1.5	n/a	2
	1986	2.8	2	n/a	n/a
	1991	5	2.5	n/a	n/a
	1978	0.5	0.6	n/a	n/a
Argentina	1978	n/a	-0.4	n/a	n/a
Brazil	1978	n/a	0.6	n/a	n/a
India	1978	n/a	0.6	n/a	n/a
Korea	1973	n/a	0.4	n/a	n/a
Argentina	1973	n/a	0.3	n/a	n/a
Brazil	1973	n/a	0.4	n/a	n/a
India	1973	n/a	0.4	n/a	n/a
Mexico	1973	n/a	0.2	n/a	n/a

Sources: Data for Korea and the developed countries/Government of Korea, Ministry of Science and Technology (MOST), Annual on Science and Technology, Seoul, 1979; and 'Report to the President by the Minister of Science and Technology,' Report no. 84-2-1, Seoul, November 1984. Data for developing countries/Westphal, Kim, Lin-Su and Dahlman (1984), Table 3, p. 26.

Incomes of research workers in Korea are less than those in the developed countries, as are most of the other prices of resources necessary to undertake R&D. Additional data from KIRI provide estimates of national expenditure, in US dollars per research worker per year, for the three developed countries in Table 15.5, plus France and England; the results are, in descending order, $230,000 per year for West Germany (1979), $184,000 for France (1979), $89,000 for the USA (1979), $79,000 for Japan (1982) and $27,300 for the UK (1978) versus $24,300 for Korea (1983). The comparison in which Korea comes out in the best light is that of the fraction of the population engaged in R&D. Per 10,000 citizens, the figures for the developed countries listed in the same order and during the same years as above are 18, 14, 28, 28 and 15, versus eight for Korea. On this last basis, as on the first (namely, the fraction of GNP allocated to R&D, Table 15.4), the figure for Korea is currently about one-half to one-third that of the developed countries and, relative to theirs, is increasing rapidly. Some five years earlier, the newly industrialized countries in Westphal, Kim, Lin-Su and Dahlman's sample (1984, Table B) recorded per 10,000 citizens, three scientists and engineers in R&D in Argentina (1978), two in Brazil (1978) 0.5 in India (1976), and 0.1 in Mexico (1974), versus four in Korea (also 1978), similar to the ranking in Table 15.4.

The preceding tables provide measures of the use and costs of technical resources by Korean R&D establishments, but say nothing about the outputs that these inputs provide. Of course, it is notoriously difficult to attribute specific outputs to such generalized inputs as R&D, but it is still worthwhile attempting the task. Three partial measures are available of the contribution of R&D to the output of Korean industries; the first of these gives the numbers of patents registered in Korea, in various years between 1960 and 1983, by both Koreans and foreigners: over the 23 years the number granted to foreigners has increased fairly steadily from 45 in 1960 to 2,203 in 1983, whereas those grand to Koreans have fluctuated between a low of 104 in 1977 to a high of 258 in 1979 without any noticeable trend (Government of Korea, Ministry of Science and Technology, Science and Technology Annual, Seoul: 1984).

The second measure focuses not on quantity of output of R&D but on the quality of the products that are manufactured in Korea with its assistance. In an inquiry into product quality conducted by the Korea Industrial Research Institute and published in The Eleventh Study on Trends in Industrial Technology Development (Seoul: KIRI, May 1985), KIRI asked the managers of the institutes it represents to categories the products of their industries according to their international competitiveness. The distribution of answers along the product's dimensions of quality, design, durability, precision and practicability were remarkably similar − approximately 10 percent of the products were classified as being at the highest level in the world, approximately 50 percent as being at the same level as those of the developed countries, and approximately 40 percent as being at the same level as those of the rest of the world. The final category, below the level of those of the rest of the world, contained very few observations, too few to be statistically significant.

The third partial measure of the contribution of R&D to Korea's development is that derived from econometric analyses of the sources of a country's economic growth, applying the methodology of E.F. Denison (Denison and Chung, 1976). The results for Korea are given in Table 15.6: a comparison with the US and Japan reveals that Korea's growth has stemmed proportionally more from increases in labor supply and proportionally less from advances in technology. The relative contribution of technological advance to growth in Korea, vis-a-vis the two developed countries, corresponds closely to the relative fraction of its resources devoted to research and development (from Table 15.4).

Table 15.5
Ratio of R&D expenditures to total sales of industrial firms in the US, Japan, West Germany and Korea, late 1970s and early 1980s

Late 1970s	USA (1975)	Japan (1970)	W Germany (1975)	Korea (1978)
Total manufacturing	3.1	1.6	3.3	0.75
Chemical industry	3.6	2.4	3.3	0.5
Electric machinery	7.1	3.7	6.7	1.34
Precision machinery	5.3	2.4	4.5	0.94
General machinery	4.1	1.6	3.1	0.94
Airplanes	13.8	-	44	-
Early 1980s	**USA (1980)**	**Japan (1982)**	**W Germany (1979)**	**Korea (1983)**
Total manufacturing	3.1	2.15	3.2	0.8
Chemical industry	3.5	3.05	4.4	0.56
Electric machinery	6.5	4.52	7.2	3.01
Precision machinery	6	3.97	4.7	1.28
General machinery	5.6	2.34	3	2
Automobiles	5	3.02	3.1	1.48
Airplanes	11.6	-	30.3	-

Source: Korea Industrial Research Institute (KIRI), 1985.

Table 15.6

**Contributions of technological advance and other factors
to the growth of GNP in the US, Japan and Korea**

Source of growth	US (1948-69) %	Japan (1953-72) %	Korea (1963-83) %
Labor	22	17.1	35.8
Capital	19.8	23.8	21.4
Economies of Scale	10.5	22	18
Technological advance	29.8	22.4	11.8
Miscellaneous	17.7	14.7	13
Total	100	100	100

Source: US and Japan/Denison and Chung (1976); Korea/Government of Korea, Economic Planning Board, 'Report Presented to Consultative Meeting on Industrial Structure and Strategy of Technological Development for the Formulation of the Sixth Five Year Plan', July 12, 1985 (in Korean).

Promotion of R&D capacities

During the 1970s, the main strategies for science and technology development were the establishment of R&D institutions such as government-supported research institutes (GRIs) and the development of indigenous R&D capabilities through the absorption and improvement of imported advanced technology. Since the 1980s, the government has strengthened its strategies to develop future-oriented, long-term research and development projects.

Entering the 1990's, Korea has set the national goal so as to enhance the levels of S&T in some priority areas similar to those of G7 advanced countries by the year 2001. To this end, specifically, more emphasis has been given to technology rather than science. Available resources are to be allocated for the promotion of science and technology in a preferential manner. It is expected now that technological development will take precedence over economic development in the future.

During the last 10 years from 1980 to 1990, the Korean government and firms drastically increased R&D expenditures; R&D expenditure was increased 14 times from $321 million (1980) to $4,481 million (1990). The private sector played the leading role in rapidly augmenting R&D expenditures, while the government portion of R&D expenditures has decreased significantly from 50 percent (1980) to 16 percent (1990). According to the long-term plan, Korea has set the goal of boosting R&D investment to five percent of GNP in the year 2001.

The Korean government placed also a special emphasis on the securing and nurturing of high caliber S&T manpower in order to meet the rapidly increasing demand for R&D, both in the public and private sectors. As of 1990, the number of researchers reached 70,503 (16.4 persons per 10,000 population), including 17,662 PhD's.

The Korean government again undertook national R&D projects after 1982 which normally could not be pursued by industry alone, to develop key industrial technology for industrialization. Among the projects of this nature, industry-oriented projects were carried out via the joint efforts of industry, public institutes, and the government.

In order to effectively utilize R&D resources and to push ahead with policies systematically, the roles of R&D performing institutes were redefined. The R&D capability of universities and private enterprises was nominal in the 1960s, with most R&D activities being implemented by government-supported research institutes (GRIs). This was changed drastically, particularly in the 1980s. Private businesses set up their own in-house R&D facilities numbering over 1500, greatly enhancing R&D capability while universities increased their R&D capacity by allocating more expenditures for R&D.

In order to foster industrial technology development, the Korean government provided various incentives to private enterprise, such as tax exemptions, special depreciation, financial grants, availability of long-term low-interest development loans, and government procurement among others.

Externally, to better cope with the growing interdependence of the world economy, Korea expanded both bilateral and multilateral international cooperation activities, especially since 1980. Sixty-six international joint research projects were in full swing with financial support from the government amounting to $4 million in 1989.

Domestically, the government has established industrial complexes in major regions of the country since the 1970s, and finished the construction of the Daeduk Science Town, in the city of Taejon, located at 150km south of Seoul.

Recently, several institutes located at the different regions are planning the establishment of such functions with different names such as the Technology Innovation Center (TIC), Technology Business Incubators (TBI), Technology Business Development Centers (TBDC), Technopolis, Techno-complex and so on. Through promoting these centers, small and medium industries and local universities can be revitalized together, and contribute greatly to the local economies.

Despite remarkable development in S&T, Korea has still many problems to be solved for further development, such as poor consensus on the future directions and priorities of S&T development, insufficient S&T investment, particularly in the government sector, poor quality and unbalanced output of technical manpower, unclear strategic focus in R&D project planning and selection, lack of cooperation and role adjustments among R&D performing institutes, poor and insufficient international cooperation, and centralized and unbalanced regional S&T development.

As the scale of the economy grows, government initiative is giving way to private-sector initiative. Accordingly, the government's role shifts from that of a supporter rather than an initiator. Within the government sector, coordination and cooperation among concerned ministries are of major importance. To promote such activities, political support should be developed.

R&D performing institutions, such as universities, GRIs, and private companies should shift their roles, adapting to the environmental change. GRIs have primed the pump in developing S&T levels of Korea, and played the role of a bridge linking universities and private institutes with some supporting and coordinating functions. They are responsible for the areas which private institutes cannot afford, due to heavy financial burdens and high risk, along with commonly based technology areas, having a great impact on socio-economic sectors. Recently, successive technical innovations in advanced countries and interdisciplinary characteristics of large-scale R&D programs have shown that a more systematic approach, more advanced technology and a higher level of technical information are required for the success of R&D projects.

To cope with fierce competition in the world market, the Korean government has launched 11 'Highly Advanced National (HAN)' Projects (so-called G7 Projects), to develop strategic industrial technologies such as development of highly integrated semiconductors, Integrated Services Digital Network (ISDN), High Definition TV (HDTV), new medicine and new agricultural medicine, advanced production systems, new advanced materials, next-generation vehicle, new functional bio-materials, environmental

276

engineering, new energy resources, and next-generation atomic reactor and verification. Active utilization of intranational and international cooperation in carrying out these projects is the key to success.

Korea inaugurated a new president in February 1993. The focus of President Kim's 'New Economy' is fourfold; to strengthen the competitive position of the Korean economy and to implement new institutional change. The first part of the new economic policy is burden-sharing through belt tightening measures, which include a wage freeze for government workers. The second is to assist the private sector by cutting the cost of financing such as lowering the interest rate and opening up the financial sector. The third is to achieve overall deregulation of the country's economy. The fourth step is to improve industrial productivity: to do so, Korea needs to make a concerted effort to invest in high-skilled human resources. Technology is the crucial ingredient in the economic and industrial policy.

To date, the Kim's government has aimed to provide an effective technology policy as follows:

1 The government has pursued a technology-led policy to raise the level of science and technology in some priority areas into those of G7 advanced countries by the year 2001.
2 R&D expenditures will be increased up to the level of five percent of GNP in the year 2001, and the number of researchers will be 150,000 scientists and engineers by 2001.
3 The new government is placing top priority on securing self-reliance in science and technology, which it believes will determine the success of the president Kim's policy to build a 'New Korea.' To that end, funds for R&D are being sharply increased, the budget of which remained at a meager two percent of GNP in 1991 will be up to four percent by 1998.
4 So far, the Korean government has placed priority on the development of high technologies in the so-called G7 projects as noted above. Now, however, the government is turning into a double-track strategy for R&D activities. Along with the continued support for G7 projects, the government will also provide intensive financial assistance for the development of medium technologies in 13 fields, to help improve the international competitiveness of the small and medium-size businesses, and to recover the international competitive edge of major Korean export industries.
5 Some 785 patents and technical knowhow hold by government-invested research institutes will be provided free to small enterprises, and more

researches and technicians of the institutions will be dispatched to industrial fields to conduct joint research and to serve the commercialization of technology already developed. More funds of 400 billion won and more chances of training researchers and technicians will be fueled into R&D activities of small firms. The list of Korean engineers abroad will also be filed so that local institutes & enterprises may get technical cooperation from them.

A proposal for Korea-US technological alliance

One of the most vital considerations in advancing Korea's economy is the necessity of its domestic high technology. As a newly developing country, however, Korea must still rely on other advanced countries for R&D assistance. A rough estimate indicates that Korea has less than one percent of the world's R&D resources, so that it is crucial that Korea should take advantage of the other 99 percent. With this in mind, international cooperation such as technological transfer, licensing public joint-research effort, foreign direct investment embodying foreign high-technology seems to be one of the most viable solution for maximizing Korean productivity and economic growth.

At the Korea-US summit meeting in Seoul in 1993, the establishment of 'Dialogue for Economic Cooperation' (DEC) was agreed to secure official diplomatic channel for the discussion on current bilateral economic issues. EDC takes the form of a comprehensive council for practical business affairs, where the assistant ministers of the foreign affairs in both countries will be the chairman. The council is subjected to the existing Korea-US Economic Council. Through this system, two nations decided to moderate various regulations which could affect the economic relationship between two countries and to reform many systems of trade, investment and industrial property rights, and also to seek the method for the cooperation of industrial technology. Korea should notice that this Korea-US summit meeting provided the opportunity to build up new relationship.

The future relationship in trade between the countries must be developed from the level of settling the past conflicts in trade to the level of industrial cooperation. By grafting the American high-tech on Korean manufacturing technology, trade between two nations will be enlarged and the joint advance into the third nation will also be promoted.

In fact, in the Clinton government, the favorable atmosphere for this kind of cooperation is being made in the government level. On the threshold of the dawn of the era of Asian-Pacific, US policy for the industrial and technological cooperation with Korea is to set up the ground work on which the US can continually keep its influences over the Asian-Pacific area. On the other hand, it is felt urgent in Korea to strengthen the competitiveness in the world market by acquiring the advanced technology from abroad such as the United States. Therefore, for the economic coprosperity of two nations, it is very important to enlarge the industrial and technological cooperation, by:

1 establishing the cooperative system between major institutes and database,
2 setting up the channel of cooperation between private enterprises of two nations,
3 forming the official forum,
4 installing the region to induce investments,
5 opening the techno-mart.

Indeed, combining the US high technology with Korea's production efficiency to create a mutually beneficial alliance is very appealing and viable. This idea has already been proposed at several occasions quite recently, by Korea's Science and Technology Minister Jin-Hyun Kim, Trade and Industry Minister Chulsu Kim, Trade and Industry Assistant Minister Un-suh Park, National Assembly Member Sang-Mok Suh and Lucky-Goldstar Chairman Pyong-Hwoi Koo.

The Kim administration's 'New Economy' program will give a strong impetus to this industrial and technological alliance idea. To help launch this concept, the Korean government proposed the creation of 'Korea-America Fund for Industrial Cooperation' and already contributed $300,000 as seed money for feasibility studies and related research. To support further such cooperative ventures, it has been established under the name of 'US-Korea Technology Foundation' which will facilitate more productive cooperation in the fields of joint exchange of top-level scientists & engineers, sponsoring joint R&D programs, and for commercialization.

The Korean government is determined to take all measures, legal as well as institutional, to provide an environment that is conducive to productive technological cooperation between two countries. The protection of intellectual property rights (IPR) will be ensured by strengthening the domestic measures to the level of the US IPR protection may well be the key to inducing foreign investment, especially technology-intensive investment, to Korea. A new Trade Secrets Protection Law was implemented, and

Computer Program Protection Law and the Copyright Law will be submitted to the National Assembly soon. Korea will also liberalize in full breadth direct foreign investment in Korea. Businesses will be widely open to foreign investors under the Korean government's five-year liberalization program. Upon completion of this program, 93.6 percent of the 1,148 business lines listed in the Korean standard industrial classification will be eligible for foreign investment. Beginning in late 1994, a network of 'free investment zones' will be created in which foreign investors having high technologies will be able to lease factory sites and lending in offshore capital, along with the benefit from the streamlining of the approval procedure for starting operations.

The government is currently drawing up a comprehensive deregulatory program. Already in the first hundred days of the new government, more than four hundred regulations have been revised and abolished. These deregulatory measures will be applied equally to both Korean and foreign investors.

Possible areas for industrial and technological cooperation are semiconductors, telecommunication, computers, machine tools, aerospace, medical equipment, environment facilities, laser, HDTV and electric automobiles.

The semiconductor industry is one area where the partnership is not only beneficial for both sides but complementary in nature. There are a number of companies which have the technology such as ASIC but lack the capital to get the project off the ground. On the contrary, capital is available for Korean companies but reluctant to be used for risky investments. The Korean computer industry is at a crossroads. The only strategy for survival would be through enhanced technology in computer design, in a higher level of structural quality, and in increased localization of parts and components, where the US industrial technology can be helpful.

Demands for telecommunications are forecast to explode in the near future. The localization should be accelerated for digital cellular telephones, personal communications services, mobile telecommunications services, and tele-terminals. The Korean machine tool industry is expected to grow steadily mainly due to the increasing demand for sophisticated, high precision and high technology machine tools. But the level of technology is considered to be competitively advanced only in such functional technologies as machining and assembling processes, but the capability for designing the versatile, ultra-precise and automated machine tools still lag behind those of advanced countries. The Korean government has made public its plan to develop Korea into one of the world's 10 major aerospace makers early in the next century, by investing W1.4 trillion for facilities investment and W1.9 trillion for R&D. New corporate investments are actively being made in the environment facilities sector as the government is vigilant against environment-damaging and pollution-emitting industries. It is estimated that the size of market for facilities and equipment is about W1.5 trillion.

The United States was the leader in these fields at one time, but lost its lead to Japan. Korea is especially concerned with the US decline, particularly in semi-conductor equipment and material, which is translated directly into a decline in the Korean industry and make it inevitable for Korea to depend more on Japan. The US semiconductor and related equipment and material manufactures are hurrying to increase their presence in Korea; Applied Material of the US in a wafer processing equipment plant, LAM Research in water etching subsidiary, Motorola in cathode ray tube driver. As a means of accelerating more US transfer of technologies, the Korea Trade Promotion Corporation (KOTRA) sponsored a techno-mart, in September 15-17, 1993, which is the first US-Korea exchange of technologies held in Korea.

Conclusion

Approaching 21st century, Korea is trying to develop high technologies as well as basic sciences in some priority areas. Increasing the level of S&T through expanding material and human resources are crucial targets of Korea. S&T development is expected to lead and determine the economic and industrial development, but there are many problems to be solved further.

Korea is facing a turning point towards the 21st century, and new thoughts and philosophy for S&T policy are required for the sustained growth of the Korean economy in the future. As a small country with poor resources and little land, Korea should pursue a dynamic S&T policy to cope with the rapidly changing world, particularly with regard to the transfer of the US high-technology. Korea-US technological alliance is required for the benefits of Korea as well as the US.

281

References

Amsden, Alice H. and Kim, Lin-Su (1982), 'Korea's Technology Exports and Acquisition of Technological Capability', World Bank Productivity Division, Development Research Department, Washington, D.C.

Amsden, Alice H. and Kim, Lin-Su (1984), 'A Technological Perspective on the General Machinery Industry in the Republic of Korea', Division of Research, Harvard Business School, Working Paper 9-784-075, Boston, Mass. (forthcoming in Fransman, Marin, ed.)

Baranson, J. (1978), *Technology and the Multinationals,* Lexington Books, Lexington, MA.

Bell, R.M. (1984), 'Learning and the Accumulation of Industrial Technological Capacity in Developing Countries', in M. Fransman and K. King (eds), *Technological Capability in the Third World,* Macmillan, London.

Berman, J.A. (1976), *Transfer of Manufacturing Technology within Multinational Enterprises,* Ballinger, Cambridge, MA.

Cole, D.C. and Lyman, P.N. (1971), *Korean Development: the Interplay of Politics and Economics,* Cambridge: Harvard University Press, Ambridge, MA.

Davies, S. (1979), *The Diffusion of Process Innovations,* Cambridge University Press, Cambridge, UK.

Denison, E.F. and Chung, W.K. (1976), *How Japan's Economy Grew So Fast,* The Brookings Institute, Washington, DC.

Enos, J.L. (1958), 'A Measure of the Rate of Technical Progress in the Petroleum Refining Industry', *Journal of Industrial Economics,* June.

_____ (1985), 'A Game-Theoretic Approach to Choice of Technology in Developing Countries', in J. James and S. Watanable, *Technology, Institutions and Government Policies,* Macmillan, London, pp.47-80.

Enos, J.L. & Park W.H. (1989), *The Adoption and Diffusion of the Imported Technology: The Case of Korea,* Croom Helm, London.

Franks, C., Kim, K. and Westphal, L. (1975), *Foreign Trade Regimes and Economic Development: South Korea,* National Bureau of Economic Research, Washington, DC.

Griliches, Z. (1957), 'Hybrid Corn: An Exploration in the Economics of Technological Change,' *Econometrica,* October, pp.501-22.

Hirsch, W.Z. (1956), 'Firm Progress Ratios,' *Econometrica,* April.

Hollander, S. (1965), *The Sources of Increased Efficiency: A Study of du Pont Rayon Plants,* MIT Press, Cambridge, MA.

Jones, L.P. and Sa-Kong, Il. (1980) *Government, Business and Enterpreneurship in Economic Development: the Korean Case,* Harvard University Press, Cambridge, MA.

Kamien, M.I. and Schwartz, N.L. (1982), *Market Structure and Innovation,* Cambridge University Press, Cambridge, UK.

Katz, Jorge et al. (1978), 'Productivity, Technology and Domestic Efforts in Research and Development', IDB/ECLA Research Programme in Science and Technology Working Paper no.13, Buenos Aires, July.

Kim, Lin-Su (1980a), 'Stages of Development of Industrial Technology in a Developing Country: a Model', *Research Policy,* 9, pp.254-77.

_____ (1980b), 'Organizational Innovation and Structure', Journal of Business Research, pp.225-45.

_____ (1982), 'Technological Innovations in Korea's Capital Goods Industries: A Micro Analysis', ILO Working Paper WEP 2-22/WP92, Geneva.

Kim, Lin-Su and Utterback, J.M. (1983), 'The Evolution of Organizational Structure and Technology in a Developing Country,' *Management Science,* 29, 10, pp.1,185-97.

Kim, Lin-Su and Young-Bae Kim (forthcoming) 'Innovation in a Newly Industrializing Country: A Multiple Discriminant Analysis,' Management Science.

Lee, J.J. (1981) 'Development of Engineering Consultancy and Design Capability in Korea,' in A. Araoz (ed.), *Consulting and Engineering Design in Developing Countries,* International Development Research Center, Ottawa.

Lee, Jin-Joo and Sharan, H.N. (1985) 'Technological Impact of the Public Procurement Policy: The Experience of the Power Plant Sector in the Republic of Korea,' UNCTAD programme on technology issues in the energy sector of developing countries, UNCTAD/TT/60, Geneva: United Nations.

Lee, J.J. (1993), 'Korean Technology Strategy towards the 21st Century,' KIET, Seoul.

Mansfield, E. (1971) 'Technical Change and the Rate of Limitation,' *Econometrica,* pp.741-66.

Michell, T. (1984) 'Trade, Industrialization and Employment in the Republic of Korea', ILO World Employment Programme, Geneva.

Moritani, Masanori (1984) *Advanced Technology and the Japanese Contribution,* Nomura Securities Co. Ltd., Tokyo.

Moxon, R.W. (1979) 'The Cost, Conditions and Adaptation of MNC

Technology in Developing Countries,' in R.G. Hawkins (ed.), *The Economic Effects of Multinational Corporations,* JAI Press,Greenwich, CT.

Nabseth, L. and Ray, G.F. (1974) *The Diffusion of New Industrial Processes: An International Study,* Cambridge University Press, Cambridge, UK.

Nelson, R.R. (1981) 'Research on Productivity Growth and Productivity Differences: Dead Ends and New Departures,' *Journal of Economic Literature,* 19, 3 (September), pp.1,029-64.

Nelson, R.R. and Winter, S. (1980) 'The Schumpeterian Tradeoff Revisited.' *American Economic Review,* vol.70, pp.114-32.

Ozawa, Terutomo, 'Transfer of Technology from Japan to Developing Countries', UNITAR Research Reports no.7, United Nations Institute for Training and Research, New York.

Park, W.H. (1990), 'Science, Technology and Korean Economic Growth.' Seoul National University, Seoul.

Ramaer, J.C. (1979), 'The Choice of Appropriate Technology by a Multinational Corporation: A Case Study of Messrs. Philips, Eindhoven,' in A. Robinson (ed.), *Appropriate Technologies for Third World Development,* Macmillan, London.

Ray, G.F. (1984) *The Diffusion of Mature Technologies,* Chapter 2 ('Oxygen Steelmaking,' pp.21-7) and Chapter 3 ('Continuous Casting of Steel,' pp.28-37), Cambridge University Press, Cambridge, UK.

Ray, George et al. (1985) *Technological Trends and Employment: Two Basic Process Industries,* Gower, Aldershot, Hampshire.

Rosenberg, Nathan (1976) *Perspectives in Technology,* Cambridge University Press, Cambridge, UK.

Stewart, F. (1978) *Technology and Underdevelopment*, 2nd edition, Macmillan, London.

Teece, D.J. (1976) *The Multinational Corporation and the Resource Costs of International Technology Transfer,* Ballinger, Cambridge, MA.

Tilton, J.E. (1971) *International Diffusion of Technology: The Case of Semiconductors,* The Brookings Institute.Washington, DC.

Turner, T. (1977) 'Two Refineries: A Comparative Study of Technology Transfer to the Nigerian Refining Industry,' *World Development,* Vol. 5, No. 3 (March), pp.235-56.

Utterback, J.M. and Kim, Lin-Su (forthcoming) 'Invasion of a Stable Business by Radical Innovation,' in P.R. Kleindorfer (ed.), *Productivity, Technology and Organizational Innovation,* Plenum Press, London.

Veldhuis, K.H. (1979) 'Transfer and Adaptation of Technology: Unilever as a Case Study', in A. Robinson (ed.), *Appropriate Technologies for Third*

World Development, Macmillan, London.

Westphal, L.E., Rhee, Yung-W., Kim, Lin-Su and Amsden, Alice H. (1984) 'Exports of Technology by Republic of Korea', *World Development,* 12, 5/6, pp. 505-33.

Westphal, L.E., Kim, Lin-Su and Dahlman, C.J. (1984) 'Reflections on Korea's Acquisition of Technological Capability,' World Bank, Development Research Department, Economics and Research Staff Paper, April (forthcoming in Nathan Rosenberg, ed., *International Transfer of Technology: Concepts, Measures and Comparisons,* Pergamon Press, NY.

16 Changes in Korea's bilateral trade structure with Japan and the US

Dong K. Jeong

Since the early 1960s, the Pacific basin has emerged as the world's most dynamic economic region, and its phenomenal growth in production and international trade have transformed the region into the world's political and economic center of gravity (Linder, 1986, p.1). In 1981, for the first time in its history, the United States' trade with Asian countries across the Pacific Ocean had exceeded its trade with European countries across the Atlantic Ocean (Datta, 1988, p. xiii). The Asian and Pacific region has $1 trillion a year in intra-regional trade alone.

Korea's export-led industrialization strategy from the early 1960s heavily relied on the US and Japanese markets. In 1970 Korea exported 47.3 percent of its total exports to the United States and 28 percent to Japan, while Korea imported 29.5 percent of its total imports from the US and 40.8 percent from Japan. As Korea expanded its exports markets in other countries, the figures began to decrease. In 1990, Korea's export dependency rate to the US market declined to 29.8 percent from 40 percent in 1986. The lack of competitiveness of Korean products has also substantially contributed to the decline.

In 1993, the bilateral trade between Korea and the US grew to 0.9 percent to $36.1 billion after a 2.9 percent decline in 1992. Exports to the US increased 0.3 percent to $18.1 billion, while imports decreased 2.0 percent to $17.9 billion during the period. Korea's bilateral trade with Japan grew to $31.6 million in 1993. Exports to Japan decreased to $11.6 billion in 1993 from $12.4 billion in 1991, while Korea's imports have increased to $20.0 billion in 1993 from $19.5 billion in 1992. Korea still maintains chronic trade deficits with Japan.

Korea's imports from the US has recently increased substantially, in part because of US pressures to open the Korean market. Although Korean's exports to Japanese markets have steadily increased until 1989, there has been a dramatic decrease in Korea's exports to Japan since then, especially light industry products and electronic appliances. This may be attributed to the fact that Japanese firms are producing those products in ASEAN countries.

Korea's trade deficits with Japan have been steadily increasing. This is because Korea imports most of the raw materials, parts and machineries needed for production of its export goods. The Korean economy is still characterized by the underlying import-inducing economic structure as its exports expand.

The purpose of this study is to examine Korea's bilateral trade pattern with Japan and the US since the early 1960s. This study also presented estimates of a set of crude econometric models to explore the interdependence among Korea, Japan, and the US.

In what follows, Section II examines Korea's bilateral trade structure and its changes with Japan and the US. In an attempt to analyze the degree of economic interdependence among Korea, Japan and the US, a set of four rough export functions are estimated along with a set of indices of the bilateral export nexus among the three countries. In Section III, some conclusions are given.

Trade structure: 1960-1990

Korea's economic policy during the 1950s remained inward-looking, although some incentive measures such as a preferential export system and direct subsidies to promote exports were taken by the policy makers. Top priority was given to reconstructuring the war-torn infrastructure and to producing enough consumer nondurables and construction materials for basic needs. The GNP in 1953, the year the Korean War (1950-1953) ended, amounted to $2.7 billion at 1970 constant prices. Agricultural, forestry and fishery products accounted for 47 percent of GNP and manufacturing for less than nine percent.

Korea's exports in the 1950s were limited to a small number of primary commodities which fluctuated depending on the demand and supply in the world market. Korea's exports averaged only $20 million in the 1950s. Rapid export expansion began in the early 1960s, when Korea adopted the vigorous export-oriented growth strategy. The exported industrialization strategy enabled Korea to take advantaged of its well-educated labor force and highly motivated entrepreneurs during the 1960s 'golden age' of global free trade.

Today, Korea is emerging as the most dynamic and fastest growing new industrial power of the Pacific Rim. The Korean economy has successfully maintained a high rate of economic growth for the past thirty years. From 1961 to 1980, manufacturing products grew by an average of 16 percent annually. From 1985 to 1991, the real GNP continued to grow at an annual rate of 10 percent, with remarkable stability in the price level. The per capita GNP in 1993 was 7,435 in current US dollars. It was only $87 in 1962. The gross domestic savings ratio grew to 34.5 in 1993. The high savings rate enabled the Korean economy to expand its foreign investment. The savings rate exceeded the investment demand from 1986 until 1989.

The Korean economy has achieved a phenomenal expansion in foreign trade volume as a result of a successful implementation of an outward-oriented development strategy since the early 1960s. In 1961, which was the base year of the First Five Year Economic Development Plan, Korea exported only $41 million worth of its products of which 18.2 percent was manufactured goods, importing more than $316 million worth of foreign products in the same year. Exports continued to soar dramatically at an annual average rate of 37.6 percent from 1961 to 1980 and reached $65 billion in 1990 of which 94.9 percent was manufactured goods.

In 1961, Korea exported $6.9 million worth of its products to the US market, while it imported $143.3 million worth of the US products. Today, Korea ranks seventh among the US trading partners. Korea's exports peaked at $21.4 billion in 1988, and its imports peaked at $18.9 billion in 1991. Korea's trade with the US grew from $150 million in 1960 to $36.4 billion in 1992.

Historically, as seen in Table 16.1, Korea suffered from large and chronic trade deficits with the US until the 1970s, when a rough balance between the two trading partners emerged. During the two decades from 1961 to 1981, Korea incurred a cumulative trade deficit of $3.8 billion with the US. Beginning 1982, the trade imbalance between the two countries finally turned around to Korea's favor. In 1987, Korea's trade surplus with the US peaked at $9.6 billion. It declined to $4.7 billion in 1989. The dramatic increases in wage costs and progressive opening of its market, resulted however, in a dramatic reverse shift in the Korea-US trade relationship.[1] From 1988 to 1991, Korea's exports to the US market declined for three consecutive years by an annual average rate of 4.7 percent, while US exports to Korea climbed at an annual average rate of 14 percent during the period as shown in Table 16.2. By the end of 1991, Korea's external debt increased to $39.2 billion, up from 1989's $29.4 billion. Yet, the most recent trade statistics indicate that the Korean trade surplus has dissipated, and the balance in Korea-US trade has been restored. In 1992, Korea's trade deficit with the US was $0.2

billion. The US took in the largest share of Korea's exports amounting to 23.6 percent in 1992 and ranked second as a source of Korean imports. Korea imported $2.5 billion worth of US agricultural products, ranking fourth in 1992, behind Japan, Canada and Mexico.

Table 16.1
Current and trade account balances
of Korea, the US and Japan: 1961-1991
(US$ billions)

	Korea				US		Japan		
	Current Acct	Trade Balance	Trade Balance With US	Trade Balance With Japan	Current Acct	Trade Balance	Current Account Balance (Billion)	Trade Balance	Trade Balance With US
1961	-0.03	-0.24	-0.14	-0.05	3.82	5.57	-0.98	-0.56	-1.03
1962	-0.06	-0.34	-0.21	-0.09	3.38	4.52	-0.04	0.4	0.41
1963	-0.14	-0.41	-0.26	-0.13	4.4	5.22	-0.77	-0.16	-0.57
1964	-0.03	-0.25	-0.17	-0.07	6.82	6.8	-0.48	0.37	-0.49
1965	0.01	-0.24	-0.12	-0.12	5.41	4.95	0.92	1.9	0.11
1966	-0.1	-0.43	-0.16	-0.23	3.03	3.82	1.25	2.27	0.31
1967	-0.19	-0.57	0.17	-0.36	2.59	3.8	-0.18	1.16	-0.2
1968	-0.44	-0.84	-0.21	-0.52	0.59	0.64	1.03	2.53	0.56
1969	-0.55	-0.99	-0.21	-0.62	0.42	0.6	2.12	3.69	0.87
1970	-0.62	-0.92	-0.19	-0.58	2.33	2.59	2	3.96	0.38
1971	-0.85	-1.04	-0.15	-0.69	-1.45	-2.27	5.81	7.76	2.52
1972	-0.37	-0.57	-0.11	-0.62	-5.78	-6.42	6.67	8.94	3
1973	-0.31	-0.57	-0.18	-0.49	7.07	0.91	-0.12	3.64	0.18
1974	-2.02	-1.94	-0.21	-1.24	1.92	-5.51	-4.72	1.35	0.12
1975	-1.89	-1.67	-0.52	-1.14	18.13	8.91	-0.69	4.94	-0.46
1976	-0.31	-0.59	-0.53	-1.3	4.17	9.49	3.74	9.8	3.88
1977	-0.01	-0.48	-0.67	-1.78	-14.5	-31.1	10.91	17.16	7.32
1978	-1.09	-1.78	1.03	-3.35	-15.4	-33.95	16.53	24.3	10.13

Table 16.1, *continued*

Current and trade account balances
of Korea, the US and Japan: 1961-1991
(US$ billions)

	Current Acct	Trade Balance	Trade Balance With US	Trade Balance With Japan	Current Acct	Trade Balance	Current Account Balance (Billion)	Trade Balance	Trade Balance With US
1979	-4.15	-4.4	-0.23	-3.3	-0.97	-27.54	-8.74	1.74	5.97
1980	-5.32	-4.38	-0.28	-2.82	1.84	-25.5	-10.75	2.13	9.96
1981	-4.65	-3.63	-0.39	-2.87	6.87	-27.97	4.77	19.96	13.31
1982	-2.65	-2.59	0.29	-1.92	-8.64	-36.45	6.85	18.08	12.15
1983	-1.61	-1.76	1.97	-2.83	-46.3	-67.08	20.8	31.46	18.18
1984	-1.37	-1.04	3.6	-3.04	-107	-112.5	35	44.26	33.08
1985	-0.89	-0.02	4.26	-3.02	-122	-122.2	49.17	55.99	43.51
1986	4.62	4.21	7.34	-5.44	-145	-145.1	85.83	92.82	54.42
1987	9.85	7.66	9.55	-5.22	-160	-159.5	87.02	96.42	56.94
1988	14.16	11.45	8.65	-3.93	-126	-127	79.61	95	52.61
1989	5.06	4.6	4.73	-3.99	-106	-115.9	56.99	76.89	49.1
1990	-2.17	-2	2.42	-5.94	-92.2	-108.1	35.87	63.58	44.5
1991	-8.83	-7.07	-0.34	-8.76	-8.76	-73.6	72.91	103.09	46.9

Sources: International Financial Statistics, IMF, June 1992; *Korea Statistical Yearbook*, EPB, Republic of Korea, 1991; *Economic Report of the President*, 1992; *The Statistical History of the US From Colonial Times to Present* (1970), Bureau of Census, 1975; *Survey of Current Business*, US Department of Commerce; *Economic Statistics Annual*, Various Issues, The Bank of Japan; *Major Statistics of Korean Economy*, KFTA, Seoul, 1991; *KOREA Trade Focus*, Office of KFTA, Washington, DC, March, 1992; *Major Statistics of Korean Economy*, EPB, Seoul, 1977.

Japan's rapid postwar economic growth after World War II has brought about both envy and alarm in the world. Japan's per capita income in 1950 was less than three-fourths its pre-war level. In 1952, Japanese per capita GNP was below that of Malaysia and Chile. By the mid-1950s Japan had already attained its prewar level per capita income, had doubled its level by 1963, and had entertained the ranks of industrialized countries.[2] Japan's growth momentum has been steadily sustained since 1963. Its trade surplus has been solidly maintained after that year and has even begun to escalate since 1981.

Table 16.2
US merchandise trade with Korea and Japan (1980 - 1990)

Yr	Total US				With Japan				With Korea			
	Exports	Imports	Balance	Exports	Share (%)	Imports	Share (%)	Balance	Exports	Share (%)	Imports	Share (%)	Balance
'80	220781	256,959	- 36,198	20,790	9.4	32,973	12.8	- 12,183	4,685	2.1	4,433	1.7	252
'81	233739	273,351	- 39,613	21,823	9.3	39,904	14.6	- 18,081	5,116	2.2	5,474	2	-358
'82	212274	254,882	- 38,462	20,966	9.9	39,931	15.7	- 18,965	5,529	2.6	6,011	2.4	-482
'83	200528	269,880	- 64,239	21,894	10.9	43,559	16.1	- 21,665	5,925	3.0	7,657	2.8	-1732
'84	217889	341,170	-122,388	23,575	10.8	60,371	17.7	- 36,796	5,983	2.7	10,027	2.9	-4,044
'85	213146	361,620	-133,648	22,631	10.6	72,380	20.0	- 49,749	5,956	2.8	10,713	3	-4757
'86	217292	387,075	-154,988	26,882	12.4	85,457	22.1	- 58,575	6,355	2.9	13,497	3.5	- 7,142
'87	252884	424,068	-169,958	28,249	11.2	88,074	20.8	- 59,825	8,099	3.2	17,991	4.2	- 9,892
'88	319413	459,775	-137,970	37,620	11.8	93,128	20.3	- 55,436	11,257	3.5	21,164	4.6	- 9,919
'89	363807	493,324	-108,994	44,584	12.3	97,110	19.7	- 49,002	13,478	3.7	20,543	4.2	- 6,264
'90	394045	495,042	-100,997	48,585	12.3	89,655	18.1	- 41,071	14,399	3.7	18,493	3.7	- 4,095

Source: IMP, Direction of Trade Statistics; US Commerce News; Korea and World: Key Statistics 1991. KFTA, Seoul, Korea.

In 1985, Japan's per capita GDP, estimated in terms of 1975 purchasing power parities, exceeded France's per capita income by 2 percent and the United Kingdom's by 28 percent, reaching 81 percent of the US level and 94 percent of per capita income of West Germany in the same year.

In 1960, Japan's nominal GNP represented only 4.5 percent of the gross world product; by 1980 it reached 9.0 percent, and 13.6 percent by 1989, while the US share declined to 24.5 percent in 1989 from 25.9 percent in 1960.[3] The rapid growth in Japanese income level has been achieved primarily by improving its labor productivity. The period from 1964 to 1973 was the most rapid economic growth period, just prior to the first oil crisis, labor productivity in terms of real GNP grew by an annual rate of 9.0 percent. This is a remarkably high figure compared with 1.9 percent for the US and 4.7 percent for West Germany. The rate of productivity growth, however, substantially decreased following the first oil crisis in 1974-75 to the annual average rate of 3.9 percent during 1969-79. The productivity growth is still considerably higher than 0.7 percent for the US, 3.0 percent for West Germany, and 1.4 percent for the United Kingdom (Okita,1989, p.5).

The rapid economic growth of the Japanese economy, resulting particularly from unmatched productivity growth, replaced the glory days of unchallenged economic superiority of the US The mounting imbalance of the US with Japan, especially after the 1985 Plaza Accord, has escalated trade friction between the US and Japan.

Lately, negative voices of 'cynicism and anger among some Americans against Japan appear to be heaping scorn on the Japanese for their industriousness and thrift.'[4] It is unfortunate that many Americans seem to be ignoring the profound economic interdependence among the US, Japan, Korea, and other Asian NICS that have arisen over the past 30 years. One cannot overemphasize the gravity of the reality that neither the US, Japan, Korea nor any other country can sustain economic prosperity without the healthy economy of the other trading partners.

The trade volume between Korea and the US has expanded 250-fold in the past three decades, from an anemic $150 million in 1960 to approximately $37.4 billion in 1991. The US has consistently been Korea's largest trading partner since the mid-1960s.

Rapid export expansion first initiated from a paltry based of $33 million in 1960 and has persistently continued to grow. By 1965, the nominal value of commodity exports reached $175 million. From 1965 to 1977, exports grew by 40 percent annually, and Korea's commodity exports reached $10 million.

The dynamic growth of export activities accompanied by a remarkable change in the structure of export commodity composition. As shown in Table 16.3, Korea's exports in the early 1960s consisted of mostly primary products such as tungsten, iron ore, raw silk, fish and rice. The proportion of manufactured commodities with SITC code number 5 through 8 in total exports was less than 20 percent in 1962. It expanded to more than 90 percent of Korea's total commodity exports in 1980, and it reached almost 94 percent in 1990.

During the period of 1953-1961 when Korean economic policy largely adhered to the inward-looking strategy, the export share of Korea's GNP amounted to a meager 3 percent. With the vigorous implementation of the outward-looking growth strategy in the early 1960s, the exports-to-GNP ratio increased rapidly from approximately 8 percent in 1962-1966 to about 35 percent in 1980, and it reached over 40 percent in the late 1980s. In 1961, the trade-to-GNP ratio was only 1.2 percent and it grew exponentially reaching almost 85 percent in 1981. As shown in Table 16.5, the trade-to-GNP ratio decreased to about 66 percent in 1990.

Table 16.6 presents the trend of Korea's exports by regions from 1962 to 1990. More than 65 percent of its exports were made in Asia, of which two-thirds of the exports were directed in Japan. In 1962, approximately 22 percent of Korea's exports were absorbed by the US. Korea's exports expanded dramatically from $54.8 million in 1962 to $65 billion in 1990. Because of Korea's efforts to diversify export commodities and markets, the proportion of Korea's exports to Japan declined from 42.9 percent in 1962 to 19.4 percent in 1990, although exports to Japan increased from only $23.5 million to $12.6 billion during that period. on the other hand, Korea's exports to the US has increased from 22.8 percent of its total exports in 1962 to 29.8 percent in 1990, while Korea's exports to the US increased from only $12 million to 19.4 billion during the period. As Korea expands its exports to China, ASEAN countries, Russia and East European countries, heavy reliance of Korea's exports on Japanese and US markets is expected to decline further.

Table 16.7 presents the trend of Korea's import by regions. In 1962, more than half of Korean imports were from the US, while more than a quarter of Korean imports were from Japan. In 1990, approximately one-fourth of Korean imports were from each Japan and the US. Korean exports and imports to and from Europe has noticeably increased during the same period.

The rapid expansion of exports of manufactured goods necessitated the corresponding increase of imports for production of export goods. Until 1963 the imports of commodities primarily for export production had been negligible. However, as the rate of growth of Korean exports accelerated, the direct import content of exports increased rapidly to about 47 percent by 1969. Thereafter, the import content of exports roughly increased from 37 percent to 50 percent (Mason, et al., 1980, p.136). As shown in Table 16.4, the imports of crude material increased form $405 million in 1962 to $8.6 billion in 1990, while machinery imports rose from $590 million to $24 billion during the period. Table 16.8 presents the commodity structure of Korea's trade with the US, Japan and the European community for the year 1990. It is interesting to note that the values of exports and imports of electronic parts to these three trading partners were almost identical in 1990. Furthermore, Korea's exports of industrial electronics to the US, Japan and the EC exceeded its imports from them by about $3 billion. Meanwhile, Korea's imports of iron and steel products exceeded its exports of iron and steel products by about $3 billion in 1990.

In order to examine the strength of the triangular trades among Korea, Japan and the United States, the indices of the bilateral export-nexus are computed. If the index exceeds 1, it indicates that the proportion of the Country A's exports to Country B out of Country A's total exports is greater than the proportion of Country B's total imports out of world's total import. Table 16.9 shows that Korea's index of export-nexus with Japan is substantially increased from 1985 to 1989, and it is almost comparable to Japan's index of export-nexus with Korea's in 1989. It is also to be noted that Japan's index of export-nexus with the US is much grater than the US index of export-nexus with Japan. They are all greater than 1, which indicates strong trade relations among the three trade partners, and they are rapidly growing. These figures clearly indicate the growing interdependency in their triangular trade relations.

It is to be noted that on the basis of recent indices of the export nexus, the market share of the US exports in Korea became more favorable compared to the market share of Korea's exports in the US market. In the event that the differential in the index of the bilateral export nexus favoring the US continues to prevail, the US policy makers will lose their theoretical ground to put further pressure on Korea to open its domestic market for US products. Comparing the export-nexus indices between the US and Japan, on the other hand, one can readily see that the US export-nexus index in the Japanese market is approximately 20 percent less than Japan's export-nexus index in the US market.

Table 16.3
Trend of structure in Korea's
major export commodities:1962-1990

($US millions, %)

Commodities (SITC Code)	1962	1965	1970	1975	1980	1985	1990
Food Stuff (0)	21.9	28.2	66	602	1,153	1,136	2,037
	(40.0)	(16.1)	(7.9)	(11.8)	(6.6)	(3.8)	(3.1)
Chemicals (5)	1.0	0.4	11	74.8	755	936	2,511
	(1.8)	(0.2)	(1.3)	(1.5)	(4.3)	(3.1)	(3.9)
Fabrics, textile, yarns (65)	-	-	85	648.9	2,216		6,076
				(12.8)	(12.7)	2,544	(9.3)
						(8.4)	
Iron & steel (67)	0.5	10.2	13	232	1,658	1,811	3,605
	(0.9)	(5.8)	(1.6)	(4.6)	(9.5)	(6.0)	(5.5)
Office machinery (75)	-	-	-	-	89	588	2,702
					(0.5)	(1.9)	(4.2)
Thermionic valves (776)	-	-	-	-	517	1,137	5,364
					(3.0)	(3.8)	(8.3)
Passenger cars (781)	-	-	-	-	50	519	849
					(0.3)	(1.7)	(0.3)
Ships (793)	-	-		-	618	5,040	2,801
					(3.5)	(16.6)	(4.3)
Apparel (841)	-	-	214	1,148	2,950	4,450	7,879
			(25.6)	(22.6)	(16.9)	(14.7)	(12.1)
Footwear (851)	0.2	4.2	17	92	874	1,538	4,307
	(0.4)	(2.4)	(2.0)	(1.8)	(5.0)	(5.1)	(62.0)
Toys (8942-3)	-	-	-	-	209	482	758
					(4.2)	(1.6)	(1.2)
Manufactured goods (5-8)	10.6	106.8	646	4,144	15,791	27,756	60,985
	(19.3)	(61.0)	(77.3)	(81.6)	(90.2)	(91.7)	(93.8)
Total	54.8	175.1	835	5,081	17,505	30,283	65,016

Note: Export figures are based on SITC Code. *Sources: Major Statistics of Korean Economy 1977*, Economic Planning Board, Seoul, Korea; *Korea and the World: Key Statistics* 1991, Korea Foreign Trade Association; *Major Statistics of Korean Economy 1991*, KFTA.

Table 16.4
Trend structure in Korea's
major import commodities: 1962-1990

($US millions, %)

Commodities (SITC Code)	1962	1965	1970	1975	1980	1985	1990
Food stuff (0)	48.6 (11.5)	63.5 (13.7)	319 (16.1)	947 (13.0)	1,789 (8.0)	1,398 (4.5)	3,245 (4.6)
Wheat (04)	26.1 (6.2)	35.9 (7.7)	80 (4.0)	294 (4.0)	367 (4.6)	442 (1.4)	419 (0.6)
Crude material (2)	89.7 (21.3)	110.0 (23.7)	405 (20.4)	1,118 (15.4)	3,632 (16.3)	3,857 (12.4)	8,648 (12.4)
Raw cotton (2631)	34.2 (8.1)	40.8 (8.8)	63 (3.2)	249 (3.4)	604 (2.7)	531 (1.7)	786 (1.1)
Mineral fuels (3)	30.6 (7.3)	31.3 (6.8)	136 (6.9)	1,387 (19.1)	6,660 (29.9)	7,363 (23.6)	11,023 (15.8)
Petroleum (333)	0.5 (0.1)	23.1 (5.0)	125 (6.3)	1,271 (17.5)	5,633 (25.3)	5,572 (17.9)	6,386 (9.1)
Chemicals (5)	94.3 (22.4)	103.4 (22.3)	164 (8.3)	790 (10.9)	1,800 (8.1)	2,789 (9.0)	7,424 (10.6)
Mfg goods by material (6)	73.1 (17.3)	70.8 (15.3)	306 (15.4)	866 (11.9)	2,450 (11)	3,555 (11.4)	10,581 (15.1)
Machinery (7)	69.8 (16.5)	73.5 (15.9)	590 (29.7)	1,909 (26.2)	4,999 (22.4)	10,648 (34.2)	23,940 (34.3)
Thermionic valves (776)	-	-	-	294 (4.0)	527 (2.4)	1,130 (3.6)	4,560 (6.5)
Miscellaneous goods (5-8)	10.2 (2.4)	6.8 (1.5)	47 (2.4)	188 (2.6)	665 (3.0)	1,233 (4.0)	4,242 (6.1)
Manufactured goods (5-8)	247.4 (58.7)	254.5 (54.9)	1,107 (55.8)	3,753 (51.6)	9,914 (44.5)	18,225 (58.5)	46,196 (66.1)
Total	421.8	463.4	1,984	7,274	22,292	31,136	69,844

Note: Import figures are based on SITC Code. *Sources: Major Statistics of Korean Economy* 1977, Economic Planning Board, Seoul, Korea; *Korea and the World: Key Statistics* 1991, KFTA; *Major Statistics of Korean Economy* 1991, KFTA.

Table 16.5
Ratio of Trade to GNP[1]: 1972-1990

	United States	Japan	Germany[3]	United Kingdom	France[4]	Taiwan	Korea
1972	(4.)[2].90	17.4 (9.5)	33.7 (18.1)	38.7 (14.8)	15.3 (7.5)	70.1 (38.0)	46.1 (20.5)
1973	10.7 (5.3)	18.2 (8.9)	35.6 (19.6)	45.4 (16.1)	16.4 (8.1)	77.7 (42.1)	63.2 (29.7)
1974	14.2 (6.7)	25.6 (12.1)	41.8 (23.5)	45.8 (19.1)	18.8 (8.8)	87.9 (39.3)	68.2 (28.1)
1975	13.4 (6.8)	22.8 (11.2)	39.5 (21.6)	41.7 (18.3)	17.4 (8.7)	73.6 (34.7)	66.1 (28.0)
1976	13.9 (6.5)	23.6 (12.0)	42.6 (22.8)	47.0 (19.6)	17.8 (8.4)	86.1 (44.6)	65.5 (31.2)
1977	14.1 (6.1)	22.1 (11.7)	42.5 (22.9)	51.7 (21.9)	17.5 (8.4)	83.3 (43.6)	65.6 (31.7)
1978	14.7 (6.4)	18.0 (10.2)	41.1 (22.2)	51.7 (21.0)	17.0 (8.4)	89.8 (48.1)	64.7 (29.9)
1979	16.1 (7.3)	21.0 (10.2)	43.5 (22.5)	48.2 (20.6)	18.4 (8.9)	94.3 (49.2)	64.6 (28.1)
1980	17.5 (8.1)	25.7 (12.2)	46.6 (23.6)	39.8 (20.6)	19.3 (8.9)	97.0 (48.6)	80.6 (34.7)
1981	16.6 (7.7)	25.3 (13.0)	49.7 (25.8)	28.3 (14.3)	15.4 (7.2)	117.0 (60.4)	84.9 (37.7)
1982	14.8 (6.8)	24.9 (12.8)	50.4 (26.8)	40.6 (20.0)	12.7 (5.8)	86.6 (46.8)	78.4 (35.7)
1983	13.8 (6.0)	23.1 (12.4)	49.2 (25.8)	42.8 (20.0)	10.8 (5.1)	89.0 (49.2)	77.0 (36.5)
1984	14.8 (5.9)	24.3 (13.5)	52.6 (27.8)	47.2 (21.9)	10.1 (4.9)	91.1 (52.9)	77.5 (37.0)
1985	14.6 (5.5)	23.1 (13.2)	54.8 (29.5)	57.1 (22.2)	10.1 (4.9)	84.6 (51.1)	73.8 (35.8)
1986	14.6 (5.4)	16.9 (10.7)	48.4 (27.1)	42.3 (19.4)	32.2 (17.3)	88.2 (54.8)	76.9 (40.0)
1987	15.0 (6.6)	16.0 (9.6)	46.4 (26.1)	42.1 (19.3)	34.9 (16.9)	90.6 (55.1)	79.1 (42.5)

Table 16.5 *continued*
Ratio of trade to GNP[1]: 1972-1990

Year							
1988	15.6	15.9	47.4	40.2	36.4	92.0	73.9
	(6.6)	(9.3)	(26.7)	(17.4)	(17.6)	(50.5)	(40.5)
1989	16.0	17.1	50.9	42.1	38.9	78.9	67.3
	(7.0)	(9.7)	(28.4)	(18.3)	(18.7)	(44.1)	(34.7)
1990	16.3	17.6	49.0	42.3	-	75.4	65.7
	(7.2)	(9.7)	(26.3)	(19.2)	(-)	(41.6)	(32.2)

1. Trade to GNP Ratio = (Exports + Imports)/GNP
2. The figures in the parentheses are exports to GNP ration = exports/GNP
3. The figures are from former West Germany
4. Figures from 1986 are (exports + imports)/GDP and exports/GNP respectively
Source: Major Statistics of Korean Economy, KFTA, 1991, pp. 314-315

Table 16.6
Trend of Korea's exports by regions: 1962 - 1990

(US$ millions, %)

	1962	1967	1972	1977	1982	1987	1990
Asia	35.7	129.2	591.0	4,250.5	8,244.2	15,918.9	24,639.0
	(65.1)	(40.3)	(36.4)	(42.3)	(37.1)	(33.7)	(37.9)
(Japan)	23.5	84.7	409.6	2,148.3	3,388.1	8,436.8	12,638.0
	(42.9)	(26.5)	(25.2)	(21.4)	(15.5)	(17.8)	(19.4)
America	12.5	146.1	831.2	3,594.1	7,426.6	19,761.6	23,195.0
	(22.8)	(45.6)	(50.9)	(5.8)	(34.0)	(41.8)	(35.7)
(US)	12.0	137.4	765.6	3,118.7	6,243.2	18,310.8	19,360.0
	(21.9)	(42.9)	(46.7)	(31.0)	(28.6)	(38.7)	(29.8)
Europe	6.3	33.2	164.9	1,759.9	3,740.7	7,848.6	12,034.0
	(11.5)	(10.4)	(10.2)	(17.5)	(17.1)	(16.6)	(18.5)
Africa	0.0	8.8	19.9	291.0	1,053.4	879.4	915.0
	(0.0)	(2.7)	(1.2)	(3.0)	(4.8)	(1.9)	(1.4)
Oceania	0.2	3.0	15.0	186.8	408.3	823.1	1,214.0
	(0.4)	(0.9)	(0.9)	(1.1)	(1.9)	(1.7)	(1.9)
Others	0.1	0.0	0.0	8.3	978.9	1,226,9	3,019.0
	(0.2)	(0.0)	(0.1)	(0.08)	(4.5)	(2.6)	(4.6)
Total	54.8	320.2	1,624.1	10,046.4 5	21,616.1	47,280.9	65,016,0
	(100.0)	(100.0)	(100.0)	(100.0)	(100.0)	(100.0)	(100.0)

Source: Major Statistics of Korean economy 1977, E.P.B., Seoul, Korea; *Major Statistics of Korean Economy* 1991, KFTA.

298

Table 16.7
Trend of Korea's imports by regions: 1962 - 1990

(US$ millions, %)

	1962	1967	1972	1977	1982	1987	1990
Asia	141.5	573.6	1,474.9	6,731.3	11,997.5	18,890	28,514.6
	(33.5)	(57.6)	(58.5)	(62.3)	(49.5)	(46.1)	(40.8)
(Japan)	109.2	443.0	1,031.1	3,926.6	5,305.3	13,657	18,573.9
	(25.9)	(44.5)	(40.9)	(36.3)	(29.9)	(33.3)	(26.6)
America	228.9	317.8	690.5	2,686.40	8,413.0	10,889	21,696.6
	(54.3)	(31.9)	(27.4)	(24.8)	(34.7)	(26.5)	(31.1)
(US)	220.3	305.2	647.2	2,447.4	5,955.8	8,758	16,942.5
	(52.2)	(30.6)	(25.7)	(22.6)	(24.6)	(21.4)	(24.3)
Europe	41.4	84.3	280.2	985.8	2,126.2	5,661	10,512.1
	(9.8)	(8.5)	(11.1)	(9.1)	(8.8)	(13.8)	(15.1)
Africa	1.9	8.7	13.7	33.6	29.3	90	363.0
	(0.5)	(0.9)	(0.5)	(0.7)	(2.0)	(0.2)	(1.0)
Oceania	7.9	11.1	53.7	328.2	1,058.1	1,648	3,200.6
	(1.8)	(1.1)	(2.1)	(3.1)	(4.4)	(4.0)	(4.6)
Others	0.2	0.8	9.0	0.3	1,143.2	3,842	5,556.8
	(0.0)	(0.0)	(0.4)	(0.0)	(4.7)	(9.4)	(8.0)
Total	421.8	996.2	2,522.0	10,810.5	24,250.6	41,020	69,843.7
	(100.0)	(100.0)	(100.0)	(100.0)	(100.0)	(100.0)	(100.0)

Source: Major Statistics of Korean Economy 1977, Economic Planning Board; *Major Statistics of Korean Economy* 1991, Korea Foreign Trade Association.

Table 16.8 Korea's commodity structure of trade with the US, Japan and EC: 1990

Commodity	US	Japan	E.C.	US	Japan	E.C.
Textile products	3,487	2,596	1,403			
	(18.0)	(20.5)	(15.8)			
Footwear	2,561	429	728			
	(13.2)	(3.4)	(8.2)			
Parts of electronics	2,309	1,878	952	1,373	3,484	329
	(11.9)	(14.9)	(10.7)	(8.1)	(18.8)	(3.9)
Industrial electronics	1,748		974	1,230	988	276
	(9.0)		(11.0)	(7.2)	(5.3)	(3.3)

299

Table 16.8 *continued*

Commodity	US	Japan	E.C.	US	Japan	E.C.
Home appliance electronics	1,597 (8.2)		1,199 (13.5)			
Transportation equipment	1,515 (7.8)					287 (3.4)
Iron & steel products	784 (4.0)	1,553 (12.3)		831 (4.9)	1,514 (8.2)	290 (3.4)
General machinery	600 (3.1)		204 (2.3)	2,434 (14.4)	3,897 (21.0)	2,598 (30.9)
Container	417(2.2)					
Agricultural forestry & fisheries		1,636 (12.9)		3,099 (18.3)		396 (4.7)
Petroleum products		484 (3.8)		620 (3.7)		
Organic chemicals		363 (2.9)	191 (2.2)	1,328 (7.8)	1,703 (9.2)	850 (10.1)
Plastic products		328 (2.6)				
Ships			515 (5.8)			
Textile fabrics			399 (4.5)			
Aircrafts & parts				886(5.2)		
Paper products				756(4.5)		
Precision machinery					844 (4.5)	367 (4.4)
Tools					755 (4.1)	
Raw material For pharmaceuticals					685 (3.7)	546 (6.5)
Heavy electric equipment					575 (3.1)	
Total	19360	12638	8876	16942	18574	8421

Source: Korea and the World: Key Statistics 1991. KFTA, Seoul, Korea, pp. 43-45.
Note: Figures are based on MTI Code 2 digit and customs clearance basis.

300

to 1989, and it is almost comparable to Japan's index of export-nexus with Korea's in 1989. It is also to be noted that Japan's index of export-nexus with the US is much grater than the US index of export-nexus with Japan. They are all greater than 1, which indicates strong trade relations among the three trade partners, and they are rapidly growing. These figures clearly indicate the growing interdependency in their triangular trade relations.

It is to be noted that on the basis of recent indices of the export nexus, the market share of the US exports in Korea became more favorable compared to the market share of Korea's exports in the US market. In the event that the differential in the index of the bilateral export nexus favoring the US continues to prevail, the US policy makers will lose their theoretical ground to put further pressure on Korea to open its domestic market for US products. Comparing the export-nexus indices between the US and Japan, on the other hand, one can readily see that the US export-nexus index in the Japanese market is approximately 20 percent less than Japan's export-nexus index in the US market.

In an effort to estimate a quantitative measure of the interdependence of the trade structure among Korea, Japan, and the US, a set of four crude econometric export functions are estimated. As shown in Table 16.10, in contrast to the relatively low magnitude of import income elasticity (5.02) in the US for Korean products, the relative export price elasticity of Korean products in the US market is unusually high (7,083.23). The import income elasticity of Japan for Korean products is about one-half of that of the US, while relative price elasticity of Korea's exports to Japan is roughly compatible to the relative export price elasticity of Korean exports to the US.

Table 16.9

Index of export-nexus among Korea, Japan and the US: 1985-1989

Import Country / Export Country	Korea	Japan	US
Korea		(2.14) 3.07	(1.89) 2.00
Japan	(2.57) 3.08		(2.01) 2.97
US	(1.79) 2.12	(1.49) 1.74	

Country A's Index of Export - Nexus with Country B = $\dfrac{\text{Country A's Exports to Country B}}{\text{Country A's Total Exports}}$ $\dfrac{\text{Country's B Total Imports}}{\text{World's Total Imports}}$

The figures in the parentheses are for 1985 and the figures without parentheses are for 1989.

Source: The figures for Japan-US are obtained from the *Economic White Paper* (in Japanese language). EPB, Tokyo, Japan, 1991, p. 313. The figures for Korean-Japan, and Korea-US are computed from *Korea and World: Key Statistics,* KFTA, 1991.

302

Table 16.10
Estimates of economic interdependence
among Korea, the US and Japan: 1972-1990

Dependent variable / Explanatory variable	Korean exports to US	US exports to Korea	Korean exports to Japan	Japan's exports to Korea
Constant	-15,476.00*** (-2.91)	1,782.67 (1.17)	-6,493.51** (-3.64)	-3,883.91* (-1.34)
US GNP	5.06*** (15.88)	-	-	-
Korean GNP	-	72.23*** (36.15)	-	60.09*** (4.94)
Japanese GNP	-	-	2.83*** (4.70)	-
Korea's relative price factor w.r.t. US	7,083.23* (1.60)	-1,317.05 (-0.99)	-	-
Korea's relative price factor w.r.t. Japan	-	-	6,827.21** (2.96)	6,055.95** (1.73)
R⁻²	.93	.98	.97	.96
D-W	.56	1.06	1.07	.78
Rho	.64	.43	.46	.54

Note: All the variables are measured in log form. The figures in parentheses are t-ratios. The relative price factor is defined as the ratio between Korea's export unit value index and the US producers price index and Japanese wholesale price index respectively.

***Significant at the one percent.

** Significant at the five percent.

*Significant at the 10 percent.

R^{-2}: The coefficient of multiple determination adjusted by the degrees of frame

D-W: The Durbin Watson Statistics

Rho: The estimate of the first order autoregressive coefficients.

Korea's import income elasticity of US products is roughly comparable to Korea's import income elasticity of Japanese products. Both of them are highly significant at the one-percent level. The estimated partial regression coefficient of Korea's relative price factor with respect to the US producers price index in the US export function to Korea has a correct sign, but it is statistically insignificant. On the other hand, the partial regression coefficient of Korea's relative price factor with respect to Japanese whole sale price index is marginally significant at the ten percent level, but it has a wrong sign. The insignificance of the regression coefficients seem to imply that Korea's imports from the US and Japan are not highly responsive to prices to both Japanese and US products. This appears to indicate that most of Korean imports from Japan and the US are structurally necessitated for production of manufactured export goods of Korea. The adjusted coefficient of multiple determinations for each estimated export function indicates a remarkable, substantial explanatory power of the empirical results.

The empirical results of the four export functions indicate that Korean exports to both Japan and US markets are much more highly responsive to Korea's relative price factor than Japanese and the US exports to Korea. On the other hand, Japanese and US exports to Korea are more responsive to Korea's level of income than to Korea's relative price factor with respect to their domestic price level.

Conclusion

Until the 1980s, imports and exports of the US accounted for about 10 percent of its GNP, and trade was approximately in balance (See Table 16.5). The very negligible portion of net investment in the US was financed by international capital flow. Americans in general paid little attention to the international linkage of the US economy. However, in 1990, imports and exports of the US accounted for more than 16 percent of its GNP.

The mounting trade deficits coupled with huge Federal budget deficits of the 1980s had suddenly changed all of that economic equanimity in the US By 1984, the trade deficit exceeded $100 billion and was inflicting a pain to workers who lost jobs and firms, which exported products to foreign countries or competed with imported foreign products. It is not surprising, therefore, to find the problem or rising protectionism and pressure for access to foreign markets by US policymakers on the US trading partners, especially Japan and Korea including other Asian NIEs.

As shown in Table 16.5, the foreign trade of the US and Japan account for more than 16 percent of their respective GNP, while Korea's foreign trade account for more than 65 percent of its GNP. On the multilateral level, Korea, the US and Japan have a common interest in the maintenance a strong, open triangular trade system by mitigating existing trade frictions.

The phenomenal expansion of Korea's exports accompanied by its export-led growth strategy produced a remarkable change in the structure of export and import commodity composition. Korea's exports in the early 1960s consisted of mostly primary products. The proportion of manufactured commodities with STIC code numbered 5 through 8 in total exports was less than 20 percent in 1962. It rose to more than 90 percent of Korea's total commodity exports in 1980, and it reached almost 94 percent in 1990.

The expansion of exports of manufactured goods necessitated a corresponding expansion of import content of export production. Until 1963, the imports of commodity for export production had been negligible. However, ensuing accelerated growth of Korean exports rapidly increased the direct import content of exports to about 47 percent by 1969. Thereafter, the import content of the exports rose approximately from 37 percent to 50 percent. The relative share of food stuffs declined sharply during 1962-1990, while the share of mineral fuels, mainly crude oil, rose from 7.3 percent in 1962 to about 30 percent in 1980. It then declined to 15.8 percent in 1990. Imports of machinery and transport equipment also increased significantly from 16.5 percent to 34.3 percent during 1962-1990.

On the basis of indices of the export nexus among Korea, Japan and the US, the interdependent triangular trade relations remain strong and they are growing rapidly. The comparison of the export-nexus indices indicated that in contrast to the unfavorable share of the Japanese market by US export industries, the share of the Korean market by the US export industries has recently turned around to favor the US.

The empirical results of a set of four export functions suggest that Korea's import income elasticity of the US products is roughly comparable to Korea's import income elasticity of Japanese products. Korea's imports from the US and Japan are not responsive to prices of both Japanese and the US products. Korea's imports from the two major trading partners appears to be structurally necessitated for continuing expansion of Korea's manufactured exporting products.

On the other hand, Korean exports to both Japan and the US are more responsive to Korea's relative price factor than Japanese and the US exports to Korea. Japanese and US exports to Korea are, however, more responsive

to Korea's level of income than to Korea's relative price factor with respect
to their domestic prices.

Notes

1 The contributing factors of Korea's return to its balance of payments
   deficits are: (1) appreciation of the Korean Won, (2) trade frictions with
   Korea's trading partners particularly the US, (3) the sharp rise in wages,
   (4) shortage of manpower in the manufacturing section, (5) widespread
   labor disputes after Korea's democratization of political process in 1987,
   (6) the failure of Korean firms to increase investment in R&D and
   production facilities during the trade surplus period (1986-1989), (7) US
   recession after 1989.
2 Bela Balassa and Marcus Noland, *Japan in the World Economy,* Institute
   for International Economics, 1988, p. 3. However, in 1987, at December
   1987 exchange rates, Japan's per capita income ($23,022) surpassed
   France's ($17,657), West Germany's ($21,022), United Kingdom's
   ($13,395), and the US ($18,163) levels. See also Table 1.1, p. 4.
3 Paul Kennedy, *The Rise and Fall of Great Empires* (1987), Random
   House, Table 43, p. 436. Economic Planning Board, *Economic White
   Paper,* (In Japanese), Tokyo, Japan, 1991, p. 35.
4 *EWC News,* January - April 1992, East-West Center, Honolulu, Hawaii,
   Vol. 2, No. 1-2, p. 4. This is quoted from a speech given by Senator
   Daniel Inouye at the East-West Center.

References

Arndtsven, W. and Lawrence Bouton (1987), *Competitiveness-The US In
   World Trade,* American Enterprise Institute Studies in Economic Policy.
   Washington, DC.
Balassa, Bela and Marcus Noland (1988), *Japan In The World Economy,* IIE,
   Washington, DC.
Bayard, Thomas O. and Soo-Gil Young (1989), *Economic Relations Between
   The US and Korea: Conflict or Cooperation?* Special Report 8, Institute for
   International Economics and Korea Development Institute, Washington,
   DC.
Bradford, C. Fred and William R. Cline (1987), *The US-Japan Economic*

Problem, Policy Analyses in International Economics #13, Institute for International Economics, Washington, DC.

Brock, William and Robert Hormats, eds. (1990), *The Global Economy America's Role In The Decade Ahead,* W.W. Norton and Company, New York .

Burstein, Daniel (1988), *Yen! Japan's New Financial Empire and Its Threat to America,* Simon and Schuster, NY.

Dutta, M., ed. (1988), *Asian Industrialization: Changing Economic Structures,* Volume 1, Part A, JAI Press, Inc., Greenwich, CT.

Economic Planning Board (1991), *Economic White Paper* (in Japanese), Tokyo, Japan.

Emmott, Bill (1989), *The Sun Also Sets-The Limits to Japan's Economic Power,* Random House, New York.

Higashi, Chikara and G. Peter Lauder (1987), *The Internationalization of the Japanese Economy,* Klumber Academic Publishers, Boston.

IMF, *International Financial Statistics Yearbook,* Washington, DC.

Kang, W. T. (1989), *Is Korea The Next Japan?* The Free Press, New York.

Kelly, Brian and Mark London (1989), *The Four Little Dragons,* Simon and Schuster, NY.

Korea Foreign Trade Association (1991), *Major Statistics of Korean Economy* (in Korean), Seoul, Korea.

_____ (1991), *Major Statistics of Trade Movement,* (in Korean), Seoul, Korea.

The Korean Economic Institute of America (1991), *US-Korean Economic Relations,* Washington, DC.

Korea Statistical Yearbook, National Bureau of Statistics Economic Planning Board, Republic of Korea (1991 and various issues), Seoul, Korea.

Lawrence, Robert Z. (1987), 'Imports of Japan: Closed Market or Minds', *Brookings Papers on Economics Activity,* No. 2.

Linder, Staffan Burenstam (1986), *The Pacific Century: Economic and Political Consequences of Asian-Pacific Dynamism,* Stanford University Press, Stanford, CA.

Ministry of Trade and Industry, Republic of Korea (February 1993), *Korea and the US: Economic Partnership & Prospects.*

Ministry of Trade and Industry, Republic of Korea (May 1992), *The Korean Economy and US-Korea Trade Relations,* Seoul, Korea.

Partnership in Progress: Korea's Record and Commitment (February 1990),Seoul, Korea.

Nakamura, Takafusa, tr. Robert A. Feldman (1983), *Economic Growth in*

Pre-War Japan, Yale University Press, New Haven, CT.

Okita, Sabro (1980), *Japan in the World Economy of the 1980s,* University of Tokyo Press, Tokyo, Japan.

The World Bank, *World Development Report-Financial Systems and Development World Development Indicators,* various issues, Washington, DC.

US Department of Commerce, *Statistical Abstract of the US and Survey of Current Business,* various issues, Washington, DC.

17 Remarks: A new partnership in the Asia–Pacific

Seung-Soo Han

In July 1993, I traveled to Korea to participate in the summit meetings between President Kim Young Sam and President Bill Clinton. The American leader's two-day visit to Korea was, I believe, a resounding success. In no uncertain terms, he reiterated America's staunch security commitment to Seoul. He also issued clear and stern warnings to North Korea regarding its military threat, including its maverick nuclear weapons development program.

Since President Clinton chose Korea as the venue for unveiling his Administration's Asia policy, this visit was important for the entire Pacific Rim. In sum, he pledged continued American political, military and economic engagement in the region. President Clinton spoke of a new Pacific community, and expressed his intention to step up Washington's efforts in building regional consensus and cooperation. In his address to our National Assembly, he emphasized the role of Korea in the region, as 'it stands at the center of Northeast Asia, within two hours by air from Singapore, Tokyo, Beijing and Vladivostok.'

Regional cooperation is of great interest to the Kim Young Sam government, as well, and I envision more and more teamwork between Korea and the US toward promoting interaction among our regional neighbors. On the bilateral economic front, we are in a period of relatively smooth sailing. At the post-summit joint press conference, President Clinton observed that, although Korea enjoyed a large trade surplus with the US just a few years ago, that account is in balance today. In my opinion, our recent liberalization efforts help explain this, and the 'new economic policy' of President Kim aims to create even more opportunities for American business in Korea.

During President Clinton's visit, both Presidents jointly announced a new forum for the future called the Dialogue for Economic Cooperation, or DEC. Its aim is to address practical economic concerns and procedures with an eye toward improving the long-term business environments both here and in Korea.

On the political side, President Clinton went on to praise President Kim for his lifetime devotion to democracy. This emphasized that we have successfully discarded authoritarianism, and, today, freedom and pluralism are the hallmarks of Korea. President Clinton even characterized the Korean experience in promoting a full democracy as a good example for all of Asia and for emerging democracies throughout the world.

Finally, the summit meetings forged an important personal bond between the two leaders. For a time, they even found themselves to be 'running mates,' so to speak. Presidents Kim and Clinton, both known for their jogging routines, found time for a morning run around the Blue House grounds.

At the 1993 Pacific Basin Economic Council conference in Seoul, President Kim Young Sam unveiled his 'New Diplomacy.' Through this 'New Diplomacy' initiative, President Kim is adjusting Korea to this new environment. Korea's international interests are becoming diversified, and we are increasingly turning our eyes toward multilateral relations and global concerns.

From the end of World War II and the division of Korea until just a few years ago, our attention was monopolized by the Cold War with North Korea and its supporters. While major disagreements between the South and North linger, that intense competition is ebbing. Reunification remains a high national priority, but so, too, are important new regional and global interests and activities.

The Republic of Korea joined the UN as a full-fledged member in 1991. There, we are making a substantial financial contribution and even participating in the body's worldwide peacekeeping efforts. We were part of the Desert Shield operation in the Persian Gulf. And, we have contributed to the Somalian relief effort.

The Korean government is now interested in promoting democracy and human rights around the world, and President Kim has spoken out on these issues. We also want to do our part in promoting arms control, nuclear and chemical weapons non-proliferation and environmental protection. Also of concern to the Korean government is the plight of nations shackled with poverty, hunger and disease.In short, it is time for Koreans to assume global responsibilities commensurate with our standing in the international community.

We have also set our sights on a more active regional role in the Asia-Pacific. The Asia-Pacific is the world's most dynamic region. And, despite its many contrasting interests and cultures, that diverse region is becoming an increasingly interactive community. Korea is expanding its presence in the Asia-Pacific through bilateral relations and cooperative organizations such as the Asia Pacific Economic Cooperation ministerial meeting, of which the US is a member.

Seoul has also expressed a willingness to explore new ideas for regional security cooperation, a matter discussed at the recent summit round in Korea. An Asia-Pacific version of NATO or the Conference on Security Cooperation in Europe is not what is envisioned, but there are certainly new possibilities for multilateral security discussions in the region.

What does all of this mean for the US? First of all, our expanding multilateralism does not diminish the importance of Korea-US ties. America remains by far Korea's most valuable ally. At the same time, Korea's significance as an American partner is also growing. In our shared democratic and free market values, for instance, we are now truly kindred spirits.

Regarding bilateral business ties, the hallmarks of President Kim's economic reform package are deregulation and liberalization. He plans to phase out strict government control over business and return the economy to market forces. His plans for fiscal, financial and administrative reform have important implications for American businesses. President Kim has stated publicly his position that it is now too difficult to do business in Korea, but he has pledged to make Korea 'the nation most hospitable to business activity.'

The new economic era he is building is one that will be more conducive to free trade and investment. Some challenges remain, but I believe that, even today, the success stories outshine the remaining problem areas. The Korea-US trade partnership today is strong – and profitable. The business prospects for American companies in Korea are bright, and the future looks even brighter.

Korea's geo-economic potential bodes well for America's future in the region. Located at the crossroads of Northeast Asia, Korea stands as a solid foundation from which American businesses can advance more effectively throughout the dynamic Asia-Pacific region.

Regarding American security concerns, Korea remains an anchor point. Regarding US trade interests, it represents a market of opportunity and a regional springboard. And, regarding global issues, the principles and policies of Seoul and Washington dovetail. As we look forward to what many anticipate will be the 'Pacific Century,' Korea stands out as a tested friend, stable ally and honest broker upon which America can continue to rely.